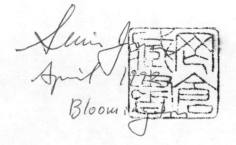

Lyotard

Geoffrey Bennington

Lyotard
Writing the event

NEW YORK

COLUMBIA
UNIVERSITY PRESS

1988

Printed in Great Britain

Library of Congress cataloguing in publication dat
Bennington, Geoffrey
   Lyotard: writing the event.
   Bibliography: p.
   Includes index.
   1. Lyotard, Jean-François I. Title
B2430.L964B46 1988   194   87-72758

ISBN 0-231-06758-5

Contents

Acknowledgements

I am grateful to students and faculty at the Universities of Essex, Sussex, and Southampton, and at Middlesex Polytechnic, for their questions and advice on early drafts of some of this book.

My greatest intellectual debt is, however, to Jean-François Lyotard himself, for encouraging this project, providing information and unpublished material, and commenting on parts of the draft. Errors and naiveties in this book are, however, entirely my own, and perhaps all that I can reasonably claim as mine. But my gratitude is not merely professional, and I thank Jean-François and Andrée Lyotard above all for their hospitality and friendship. May they forgive this gift.

Brighton
January 1987

Abbreviations

I. Works by Lyotard
(A full bibliography is to be found at the end of the book)

AE   *L'Assassinat de l'expérience par la peinture, Monory* (Paris: Le Castor Astral, 1984)

AJ   *Au Juste* (Paris: Christian Bourgois, 1979) [tr. Wlad Godzich as *Just Gaming* [JG] (Manchester University Press, 1985)]

AV   'Anamnèse du visible, ou: la franchise', in *Adami* (Paris: Musée national d'art moderne / Centre Georges Pompidou, 1985), 50-60

CPM   *La Condition postmoderne* (Paris: Minuit, 1979) [tr. Geoff Bennington and Brian Massumi as *The Postmodern condition* [PMC] (Manchester University Press, 1984)]

D   'Discussions, ou phraser "après Auschwitz"', in P. Lacoue-Labarthe and J.-L. Nancy (eds.), *Les Fins de l'homme: à partir du travail de Jacques Derrida* (Paris: Galilée, 1981), 283-310

DF   *Discours, figure* (Paris: Klincksieck, 1971)

DI   Interview with Georges Van den Abbeele, *Diacritics* Vol. 14, No. 3 (1984), 16-21

DMF   *Dérive à partir de Marx et Freud* (Paris: Union générale d'éditions, 1973) [partial tr. as *Driftworks* [DW] (New York: Semiotext(e), 1984)]

DP   *Des dispositifs pulsionnels* (Paris: Union générale d'éditions, 1973)

DW   see DMF

E   *L'Enthousiasme: la critique kantienne de l'histoire* (Paris: Galilée, 1986)

EL   *Economie libidinale* (Paris: Minuit, 1974)

FV   'Faire voir les invisibles, ou contre le réalisme', in B. Buchloh, ed., *Daniel Buren: Les Couleurs, Sculptures; Les Formes, Peintures* (Paris: Centre national d'art et de culture Georges Pompidou, 1981), pp. 26-38

IP   *Instructions païennes* (Paris: Galilée, 1977)

JG   see AJ

LD   *Le Différend* (Paris: Minuit, 1984)

MP   *Le Mur du pacifique* (Paris: Galilée, 1979)

PE   *Le Postmoderne expliqué aux enfants* (Paris: Galilée, 1986)

PMC   see CPM

PS   'Pierre Souyri, le Marxisme qui n'a pas fini', Preface to P. Souyri, *Révolution et contre-révolution en Chine* (Paris: Bourgois, 1982)

RG   Unpublished conversations with René Guiffrey (typescript)
RP   *Rudiments païens* (Paris: Union générale d'éditions, 1977)
RT   *Récits tremblants* (with Jacques Monory) (Paris: Galilée, 1977)
TD   *Les Transformateurs Duchamp* (Paris: Galilée, 1977)
TI   *Tombeau de l'intellectuel et autres papiers* (Paris: Galilée, 1984)

II. Other Abbreviations

References to works by Freud are to the Pelican Freud Library, and appear in the form 'PFL', volume number, page number.

Quotations from Kant's First and Third *Critiques* are taken from the versions by N. Kemp Smith (London: Macmillan, 1929) and by J. C. Meredith (Oxford: Clarendon Press, 1928) respectively.

With the exception of quotations from Lacan's *Ecrits,* which are taken from Alan Sheridan's selection (London: Tavistock, 1977), all translations from the French are my own.

For Rachel (something like a rigid designator)

Introduction

Jean-François Lyotard is without question best known in the English-speaking world as the author of the *The Postmodern Condition*, a short and provocative 'report' on 'the condition of knowledge in the most highly developed societies' (PMC, xxiii). Yet this is one of the least representative books from a publishing career spread unevenly over more than 30 years, and which is, at first sight, more remarkable for its shifts and breaks than for any continuity. The early work on phenomenology (*La Phénoménologie* (1953)) is criticized and displaced in *Discours, figure* (1971), which argues for the predominance of a certain psychoanalysis over phenomenology. This also involves a virulent critique of structuralism in all of its forms (including Lacanian psychoanalysis), in the name of a 'libidinal economy' which gives its name to the next major book, *Economie libidinale* (1974), which has probably suffered from being written in the shadow of Deleuze and Guattari's *Anti-Oedipus*. *Economie libidinale* extends the critique to Marxism, thus marking Lyotard's break with a long militant past (including involvement with Algerian liberation and an active role in organising the protests at the Faculty of Nanterre, at the beginning of the events known as 'May '68'). The book also lost Lyotard a lot of friends, to the extent that when the review *L'Arc* published an issue devoted to Lyotard's work in 1976, not one of his former associates in the *Socialisme ou barbarie* group would contribute an article. *Economie libidinale* is, as we shall see, a somewhat violent and scandalous book, denouncing theory as terror, and advocating and illustrating a quasi-Nietzschean monism of intensity-as-value instead. The next apparent break comes around the late 1970's, with a book of conversations (with Jean-Loup Thébaud) about justice (*Au juste* (1979), oddly translated as *Just Gaming*), and *La Condition postmoderne* itself (also 1979), which are both, in different ways, concerned to ask again the ethical and political questions which the 'libidinal' work could only exclude. Finally (though Lyotard's continuing activity makes that 'finally' very provisional), *Le Différend* (1984) is a difficult and ambitious outline of a 'philosophy of sentences', which owes much to Kant and Wittgenstein, and drops almost all of the references and arguments which supported the earlier work.

The intuitive difficulty of grasping an immediately obvious trajectory in this diverse body of work is not, at first sight, helped by the work's occasional reflections upon itself. For Lyotard sees his own intellectual career in a variety of ways. In what was to have been the final section of *Au juste*, but which was never published, he explains that he has never worked with a view to some retrospective coherence of an *œuvre*, and is untroubled by apparent inconsistencies in his writings: 'I think that inconsistency... bears witness to the life of thought, to talk a little pretentiously' (AJ, 192; see too DI,16). (And following a comment in *Les Transformateurs Duchamp*, we would need to say that the inconsistency is itself inconsistent (TD, 20-21).) Elsewhere in *Au juste,* he suggests that all of his work has nonetheless been moved by the idea that it could serve, be useful, in an ultimately, if obscurely, political sense (AJ, 34, 105-6 [JG, 17, 54-5]). At other times, he feels that all the work preceding *Le Différend* is more or less radically mistaken, and that the new book cancels and supersedes all the earlier books.

In a different vein, Lyotard sees himself as having written three 'real' books (*Discours, figure, Economie libidinale,* and *Le Différend*), and preparing to write a fourth (on the philosophy of the contemporary arts). The other work should be read as reading-notes, or analyses preparatory to these books. Thus the essays collected in *Dérive à partir de Marx et Freud*, although published in book form only in 1973, prepare *Discours, figure*; those of the *Dispositifs pulsionnels* (again published as a book in 1973) look forward to *Economie libidinale*; *The Postmodern Condition, Au juste, L'Enthousiasme* (written 1980-1, published 1986) and a number of uncollected essays anticipate *Le Différend.* On this view, *Les Transformateurs Duchamp* (1977) and *L'Assassinat de l'expérience par la peinture, Monory* (1984), plus studies of Buren, Ayme, Adami, Arakawa and others, would not be 'real' books so much as preparation for the work to come. Although this is a tempting picture, and will largely determine the structure of *this* book, it is not without its problems, and notably leaves one uncertain about what to do with two not at all negligible narrative-'fictional' texts published in 1977 and 1979, *Récits tremblants* and *Le Mur du pacifique*, and how to deal with the period of activism and overtly 'political' writing, between Lyotard's first book on phenomenology and *Discours, figure.*

Again, it sometimes seems possible for Lyotard to use the later work to re-read the earlier, if necessary against itself: thus the notion of figure elaborated in *Discours, figure* is perhaps an anticipation of the notion of presentation worked out in *Le Différend* (DI, 17). This type of manoeuvre can take place earlier: the preface to *Dérive* already discusses the essays collected in that book in terms more like those which inform *Des dispositifs pulsionnels*, and the new preface written for a second edition in 1979 wants to re-read *that* book in terms of the 'language-games' discussed in *The Postmodern Condition*.

None of these various representations, despite the signature of the

---

The signature is the fence round the terrain of writing, the grabbing by a supposed subject of products *ipso facto* raised to the dignity of an *oeuvre*. In fact the subject as 'author' is instituted by means of the exclusion of others by the signature. (DMF, 7)

---

author, could be said to be simply correct. The simultaneous desire for and refusal of an essentially narrative coherence of a 'career' is not unusual, but would at some point have to encounter Lyotard's own narrative analyses (persistent from *Instructions païennes* (1979) and *The Postmodern Condition* for a few years) and their subsequent dissolution (in *Le Différend*) into a much more complex and differentiated approach, which would induce suspicion about the effects of a narrative account. And more generally, the very notion of re-presentation has undergone persistent interrogation throughout Lyotard's work: in 1974, he gave the title 'Beyond Representation' to his introduction to the French translation of Ehrenzweig's *The Hidden Order of Art*, and that attempt to move 'beyond', or at least to name a beyond, is never repudiated.

This difficulty of representation cannot of course simply be applied from the outside to Lyotard's own occasional representations of his work: it affects the attempt to write a book such as this, which has some pretensions to introduce Lyotard's thought and therefore, whether it likes it or not, to 're-present' it as accurately and sympathetically as possible. The problems this poses are as severe in the case of Lyotard as they are in the cases of, for example, Foucault, Lacan and Derrida – and this goes some way towards explaining why introductory books on such authors have usually been so disappointing. Introductory books in general (and this one is no exception) rely on a host of well-meaning pedagogical assumptions ('pedagogical, therefore very stupid', as Lyotard says in an unpublished conversation with the painter René Guiffrey), which do not necessarily make them helpful to those for whom they are ostensibly written. On the other hand, the proliferation in recent years of such introductory books ('Modern Masters' et al.) suggests that they have some importance, and that it would be silly simply to condemn them. One of the motivations behind such books is undoubtedly a recognition of the need to 'gain time' – such books are, among other things, designed to allow their readers to make conversation (in examination-rooms if necessary) about thinkers whose work there has been no time to read. This imperative to gain time is itself analysed by Lyotard, who would see in it a basic feature of what he is (somewhat to his own regret) most famous for having analysed: the so-called 'postmodern condition'.

It would be foolish to expect to make such problems go away by simple prefatory remarks: this book will not avoid narrative and representation, pedagogy and stupidity, time-saving and post-modernity. But if there is no reasonable prospect of escaping from these constraints, Lyotard would certainly want to argue that it is the duty of thought to *resist*. These high-sounding notions (thought, duty, resistance) may already be worrying for the 'don't-worry-and-I'll-explain-it-for-you' type of introduction which this book also aims to be. In the 'Fiche de Lecture' which opens *Le Différend*, Lyotard has a note on the reader of the work: 'Reader: Philosophical, that is anybody, on condition that they accept not to get to the end of "language" and not to "gain time"' (LD, 13). Similarly for this book (in this already resisting its commercial *raison d'être*) which aims to ape its object in more than one way. Such an aping may seem both absolutely modest (letting Lyotard's work 'speak for itself' – there will indeed be very extensive quotation and paraphrase) and absolutely immodest (speaking with the 'master's voice' as though it were my own, and also, occasionally and tentatively, criticizing what that voice says). This is one of the ways in which I try to complicate the pedagogical structure, the narrative, the time-gaining. This book may make some things clearer, but also clouds some issues; it may tell a story, but that story wilfully breaks with a simple chronological presentation, and is in any case not *the* story, but only *one* story; it may seem to save the reader time, but is an invitiation to spend more time reading Lyotard rather than a replacement for his books. This book does not attempt to account for all of Lyotards's writing, but takes a largely retrospective look from the stand of the later work, presenting the earlier books in its light. I am painfully aware of the partial and lacunary presentations of *Economie libidinale* and *Discours, figure* which I have offered, and can only hope that these difficult books be more widely read, to complement and quite possibly refute what I say about them. I have aimed at a rather fuller presentation of *Le Différend* itself, at risk of over-condensing an already dense argumentation. I have also said very little directly about the so-called 'postmodernism debate', which has often scarcely deserved either name, and which is certainly not essential to an understanding of Lyotard's most vital thinking. To the extent that Lyotard's 'postmodern' is important, it means almost exactly what he means by 'philosophy', and I avoid a lot of side-issues by accepting that identification. A further reason for such evasion is that I have made no effort to provide a full account of Lyotard's strictly 'aesthetic' writing, in view of its 'work-in-progress' status – but some of what is described here will, I hope, help future reading of that work.

I have presented the major books not in chronological order, but in what I take to be the order of difficulty of exposition. The chapters are separated by brief collages or patchworks of quotations which lay down the law in a slightly parodic sententiousness, and are internally disrupted by insertions of various types, more and less than footnotes.

Lyotard's idea of a primarily political motivation for his work would seem to fit with a long tradition of French intellectuals. And yet he would not only deny that he is an intellectual in that traditional sense, but argue that that notion of the intellectual is untenable (or at least outdated). I shall present this argument at some length, partly to give a preliminary feel of his later thinking before a long detour through the earlier work, and partly to begin to complicate the idea I have so far complacently entertained, of 'Lyotard' as a substantial and unifying ground for the dispersion of texts bearing his signature.

The text in which this argument appears, 'Le Tombeau de l'intellectuel' [The Intellectual's Tomb] (TI, 11-22), was written for the newspaper *Le Monde* in the summer of 1983, in response to a disgruntled Socialist government's call for some support from those it had counted on as its 'intellectuals'. Lyotard begins by pointing out that in view of the Government spokesman's call for 'concrete implications' on social and economic matters, it would seem that the addressees of that call were not in fact 'the intellectuals' at all, but rather 'experts' with specific social, economic, cultural and administrative competences and responsibilities. An 'intellectual' is something quite different, namely someone who identifies and identifies with a collective subject given a universal or potentially universal value (humanity, the nation, the proletariat, etc.), who analyses a situation in terms of that subject and prescribes what should be done for it to flourish, accomplish its destiny, or at least proceed towards some such accomplishment. In Lyotard's view, this is not at all the position of the experts who might answer the call to debate: their role is not to embody any universal or potentially universal subject, but simply to achieve the best possible *performance* in their field – performance being judged in terms of an input/output ratio, the highest output for the lowest input defining success. The expert accepts the constitution of his or her field and attempts to succeed in these terms within it. By contrast with this, the identification of a subject with a universal vocation would lead to a questioning of the limits of constituted fields and notably ask questions about the nature of performativity as a mode of legitimation. This distinction between intellectual and expert also holds for Lyotard in the field of culture: a presupposition informing cultural activity is that the addressee ('the public') is lacking in knowledge, or taste, or sensitivity, or means to self-expression, and needs to be educated. Cultural responsibility is thus still in principle measured in terms of performativity, of public response to the activity in question. However 'good' the play, painting, music, it is a cultural failure if the public stays away.

So we have intellectuals on the one hand and experts on the other. Lyotard now introduces a third group: artists, writers, philosophers, he says, have quite different responsibilities (insofar as they are painting, writing, philosophizing): they are responsible to the questions: what is painting? what is writing? what is thought? and *only* to those questions. *As* artists, writers, philosophers, they are unmoved by the reproach that what they do is unintelligible to most people, and they are unmoved by it insofar as they have no pre-given addressee called, for example, 'the public' (they do not in fact know to whom their work is addressed). Further, they are engaged in an activity which constitutively questions accepted criteria of judgement and therefore of genres, disciplines, materials, and so on. They are not, insofar as they are artists, writers and philosophers, trying to cultivate and educate, and therefore (quite rightly according to Lyotard) find unacceptable any demand that they subordinate their experimentation to cultural purposes. Clearly, too, their activity has nothing to do with the identification and progress of a collective subject with a pretension to universalisation.

These three functions are, then, heterogeneous with respect to one another. This heterogeneity is not reduced by the fact that two or more of them might be carried out by the same 'person' (Lyotard cites André Malraux as an example). And further, this very location of a person as a possible locus for one or more of these functions suggests a fourth function, question and responsibility, namely that of 'citizen', which is again irreducible to the others: what is at stake in the function of the citizen is, roughly, the question of what the best organisation of the social might be. Nor does the acceptance of the responsibilities of intellectual, expert or 'creator' (or better, 'experimenter', which avoids the Christian overtones of 'creator') give any particular privilege in the role of citizen: nothing suggests that criteria of performativity, creativity or universality necessarily help to pose and answer questions affecting the particular citizen of a given country at a given time.

The confusion in the French government's request, then, stems from a failure to respect this sort of heterogeneity. Put differently, the intellectual could only function without obfuscation from the pont of view of the universal, dominating and hierarchizing the various responsibilities within a totalising system, or within a common teleology (for example, emancipation of the proletariat for Marxism, or universal education for Enlightenment thought). According to Lyotard (and this is something like 'the postmodern condition'), no such totalising unity is available (not, at least, to late twentieth-century thought): the signs which were to legitimate the idea of the emancipated proletariat (i.e. international solidarity of the workers) are fewer and farther between than ever, and any ideal of universal emancipation through education is nowadays apparently strictly subordinated to the production of experts and thereby to the improvement of performativity. Lyotard suggests that it is no longer possible to identify a universal subject-victim with which to identify, and that recent attempts to do so by intellectuals such as Sartre, Chomsky, Foucault and Negri show the difficulty and danger of attempting such

---

The inclusion of Foucault in this list can seem surprising, because of the manifest similarities between Lyotard's arguments here and Foucault's notion or dream of the 'specific intellectual':

'In general, I think that intellectuals – if this category exists or if it ought still to exist, which is not certain and perhaps not even desirable – are renouncing their old prophetic function

And in saying that I'm thinking not only of their pretension of saying what is going to happen but also of the legislative function to which they have aspired for so long: 'Here is what has to be done, here's what's good, follow me. In the confusion you're all in, here's the fixed point, it's where I am.' The Greek sage, the Jewish prophet and the Roman legislator are still models which haunt those who nowadays make speaking and writing their profession. I have a dream of an intellectual who destroys self-evidences and universalities, who locates and points out in the inertias and constraints of the present the weak points, the openings, the lines of stress; who constantly displaces himself, not knowing exactly where he'll be nor what he'll think tomorrow, because he is too attentive to the present' (Interview with Bernard-Henri Lévy, Le Nouvel Observateur, 12th March 1977; translation in The Oxford Literary Review, 4: 3 (1980), 3-14 (p. 14).) Lyotard would no doubt think that this account still gives too great a privilege to the intellectual, or fails to recognize that the description destroys its object: and that such a description certainly did not prevent Foucault from acting like an intellectual in the traditional sense.

identifications. It follows for Lyotard that the notion of the intellectual is no longer coherent. Injustice there is, victims there are, and there is indeed a responsibility to denounce injustice and attempt to help victims: but this can only legitimate local and essentially defensive interventions and cannot ground a narrative of emancipation or fulfilment for a universal subject.

The fact that Lyotard has welcomed this decline of universal ideas has led to accusations that he is simply endorsing techno-science and advanced capitalism. This does not of course follow from his suspicion of totalising ideas. But he is prepared to see in the obsession with totality a sort of paranoia, and to call it simply 'modernity' (starting it, for short-hand, with Descartes's fantasy of a subject 'master and possessor of nature'), and to see in its decline the beginning of possibilities of flexibility, tolerance and multiplicity. A new responsibility among the dispersion of heterogeneous responsibilities becomes that of *respecting that heterogeneity as such*, rather than, as with the intellectual, prescribing what is to be done to reclaim some lost unity and totality.

In Lyotard's case, this 'late' analysis cannot be taken as representative of his whole career: but it does seem possible to give some focus to that career by suggesting that the particular universalism with and against which most of his thought has taken place is that provided or promised

---

A sort of trouble or inhibition was invading him as reasons with which to argue went lacking and he lost the use of the dialectic. What was the purpose of refuting the other, the Marxist, if the logic of reality was not, as he believed, governed by contradiction? How could an argument prove that one was more 'realistic' than he? And in the name of what could this be done, if it were not certain that a subject, victim of a radical wrong, the proletariat, was waiting in history's unconscious for this refutation as a reparation due to it? And, finally, according to what logic could this be argued, if it was true that the contradiction between the Marxist sentence and others was not analysable or dialectisable as between true and false, but rather a difference or a *différend* to note, to describe, to meditate as lying between two equally possible genres, two perhaps equally legitimate genres? What other name could I oppose to that of the pro-letariat, what other logic to that of the dialectic? I did not know, or rather I began to imagine that it was precisely not a question of opposition. (PS, 15-16)

by Marxism. It is not at all the purpose of this book to provide an exhaustive history of Lyotard's relationship with Marxism (if only because this is not a book of history), though some decisive encounters with it will be documented and discussed. Suffice it to say for now that if it is true that much of Lyotard's most vital thinking is carried out in some sense against Marxism, his pretension has never been that of refuting Marxism, but of showing that it is *one* way of thinking (genre of discourse), and that its pretension to be *the* way of thinking (the way reality thinks itself) must be illegitimate. Various arguments around these themes will be presented in due course, but this general orientation may help to make some preliminary sense of the idea that Lyotard is fundamentally a political thinker, to the precise extent that he contests the totalisations fundamental to most ideas of politics.

It would be a gross mistake to assume that because Lyotard is engaged in questioning unities and totalities, he is necessarily promoting some form of individualism. If it is true that totality is a negatively marked term in his thought, the corresponding positive term is, rather, *singularity*. A singularity is not so much an individual as an *event*, and more than any other it is this notion of the event which I have taken as the guiding thread of this book. Perhaps the most coherent view of Lyotard's work as a whole is that it strives to respect the event in its singularity, and has experimented with various ways of achieving that respect. Such a stress on a singularity which is not an individual is itself not individual to Lyotard, of course, and he has even suggested that it might be taken as a guiding thread of what in the English-speaking countries is known as 'post-structuralism'. Many of the arguments I present in this book could usefully be juxtaposed with arguments in the work of Gilles Deleuze or Julia Kristeva or Michel Foucault; in general I have not made such juxtapositons, for fear of lengthening the book, and of suggesting identities where differences are important. I have, however, occasionally placed Lyotard's arguments in a variety of relationships with those of Derrida, without here attempting to determine that variety very closely – this is simply to suggest areas of work to be done.

Libidinal Economy

To suggest, as I did in the Introduction, that this will not be a book of history, in the sense that, if it is a story of Lyotard's work, it is just one story, another story, is already a strictly Lyotardian point, and places us in a problematic which dominates his earlier work, where representation is thematised as a problem of theatricality:

We are used to positing the following sequence: there is the fact, then the witnesses' account, i.e. a narrative activity transforming the fact into a narrative... the work proper to historical science will be to undo what is done by narration, to set out from the linguistic datum of the narrative to reach, by critical analysis (of document, text, sources), the fact that is the raw material of this production.

This way of posing the problem of history poses a theatrics: outside is the fact, external to the theatrical space; on the stage is the narrative unwinding its dramatics; hidden in the wings, in the flies, under the stage, in the auditorium, is the director [*metteur-en-scène*], the narrator, with all his machinery, the *fabbrica* of narration. The historian is supposed to undo all the machinery and machination, and restore what was excluded, having knocked down the walls of the theatre. And yet it is obvious that the historian is himself no more than another director, his narrative another product, his work another narration, even if all this is assigned the index *meta-*: meta-diegesis, meta-narration, meta-narrative. History which talks about history, to be sure, but whose claim to reach this reference to the thing itself, the fact, to establish it and restore it, is no less crazy, all in all rather crazier, than the power of literary fiction freely deployed in the hundreds of discourses from which is born the huge legend of, for example, the *Odyssey*. (DP, 180-81)

It will be useful to dwell a little on this use of the theatre as a paradigm for an analysis of representation. A theatre involves three limits or divisions or closures. First, the outside walls of the building itself. The 'real world' is outside, the theatre inside. Walking into a theatre means walking into a different sort of space: often enough the limit between the real world and that of the theatre is guarded by a place of passage, the foyer, where one prepares for theatricality by paying for a ticket, buying a programme, leaving one's coat, and so on. Within the theatre comes a second limit or division, separating the stage from the audience, marking off the place observed and the place from which it is observed. In the simplest and (for us) most familiar cases, this division is strongly accentuated by such features as a proscenium arch and an orchestra pit, and emphasised, during the performance, by a line of footlights. Conventions of various sorts govern what goes on on either side of the line: in principle the spectator sits still and silently in the dark, the actors move, talk and gesticulate in bright light.

A third essential limit separates the stage from the wings or back-stage. Again in principle, this space is invisible to the spectator and is the place of everything that might be called the theatrical *machinery:* not just of props, wind-machines and 'hands', but, structurally at least, of all the apparatus of direction, production and organisation which 'puts on' the play. The theatrical spectacle is brought forth, pro duced, from this invisi bility onto the stage. What is seen by the spectator on the stage depends on the complex support of this 'invisible' beyond.

This is a simplified description of the spatial structure of traditional 'realist' theatre. It is easy to imagine, and not difficult to verify, historically, all sorts of transgressions of these limits, invited and made possible by these limits. Selected parts of the 'back-stage' become visible to the audience, or the neat separation between audience and stage, spectator and actor, becomes more or less confused, more or less durably. Transgressing the limit between the theatre as a whole and the 'real world' outside is harder to imagine and achieve, and more disturbing to experience: and will be the whole problem.

It is impossible to limit representation to what goes on on the stage. Neither spectator nor machinery is simply a part of the 'real world' placed in connection with the stage: the *whole* of the space delimited by our first limits (the theatre-walls) is 'theatrical space', distinct from the space it places outside. Borrowing a term from the French psychoanalyst Serge Leclaire (who uses it to describe the analyst's consulting room), Lyotard describes this complex space as 'déréel', disreal, dereal. The spectator is situated in this space by its specific coordinates.

Lyotard's concern is not in general with the theatre as such (or rarely so: see discussions of Artaud and Brecht in 'La dent, la paume' (DP, 95-104); see too, on film, 'L'Acinema' (DP, 53-69)), but with a general structure of which the theatre, described in this way, is seen as exemplary. For example he links this structure to that at work in representational painting: the first limit (the theatre walls) corresponds to the place of the painting (museum, gallery, art-book), within which you are placed as a viewer of the painting, just as previously the theatre placed you as spectator of the stage. In the case of much post-Renaissance painting, this position is strongly assigned by the perspectival system of the *costruzione leggitima,* which assigns a 'right place' from which to view the painting, just as the painted backdrop in a theatre can assign an ideal place (that of the Prince) for the spectator, or, more democratically, the arrangement of the seats can make the spectator feel that the scene is organised for

I was also happy in the auditorium itself; since I had found out that – contrary to the representation with which my childish imaginings had for so long provided me – there was only one stage for everybody, I had thought that one must be prevented from seeing clearly by the other spectators, as one is in the middle of a crowd; but now I realised that, on the contrary, thanks to an arrangement which is like the symbol of all perception, each one feels himself to be the centre of the theatre. (Proust, *A la recherche du temps perdu,* 3 vols (Paris: Gallimard, 1954), I, pp. 446-7)

him or her alone. The second limit is the frame (like a proscenium arch), within which the picture gains depth, recedes from its painted surface into a 'scene' representing a 'real' scene. This visibility of the scene again depends on a supporting invisibility, which corresponds to the machinery of the theatre: the canvas and the paint must themselves be in in a sense invisible if the represented scene is to be visible – the canvas for example has a *back* which must be forgotten for the scene to gain its depth. But this invisibility also includes all the geometrically calculated marks which allow the construction of the perspective, and 'technique' in general: as Lyotard puts it, 'All that effaces and effaces itself, occults and occults itself at the same time' (DP, 266).

This model is not proposed simply with a view to an understanding and eventual critique of a certain 'realism' in the arts: it is emphatically not just a call for more honesty in exhibiting what other circles at the same time were calling, unfortunately, 'the materiality of the signifier'. Lyotard thinks he can do more with this set-up or *dispositif,* and notably extend it to the organisation of political space:

to see how this set-up relates to what is not painting, with what goes on in what is called 'reality', we should have to show how this set-up... communicates with another, the political set-up, in the proper sense of the term, i.e. the set-up which regulates a certain number of inscriptions within the Greek *polis* or the Italian city. Here again, in the set-up of the *politeia,* you have first of all the enclosure of a space... the city closes itself off as though into a circle... it is a community of men who close in on themselves as though in a circle, and... in the middle there is an empty space... 'de-reality'. So there is a first limit in the city... Movements to the inside will be filtered exactly as spectators are filtered at the entry to a play. They will be filtered according to a certain number of codes, the set of which defines what is known as citizenship. Within, there is this central space, which is found already in the communities of warriors in Homer, *es meson*, in the middle. When one speaks as a politician, one comes to speak in the middle, and when one speaks in the middle it is not the same thing as when one speaks around the middle. In the latter case, you say nothing, in certain respects. Who can speak in the middle? Those who bear arms. So here we have a re-filtering apparatus: women do not bear arms, and consequently they never speak in the middle, and thus they never say anything. Not everybody gets up on stage. And then there are also *processes of effacement:* in fact wealth, connections, pressure groups, rhetoric will be ways of getting to talk in the middle, scenographies, but they will be effaced and must be effaced for the political stage to be constituted. I believe that the modality of representational pictural inscription is profoundly isomorphic with the modality of political inscription, taken in the sense of the politeia. We have to say that the painter is like a prince and that the prince is like a painter, they are *effaced effacers,* they are people who work on the third limit and who efface themselves on the second limit, the stage; which doesn't mean that they cannot appear on it – it's possible to paint princes and even painters, but they can be on stage as models or orators, they can be in the audience as spectators or citizens, their power, strictly speaking, is effaced. The 3rd limit, the scenography, the *mise en scène,* the underside of politics, never appear: the machinery remains hidden. (DP, 268-9)

In describing the theatrical-representative set-up as it is formulated by Lyotard around 1972, I have deliberately omitted from the description, and excised from the quotations I have used, what for Lyotard is the central issue. The essay from which I have drawn most heavily (although there are many other sources) is entitled, 'De la peinture comme dispositif libidinal': not just a 'set-up' but a *libidinal* set-up. Returning to the long quotation I have just given, for example, I have failed to include two references to 'energy': the 'set-up' of representation is not simply formal (and the description of the theatre is therefore not simply a structural description), but a 'set-up which regulates the energetical transform-ations of pictural inscription' (DP, 268); and the outer limit to the city filters 'entries of energy to the inside, and particularly energy in the form of individuals (but not only that, also in the form of commodities, of language, or armed power)'.

What is the place of energy, libido and desire in these descriptions? For the Lyotard of the late 1960's and early 1970's, essential: for the Lyotard writing a new preface to *Des dispositifs pulsionnels* in 1979, 'metaphysical'. What is at stake in this investment and repudiation?

Theatricality as outlined above is described by Lyotard as fundamen-tally *religious.* What is represented on stage is an absence. The privilege of that absence (the various names of which Lyotard often distinguishes with an initial capital: Exteriority, Zero, Other, Signifier, to mark that the power given them *by their very position* is that of transcendence) is ensured by its being placed out of reach, *beyond* representation as posited *within* representation. By this transcendence, theatricality enforces its own closure, through the entirely negative excellence it confers on what it situates outside itself. Representation is an enclosure built on the

Theatre places us right at the heart of what is religious-political: in the question of absence, in negativity, in nihilism, as Nietzsche would say, and therefore in the question of power. A theory of theatrical *signs*, a practice (dramaturgy, production, interpretation, architecture) of theatrical *signs* rest on an acceptance of the nihilism inherent to representation, and they even reinforce it. For the sign is, as Peirce said, something which replaces something else for someone. Hide-show: theatricality. Now the modernity of the end of this century consists in the fact that there is nothing to replace, no standing-in-for is legitimate, or else they all are; replacement, and consequently meaning, is itself simply a substitute for displacement. (DP, 95)

strength of an exclusion; it is a 'mise en extériorité à l'intérieur', a placing outside which takes place inside (which constitutes the inside). Whatever name is given to the absence just positioned, it is theological *by virtue of that very position.*

Lyotard's first aim is simply to account for this theatrical-representational set-up (which he would describe as extending from Plato to Lacan, and which it is not difficult for us to link to Heidegger's 'onto-theology' or Derrida's 'metaphysics of presence', although the precise nature of those links is difficult to specify). To do this he needs to discover or posit something *prior* to that set-up and, in a sense, *external* to it, though in a type of externality which will not simply reduplicate the *mise en extériorité à l'intérieur.* If it is possible to describe in this way the whole set-up, with all its implications (and notably the implication of the subject, for in this description a subject is the spectator positioned by the theatre

Supposed spectators, because the notion of such a person or function is itself contemporaneous with the predominace of representation in social life, and notably with what the modern Western world calls politics. The subject is a product of the representational set-up and disappears with it. (DP, 103)

rather than the creator of the theatre) then it can reasonably be claimed that that set-up is no longer dominant or necessary or constraining: as Lyotard himself suggests in an essay on Marx, the explanation will aim to *destroy* its referent (DMF, 88-9). In short, Lyotard needs a system which it is difficult to describe as truer or more *adequate* (insofar as these notions presuppose the representation which is in question), but which might be said to be more *powerful:* and he thinks he can find one by thinking about force or power as such, in the form of energy or libido. Nietzsche is a constant underlying reference here, though only quite rarely an explicit one (but see for example 'Notes sur le retour et le capital', DP, 304-19), but Marx and Freud, the other two 'masters of suspicion' in Paul Ricoeur's phrase, are much more commonly invoked, and specifically the latter. For the Lyotard of this period, a certain Freud is the place where force or energy as libido can be seen struggling with the theatre of representation, but also accounting for its constitution. This does not mean that Lyotard pits Freud *against* representation in any simple sense, but that he reads within Freud an ambiguity in the concept of desire which seems to provide the material with which to account for and exceed theatricality and representation:

In Freud himself there is a profound and not merely circumstantial hesitation (it is probably even of decisive importance) as to the position and function of the term desire. There are two poles: desire-*Wunsch*, or desire-wish, which implies a negativity, which implies a dynamics, which implies a teleology, a dynamics with an end, which implies object, absence, lost object, and which also implies accomplishment, something like a fulfilment of the wish. All of which forms a set-up implying the consideration of meaning in desire. The other pole of the category of desire in Freud is desire-libido, desire-process, primary process. (DP, 238)

But as a passage from an almost exactly contemporary essay makes clear, it is the second of these two poles which accounts for the first, although according to Lyotard Freud tends to *reduce* the implications of the second by his recourse to a version of the doctrine of representation:

So long as Freud considers desire-force from a *mechanical* point of view (as in the *Project [for a Scientific Psychology],* in Chapter VII of *The Interpretation of Dreams,* and even in *Beyond the Pleasure Principle),* he can *reconcile* this concept of force with that of the wish, of desire seeking fulfilment. This reconciliation is performed by the theory of the dream, of the phantasy (daydream), of *representation.* This theory can be stated in a few words: the *quanta* of energy (desire as *force*) which cannot be *discharged* in a specific action relative to reality, have themselves *represented* on a *stage* [scène] opened 'inside' the psychical apparatus (or the subject?) – and opened by that impossibility, by that very lack. (DP, 136-7)

This seems to give an account of the representational set-up in terms of something more powerful than it. We should now take a little time to specify something of the nature of libido, desire-force, primary process as formulated by Freud. Lyotard draws most heavily for this on the metapsychological paper called simply 'The Unconscious' (1915), on certain parts of *The Interpretation of Dreams* (1900), and on *Beyond the Pleasure Principle* (1920), arguably Freud's most 'philosophical' writing.

In section V of the paper on the unconscious, Freud provides the following description:

The nucleus of the *Ucs.* [unconscious] consists of instinctual representatives which seek to discharge their cathexis; that is to say, it consists of wishful impulses. These instinctual impulses are co-ordinate with one another, exist side by side without being influenced by one another, and are exempt from mutual contradiction. . .

There are in this system no negation, no doubt, no degrees of certainty: all this is only introduced by the work of the censorship between the *Ucs.* and the *Pcs.* [preconscious]. Negation is a substitute, at a higher level, for repression. In the *Ucs.* there are only contents, cathected with greater or lesser strength.

The cathectic intensities [in the *Ucs.*] are much more mobile. By the process of *displacement* one idea may surrender to another its whole quota of cathexis; by the process of *condensation* it may appropriate the whole cathexis of several other ideas. I have proposed to regard these two processes as distinguishing marks of the so-called *primary psychical process.* In the system *Pcs.* the *secondary process* is dominant. When a primary process is allowed to take its course in connection with elements belonging to the system *Pcs.,* it appears 'comic' and excites laughter.

The processes of the system *Ucs.* are *timeless;* i.e. they are not ordered temporally, are not altered by the passage of time; they have no reference to time at all. Reference to time is bound up, once again, with the work of the system *Cs.*

The *Ucs.* processes pay just as little regard to reality. They are subject to the pleasure principle; their fate depends only on how strong they are and on whether they fulfil the demands of the pleasure-unpleasure regulation.

To sum up: *exemption from mutual contradiction, primary process* (mobility of cathexes), *timelessness, and replacement of external by psychical reality –* these are the characteristics which we may expect to find in processes belonging to the system *Ucs..* (PFL, 11, 190-91)

Freud sees the primary process, determined as 'mobility of cathexes' as *one* characteristic of the unconscious system: Lyotard tends to make such a mobility characteristic of the *whole* system, or to annex the other properties of the system to the description of the libido, dominated by a mobility itself 'simplified' to be essentially displacement. We should also note that Freud already has the 'wish' element (and therefore representation?) right at the heart of the primary process, insofar as the nucleus of the unconscious 'consists of wishful impulses': Lyotard will refuse the possibility of representation so 'early' in the description, summarising Freud on the libido as a force which knows nothing of the rules of negation, of implication, of alternative, of temporal succession, a force which works by means of a few elementary operations, in fact by means of *the single operation* of displacement (*Verschiebung* or *Entstellung),* of which all the others are, from the economical point of view, only particular cases. *Displacement=operation,* in Freud's topical metaphor. (DP, 138)

In this case, the 'correction' of the detail of Freud's essay draws on the later

---

This apparent 'brutality' of Lyotard's reading is entirely characteristic: 'I remain continually surprised by the surprise that my readings of works provoke in my readers. I can't seem to make myself feel guilty for any disrespect but I ought to feel that way out of incongruousness. I must be a bad reader, not sufficiently sensitive or "passive" in the greater sense of the word, too willful, "aggressive", not sufficiently espousing the supposed organic development of the other (?), in a rush to place it in the light of my own concerns. "Wild" if you wish (but my concerns are cultivated); "impious" certainly in the sense whereby Plato judges as impious the belief that the gods (here the works I read) are corruptible by petitions and gifts. . . I would say: one writes because one hears a request [*demande*] and in order to answer it; I read Kant or Adorno or Aristotle not in order to detect the request they themselves tried to answer by writing, but in order to hear what they are requesting from me while I write or so that I write. It seems to me that Diderot proceeded in this manner' (DI, 18-19). For a subtle argument against the effects of such 'brutality' in this specific case, see Philippe Lacoue-Labarthe, 'Note sur Freud et la représentation', Digraphe, 3 (1974), 70-81 [tr. 'Theatrum Analyticum', Glyph, 2 (1977), 122 43].

---

elaboration in *Beyond the Pleasure Principle,* which is essential to Lyotard if he is to avoid a simple vitalism, and thereby a theology of the form he is concerned to attack. For if desire in Freud is not simple, but divides into desire-as-wish and desire-as-force (libido), then the libido is *also* divided, though in more complicated fashion, by *Beyond the Pleasure Principle,* which introduces the mysterious notion of the 'death-drive' into psychoanalysis. Eros and Thanatos: again Lyotard 'corrects' Freud and says that these are not in fact two different drives, but two 'regimes' of force or energy:

In both cases, we have a process of affluxes of energy and the liquidation of these affluxes in what Freud calls a psychical apparatus, which is just as much the body, or even points on the body, elements, organs of the body, partial organs. And in both cases, Eros and death drive (still on the side of desire-libido, then), we are dealing with a characteristic of this process which is non-linguistic but repetitive. When Freud speaks of repetition, which is repetition just as much in the case of Eros as in the case of the *Todestrieb,* in both cases you have repetition, but it isn't repeated according to the same regime, and this category of repetition which is introduced at this moment is in 'contradiction', if the word means anything, with the category of finality which is implied in the *Wunsch.* (DP, 238-9: the syntactic incoherence of the last sentence can perhaps be attributed to the fact that the text is a transcription of a talk)

Let us accept for the moment that Lyotard has succeeded in locating some force prior to representation: the libido appears to work according to a different principle, and will itself escape theatricalisation in that it is split between Eros and Death. How then does this force allow Lyotard to account for the theatrical set-up? More simply, how is the voluminous space of the theatre created from what Lyotard would see as an essential *flatness* of the libido? In *Economie libidinale,* he attempts a passably

Open the supposed body and spread out all its surfaces: not only the skin with each of its folds, wrinkles, scars, with its great velvety planes, and contiguous with it the scalp and its mane of hair, the tender pubic fur, nipples, nails, transparent hard skin under the heel, the light frills of the eyelids, set with lashes — but open and spread, make explicit the *labia majora*, the *labia minora* with their blue network bathed in mucus, dilate the diaphragm of the anal sphincter, longitudinally cut and flatten out the black conduit of the rectum, then the colon, then the caecum, now a ribbon with its surface all striated and polluted with shit, with your dressmaker's scissors opening the leg of an old pair of trousers, go on, bring to light the supposed inside of the small intestine, the jejunum, the ileon, the duodenum, or else, at the other end, undo the mouth at its corners, pull up the tongue to its distant root and split it, spread the bat's-wings of the palate and its damp basements, open the tracheia and make of it the skeleton of a boat under construction; armed with scalpels and the finest tweezers, dismantle and lay out the bundles and bodies of the encephalum; and then the whole network of veins and arteries intact on an immense mattress, and the lymphatic network, and the fine bony pieces of the wrist, the ankle, take them apart and put them end to end with all the layers of nerve tissue wrapping aqueous humour and the cavernous body of the penis, and extract the great muscles, the great dorsal nets, spread them like smooth sleeping dolphins. (EL, 9)

parodic 'deduction of the voluminous body', with and against Freud's famous account of the child's *fort-da* game with the cotton reel in *Beyond the Pleasure Principle.* This 'deduction' begins from a particular presen-

The child had a wooden reel with a piece of string tied round it. It never occurred to him to pull it along the floor behind him, for instance, and play at its being a carriage. What he did was to hold the reel by the string and very skilfully throw it over the edge of his curtained cot, so that it disappeared into it, at the same time uttering his expressive 'o-o-o-o'. He then pulled the reel out of the cot again by the string and hailed its reappearance with a joyful *da'* ['there']. This, then, was the complete game – disappearance and return. As a rule one only witnessed its first act, which was repeated untiringly as a game in itself, though there is no doubt that the greater pleasure attached to the second act. (PFL, 11, 284)

tation of what Freud (elsewhere, earlier (see for example PFL, 7, 109)) calls the child's 'polymorphous perversity':

The so-called perverse (really simply diverse) polymorphousness of the child is in endless displacement on a surface without holes. There are no holes, but invaginations of surfaces. This is why when we open, we merely affirm what is, a vast skin with crannies, where slits are not entries, wounds, gashes or breaches, but the same surface carrying on after a pocket-shaped detour, a front folded back almost against itself, as at Stalingrad. Diverse polymorphousness knows that there are no holes, no inside, no sanctuary to respect. That there is only skin. 'The child', that phantasy of the West, the child, i.e. desire, is energetical, economical, not representational. (EL, 31-2)

Freud derives theatricality from a loss and a concomitant suffering. For the perversely polymorphous child, there is, originally, no separation of itself and the mother (but no totality either), simply the libidinal continuity of mouth and breast, for example. According to Freud's account, the mother's absence creates a distress which the child's game with the cotton-reel seeks to master through repetition. As Lyotard points out, this explanation in fact begs the question it is supposed to answer: for the reel to represent the mother, and for the mother's absence to be perceived as such, Freud has to presuppose the child's perception of her *as* a mother, as a person or a unity: 'the possibility of pain through lack, of absence, even, exists only because it has first been supposed that there was the presence of a mother, of *someone'* (EL, 33). But the child perceiving its mother could only perceive her as a person if that child were itself already 'someone' to 'have' such a perception: in short, if the child were *already* a subject and therefore no longer the 'polymorphous diversity' it is supposed to be in the first description. The 'theatre' constituted in the *fort-da* game is simply the 'external' repeat of the 'internal' theatre

Our question is: what suffers in pain? Freud's reply is: the child, therefore a subject already constituted, formed over against, symmetrically with the mother-object, so there is already the specular wall between them, already the side of the auditorium and the side of the stage; and the theatre the child makes with the edge of his bed as footlights and the string attached to the reel as curtain and scenography regulating entries and exits, this prosthesis-theatre is of the same type as that which was already hollowed out in him, it is the 'external' replica of the hollow volume in which the two poles of his own body and that of his mother, theatrical counterparts, non-existent poles, capture, hold in their field and dominate all the events of the libidinal band. Pain as caesura, fissure, split and unplugging only hurts a unitary totality. In conceiving of pain as the motor of theatricality, Freud gives it the metaphysical consistency of the nega-tive, he is thus victim of that theatricality. . . If one wishes to explain the birth of the theatre, one must not seek its secret in the pain of a loss, for there is loss only for a memory, and as so-called polymorphous perversity is acephalic, loss is for it an occasion for enjoying/suffering, that's all. (EL, 33-4)

of subjectivity, which Freud presupposes as a given. The intense libidinal *events* of contacts between mother and child become merely the *signs* of a nostalgia for a lost unity. Lyotard's own account, which attempts to avoid the question-begging located in Freud's, is quite brief and, for pre-cise internal reasons, frustrating. Further, if it seems indeed to avoid the *petitio principii* of Freud, it seems to do so at the cost of generating a vicious circle. To present this account, we must return to the slightly earlier account of the 'libidinal band' itself. This description is best seen as an imagination or fiction, insofar as on its own terms in cannot pretend to be a description of a *reality* (for such a description would have to be a representation, and therefore still presuppose the theatre). Lyotard has already asserted that the *intensity* of libidinal energy is lessened by con-ceptuality, which is already the theatre, with its exclusions, its identity-principle, its law of the excluded middle: 'either this, or that. Not both. The bar of disjunction. Any concept thus goes along with negation, with placing in exteriority' (EL, 23). The fiction of the libidinal band begins with this 'bar of disjunction':

You take this bar which separates the this and the not-this. I.e. any segment at all. You place it in a neutral space, let's say a three-dimensional space to help the very poor intuition of the imagination. You give it a movement of rotation around a point belonging to this segment, a movement which presents the follow-ing three properties: the rotation takes place along all axes without exclusion; the central point is itself displaced along the segment in aleatory fashion, and finally it is also displaced in the neutral space we have supposed. Thus a surface is engendered, a surface which is none other than the labyrinthine libidinal band we have been talking about: this surface always has as its width the length of the segment, etc. But the important thing is not to describe the properties of the band. (EL, 24)

And indeed it is probably fruitless to wonder about the geometry of the description, and specifically about the possibility of the 'neutral space' demanded. What matters to Lyotard is that in this movement the bar of disjunction fails to disjoin, because of the *speed* of its rotation, which is, in this imagination, the mark of its intensity: in this rotation, intensity is always both this *and* not this (pleasure and pain, for example, which in view of the later work would lead me to suggest that this is already a description of the sublime), thus defying conceptual description or even confident identification. Any such identification is frustrated on the one hand by this quasi-*spatial* confusion of regions (pleasure and pain are 'in the same place'), and on the other hand by a second 'property' of the rotating bar, which has to do with its *temporality:* for this temporality is not continuous and linear, but singular and evanescent. Any 'point' or 'region' of the libidinal band is thus not only spatially indescribable, but has disappeared by the time the language that would describe it attempts that description. (And in view of the later work I would say that this is an approach to what will there be called simply 'presentation', itself to be linked with the sublime, as we shall see). These two properties (which would suggest that Lyotard is, ultimately, attempting no less than a deduction of space and time) imply that the 'imagination' of this process should not be thought of in terms of 'production'. Any such 'productive' imagination (and Deleuze and Guattari's *Anti-Oedipus* is certainly the object of this reproach) would stand in need of correction,

because it takes as its model an industrial machine, for example a wire-drawing machine or a rolling-mill, and because with this model it implies the category of an accumulation, a stock-piling, a material memory and, what comes to the same thing, a diachrony. For example, you can, I think, modify incessantly and randomly the norms of extrusion or rolling, and you will indeed obtain bars or wires with necessarily variable properties. The fact remains that they *remain,* that the marks of the variations are inscribed on these objects and transform them into monuments of a past activity, into means of determining an activity to come, they thus open the space of an 'upstream' and 'downstream' in production, a cumulative diachronic time, a capitalising history. And beware, because with the instrument and the machine you are already right in the zero [of negativity]. Whereas because the whirls of the disjunctive segment in its libidinal journey are singular, they do not make up a memory, because the segment is only ever where it is in an ungraspable time or *tense,* and because what has been journeyed 'previously' thus does not exist: acephalia, time of the unconscious. (EL, 25-6)

Now although this has been imagined on the basis of the 'bar of disjunction', it also has to be thought of as *prior* to disjunction, insofar as disjunction (inside/outside, stage/audience, subject/object) is precisely what is to be accounted for. On the basis of the imagined libidinal band, Lyotard now does this as follows:

The whirling bar slows down, the mad, aleatory movement which engenders the libidinal band brakes sufficiently for the this and the not-this (which its high speed had confused at every point in the field) now to be distinct, now the this, now the not-this, here it is, now it's gone, *fort, da.* The bar has become a frontier, not to be crossed on pain of confusion, sin against the concept, transgression, stupidity, madness, primitive thought. The bar becomes an edge, the edge of a stage: over there the not-this, here the this. End of dissimulation, beginning of value, and of ambivalence. For to go from the not-this to the this, now it will be necessary to pay: it will cost a great deal to have the not-this over there. (EL, 34-5)

We may well wonder why. Why does the bar slow down, cool off, lose intensity? This is the point of frustration mentioned above. We don't know, says Lyotard, apparently unhelpfully. Or rather, that question *itself* begs the question, insofar as such a question is only possible *because* the bar has already slowed down. 'Why?' is already in the grip of the theatre, the nostalgic search for the absent cause, the zero. And so, he would no doubt add, is any frustration caused by this evasion of the question. From within the theatre, libidinal economy will inevitably look like irrationality and inconsistency: and perhaps too this would defuse the possible objection that the derivation of the disjunctive bar from the libidinal band depends on a vicious circle, insofar as the libidinal band has itself been derived from the disjunctive bar. Thus Lyotard is able to say that Freud's begging of the question is a formal defect which in itself has no importance for 'people like us' (i.e. libidinal economists), whose discourse has no pretension to be consistent, and is the grounds for objection to Freud only insofar as Freud's writing *does* have that pretension.

Such an answer to the problem of the vicious circle would, however, be glib and unsatisfactory: for at this point at least *Economie libidinale* is trying to be as consistent as possible, drawn into being so precisely by the 'formal defect' it finds in Freud. The problem posed by the fiction of the libidinal band is that of its status as fiction. Freud himself used the term 'theoretical fiction' in his account of the primary process,

When I described one of the psychical processes occurring in the mental apparatus as the 'primary' one, what I had in mind was not merely considerations of relative importance and efficiency; I intended also to choose a name which would give an indication of its chronological priority. It is true that, so far as we know, no psychical apparatus exists which possesses a primary process only and that such an apparatus is to that extent a theoretical fiction. But this much is a fact: the primary processes are present in the mental apparatus from the first, while it is only in the course of life that the secondary processes unfold, and come to inhibit and overlay the primary ones. (PFL, 4, 763) precisely because it is by definition never observable as such. And what he elsewhere refers to famously as *ein andere Schauplatz*, another scene, is precisely not a scene or stage at all (or can be described as such only at the cost of throwing away all that might be troublesome for a philosophy of the subject in the notion of the unconscious), can never be

A suspicion can be raised here as to whether *any* account of the unconscious can in fact trouble a philosophy of the subject: 'For no doubt unconscious desire is not (re)presented to consciousness, but it is presented to the unconscious, (re)presented ("accomplished", "fulfilled") in the unconscious. And this is already sufficient to substantify the unconscious, to institute it as a subject: a subject posing itself in and through representation, a subject making sure of itself in and through thought — in short, *con-scientia*' (Mikkel Borch-Jakobsen, *Le Sujet freudien* (Paris: Aubier-Flammarion, 1982), p. 12). I must leave it to the reader to decide to what extent this brilliantly-argued book would refute the claims of a work such as *Economie libidinale*.

seen on any stage of representation by any subject or subjective agency scated in the auditorium. The primary processes are 'known' through their effects in the secondary sphere. Similarly, Lyotard cannot present the postulated 'libidinal band' for inspection, but must describe it analogically in terms of effects in the sphere of the concept. Despite a later declaration in the unpublished section of *Au juste,* Lyotard cannot really claim to write *Economie libidinale* 'on the side of the primary process' (AJ, 193: Lyotard himself modalises the claim), but on the side (which is not really a side) of its effects on thought, and can mime in his writing not the pure displacement of energy characteristic of the primary process, but the humorous or scandalous effects of that displacement on the secondary sphere. This also implies that we are not in fact dealing with an *opposition* of primary and secondary, but of a complex relationship of imbrication and dissimulation, a paradoxical version of 'the same thing':

there is no notable difference between a libidinal formation and a discursive formation, insofar as they are both formations, *Gestaltungen.* A libidinal *set-up,* considered, precisely, as a stabilisation and even a stasis or group of energetical stases is, examined formally, a structure. Conversely, what is essential to a structure, when it is approached in economic terms, is that its fixity or consistency, which allow spatio-temporal maintenance of identical denominations between a this and a not-this, work on the movement of the drives as would dams, sluices and canalisations. So one can step twice, and even innumerable times, into the same river, if the river is located by its slope, its banks, its direction, its flow, as it is by any reasonable and discriminating mind-body; but one never steps twice

into the same river, quite simply because *there is no river* – that's what is said
by the madman, lover of singularities, be his name Proust, Sterne, Pascal,
Nietzsche, Joyce, madman determined to judge a given swim as *unexchangeable*
for any other, *in spite* of its generic name, a madman ready to want a proper
name, a divine name, for each intensity, and thus to die with each of them, to
lose even his memory (river-bed and course), and certainly his own identity. (EL,
36-7)

Lyotard knows that he and his writing are irremediably, always already,
situated in discourse, in the realm of the concept, in the secondary sphere:
there can be no pure 'escape' into a 'beyond' of representation: energy
as such cannot be presented in person. It does not of course follow that
all ways of negotiating this situation are equivalent.

It may be wondered why it is important for desire-libido to be split according to Eros on the one hand and the death-drive on the other. Insofar as
Eros already works by repetition, is it not *already* contesting representation? But if the libido were *only* Eros, then it could certainly be claimed
that it worked *prior* to the theatre and representation, but it could also
be argued that it worked precisely *in the service* of the theatre and representation, that Eros was simply the name for the power that built the
theatre in the first place – or perhaps that the repetition of Eros was
something of a *répétition* in the French sense of rehearsal, which would
introduce a sort of secondary finality, that of ensuring the good working
of the machinery of representation. Eros in any case, to the extent that
it is subordinate to the pleasure-principle, seeks organisation and order
and constancy: whereas the death drive disrupts constancy and tends
towards the unsettling of unity – towards zero or the inanimate, says
Freud: towards infinity just as well, corrects Lyotard (or towards a reference point other than that of the apparatus in question) (DP, 239).
    It will be said that none of this is very disturbing for representation,
insofar as Freud and Lyotard are both happily providing representations
of the libido which is supposed to disrupt representation. Maybe so in
the case of Freud, Lyotard would reply, to the extent that he is writing a
theory. But we have already seen Freud's use of the term 'theoretical
fiction'; he also presents *Beyond the Pleasure Principle* as an exercise in
'speculation', with effects to which we shall return, and in the paper on
the unconscious, he asserts of the unconscious processes that 'in themselves they cannot be cognized' (PFL, 11, 192). This implies that their
(re)presentation in language is affected in various ways. Lyotard says of
the death drive, or of libido under the 'regime' of zero or infinite:

we call this the 'non-regime' because we speak, because in speaking we are in the system of discourse which is also a regulated system, and because, consequently, we can speak of the other regime (which is not regulated) only negatively. Of the energy which circulates according to this other regime, we can say only that it is disruptive [détraquante], it is disordered, deconstructing, it is dead (this is what Freud says). We can say only negative things about it, but this is because we are in a place with respect to which this regulation on the zero or infinity of the drive can appear only as deregulation. (DP, 240)

Lyotard wants to say that this force of desire is *positive* and *affirmative*, and that it is the same force whether under the regime of Eros (leading to order) or the 'regime' of Thanatos, leading to disorder. This positivity, knowing no negation, is inaccessible as such to language, which depends, constitutively, on negativity: in general, it is unrepresentable *except* insofar as it seems to disrupt the ordered theatre of representation. This can easily make the libido seem like a negative, critical force, *in opposition* to theatre and representation: Lyotard's writing does not always avoid giving this impression, even after the explicit rejection of critique in *Economie libidinale*. But in the logic of desire as presented so far, no such oppositional model can be sustained – if there is an energetical continuity of Eros and Thanatos, and a further continuity between desire as libido and desire as *Wunsch,* then there can be no *opposition* between, at the extreme ends of this continuity, the death-drive and the theatre. Or, to put it another way, if the theatre is in fact a product of libidinal energy, then its apparent opposition to that energy is also part of the energy itself, one of its transformations. It would follow that Lyotard's own stress on the libido cannot be seen as in opposition to theatricality and representation (and thereby to theory), despite the angry denunciations in some of this writing: if the aim is indeed that of destroying theory and theatricality, that destruction will not be achieved by operations of critique or head-on attack, but rather by dissolving the set-up of the theatre in a more general description of its 'libidinal economy', precisely. The theatre in this description becomes no more than a local effect of the modifications or metamorphoses of the libido, or, in the language of *Economie libidinale,* a particular configuration of the 'libidinal band'. Despite some appearances, Lyotard's aim cannot be that of celebrating pure energy or libido *against* representation and theory, but that of describing representation and theory as *themselves libidinal.* And although Lyotard (and therefore our discussion) will remain for some time with this language of desire and libido and force, it is worth announcing immediately that the most rigorous effect of the language of libido is that it ends up by ruining the privilege it begins by giving to libido as the name of the force exceeding theatricality.

This insistence is necessary, because any more 'optimistic' claim would, by an apparent paradox, simply reinforce the very theatrical

> No more should one confuse the closure of representation, that sarcastic dis-covery, that false blinker-removing by thinkers who come and say: what is outside is really inside, there's no outside, the exteriority of the theatre is its interiority just as much – don't mix up this sad piece of news, this cacangelism which is only the converse of evangelism, this miserable announcement. . . don't go and confuse this crestfallen message and this representation of an entirely closed theatre with our moebian-labyrinthine film, single-sided patch-work of all the organs (inorganic and unorganised) which the libido can traverse. (EL, 12)

closure it is designed to destroy. We have noted that theatricality in Lyotard's sense gives rise to transcendence: what is re-presented on stage is an absence, something lost, an object of desire in the sense of *Wunsch,* and thereby of nostalgia. The danger of Lyotard's project in *Economie libidinale* and the attendant writing is evidently that of making the libidinal band or the primary process or the death-drive into an object of desire in the sense of *Wunsch,* of making the polymorphous diversity of the child an object of nostalgia, of making *it* into another Great Zero, an absence to be re-presented on the stage of thought by the writing of *Economie libidinale.* Not all of Lyotard's writing takes as many precau-tions to avoid this impression as would have been necessary: but as we have just seen, the logic of that writing disallows such a reading, or at least defers it. For the *effects* of the libidinal band are, precisely, effects

> When we say 'effects', these are not effects of causes. It is not a matter of attributing the responsability for the effect to the cause, of saying to oneself, 'if such and such a discourse, such a face, such a piece of music produce such and such effects, this is because. . .'. It would, precisely, be a matter of not analysing (not even by 'schizo-analysis'), in a discourse which will necessarily be one of knowledge, but rather to refine ourselves sufficiently, to make ourse-lves into bodies anonymous and conductive enough not to arrest the effects, to lead them to new metamorphoses, to wear out their metamorphic force, the force of effects traversing us. (EL, 306-7)
>
> It would also be necessary to devote a systematic analysis to this word 'effect' which is so often – and this is not insignificant – used these days, and to the new concept it marks in a still somewhat indecisive fashion. Its occurrence is increasing precisely because of this active indetermination. . . This 'new' concept of effect borrows its features both from the opposition cause/effect and from the opposition essence/appearance (effect, reflexion) without

however being reducible to these oppositions. (Jacques Derrida, *Positions*
(Paris: Minuit, 1972), p. 90)

only in the sense which frustrates both representation and causality: the
libidinal band which is hypothesized or imagined only retrospectively
from the 'given' of the 'prétendu corps' or the law of non-contradiction
cannot be the object of a representation insofar as it is not an object at
all, and cannot be a cause (in any traditional sense) insofar as it escapes
the temporality constitutive of causality. The libidinal band is/was/will
be never present, and can therefore never be re-presented.

It is not Lyotard's purpose to deny the effects of a theatrical-represen-
tional type of thinking, but to suggest that it is one *dispositif* among
others, with no particular privilege among others (despite the excellence
it traditionally assigns itself): not something in opposition to libido and
primary process (though it would conceive of itself in such terms), but
a particular modification of libido or primary process. The most forcible
attempt to argue this is found in *Economie libidinale* itself:

Far from taking the great Zero to be the ontological motif, imposed on desire,
always to defer everything, re-present and simulate everything in an endless
referral, we, libidinal economists, affirm that this zero is itself a figure... we are
going to show not only that it is not necessary to pass through this zero in order
to follow the track of intensities on the [libidinal] labyrinth, but more still, that
the passage through the zero is itself a special libidinal track, that the position
of the Signifier or the Other is... *itself* a position of *jouissance*, that the 'rigour
of the law' gives more than one person a hard-on, and that we are not dealing
in the case of this Nothing with an ontological necessity, but with a religious and
therefore libidinal phantasy, which as such is quite acceptable, let's say so, were
it not, alas, terroristic and deontic. (EL, 13-14)

It is not, then, lack which creates desire, but a certain desire which produces a set-up dominated by lack.

As an example of what might be invoked against the theatrical thought
of representation, Lyotard invokes a *theatrics,* which he borrows for the
occasion from Pierre Klossowski's discussion of certain forms of popular
religion in the late Roman Empire. Here there is a paroxystic multiplica-
tion of gods and goddesses for every act and object of daily life, not
subordinating such acts and objects to a single principle or meaning or
cause (the great Zero), but naming them as intense *singularities,* 'sufficient to themselves in their self-assertion' (EL, 15). Such an assertion
does not take place according to the 'bad' model of theatre: this is not
an inside representing an outside (the Real, the Absent), but a generalised
confusion of inside and outside, of reality and representation. The walls

of the theatre are destroyed not by a denunciation of representation in terms of a superior 'reality' (which is always only constructed as an outside from 'within' representation, as absent, yet to come, always-already lost, and so on), but by a generalisation of a 'representation' which no longer re-presents anything other than itself (and is as such no longer strictly speaking a representation). Faced with this proliferation, the protest comes from St. Augustine, who demands a clear separation of appearance and essence, a re-building of the walls of theatre. Augustine

repeats the set-up by which the auditorium is ignored in favour of the stage, and the stage devoted to the representation of an Exteriority left at the doors of the theatre, and judged for its part to be non-theatrical once and for all. (EL, 16-17)

The relationship between the 'good' popular theatrics and the 'bad' theatre of representation cannot, again, be one of opposition. Bad theatre is not in fact to be *rejected* – for such a division into good and bad, such an opposition and the rejection that it implies are the very operations by which 'bad' theatrical space is instituted. The 'bad' theatre is to be *included* within the generalised theatrics of the force here named desire or libido. It follows that 'good' and 'bad' cannot be names for opposing elements or regions, but purely quantitative differences of intensity in the force of that libido. 'Libidinal economy' is not, or at least must try not to be the name of another zero from which bad theatre could be located and expelled – and this means that it cannot be a *critique:*

The representional chamber is an energetic set-up. Describe it and follow its functioning, that's someting to do. No need to perform the *critique* of metaphysics (or of political economy, which is the same thing) since critique assumes and endlessly recreates this very theatricality: rather *be inside and forget it,* that's the position of the death-drive. (EL, 11)

This poses redoutable problems for the writing of a book such as *Economie libidinale.* As we have stressed, the primary process, the libidinal band, the death drive, are not representable insofar as they exceed and precede the whole representational set-up. And insofar as *Economie libidinale* is concerned to talk of singularities (events), and insofar as language is the domain of generality, then it cannot deliver its objects as concepts without betraying them. But it is in the nature of those 'objects' not to be locatable *somewhere else,* in a different space from the theatrical space they construct and undermine: like the death-drive, they are only 'present' in an almost indiscernible co-presence with what they threaten. There is no question, says Lyotard, of simply disentangling good and bad and thereby reproducing the theatrical set-up, rather we should:

make ourselves refined enough in the place where we are to sense, in the crudeness of exchangeable signs, the unrepeatable singularities of the passage of cathexis, discriminating enough and... I'd say, out of provocation, *jesuitical* enough to grasp, *in* the general movement of pulling back and inscription onto the Zero of capital or the Signifier, the *this sides of* and the *beyonds* of this movement, the immobilities and agitations dragged and betrayed by this movement, to love inscription not because it reports and includes, not because it channels, but because it drifts. (EL, 29)

. . . a singular drift.

I've overused this word; it scarcely satisfies me. *Drift* designates too continuous a movement: rather undifferentiated, too homogeneous, it seems to move away without turbulence from a supposed origin, from a bank, still, from an edge with an indivisible line. (Jacques Derrida, 'Spéculer – sur "Freud"', in *La Carte postale de Socrate à Freud et au-delà* (Paris: Aubier-Flammarion, 1980), pp. 277-437 (p. 279))

We should write *Drifts*. But the title is already literary enough as it is.

Indeed it is not *one* bank that is left, but several together, not *one* current which drags and pushes, not *one Treiben* or *drift* [Eng.], but many pushes and tractions. No more is it an individual, nor even a collective of individuals which is *embarked*, but rather as in Bosch's *Ship*, a collection of madmen, each madman being an exaggerated part of a normal suppost [*suppôt*], libido invested in such and such a part of the body, blocked in such and such a set-up of desire, all these fragments placed side by side (the category of *neben!*) for a journey without aim, a collection of fragments never managing to unify themselves because it drifts with the ship and that drift, through the diversity of landscapes and times traversed, gives the advantage of the most intense resonance now to one madman-*Trieb*, now to another. Not a *corps morcelé*, since there have only ever been bits of body and there never will be a body, this wandering collection being the very affirmation of the non-body. Plurality, the collection of singularities, that's precisely what power, kapital, the law of value, personal identity, ID card, the University, responsibility, family and hospital repress and put down. (DMF, 8-9 [DW, 10])

This complex 'drift' marks the writing of *Economie libidinale* and calls for repeated comment in the book (which, to the extent that it can discuss its own drift, is not *purely* adrift). For example, at the beginning of the section entitled 'The desire named Marx', on which we shall spend some time, Lyotard starts by drawing from the 'destruction' of theatricality some of the implications for a reading of Marx:

We must not criticize Marx, and even if we do criticize him, understand that it is not a critique: we have already said and repeated that we don't give a damn for criticizing, since to criticize is to remain in the field of the thing criticized and in the dogmatic or even paranoid religion of knowledge. Marx's desire interests us, in as much as it informs the themes of the writings which are metamorphosed into the themes of social and political 'practices'. . . We do not interpret, we read, and we effectuate by writing. . . Nor do we want to correct Marx, re-read him or read him in the sense in which the little Althusserians want to make us 'read *Capital*': interpret it according to its 'truth'. We do not plan on being true, on giving the truth of Marx, we are wondering how it is with libido in Marx, and 'in Marx' means in his text and his interpretations, and principally his practical interpretations. We shall treat him, rather, as a 'work of art'. (EL, 118)

All of which follows clearly enough from the destruction of the theatre of representation, but is stated in a language which that destruction ought perhaps to have made impossible, or at least which it cannot fail to render difficult: whence, in the following paragraph, a reflexion on this type of declaration:

We almost felt ourselves obliged, you've just heard it, to make a sort of declaration of intention, slightly solemn, vaguely epistemological (as little as possible, recognise that fact), on the shores of this continent. No other continent would drag such declarations from us – declarations which are, what's more, rather stupid and certainly useless. We could say that it is out of wariness and feeling intimidated, warned as we are by a militant past to what extent laying your hands on Marx, even if it were to screw with him (especially then) is closely watched over by the paranoids who call themselves Marxist politicians and in general by all the Whites of the Left. (EL, 118)

It might seem that all of this is merely a prelude to the 'real' libidinal writing which would follow from the destruction of the theatre: this is not the case, although not all of *Economie libidinale* is written in quite the same tone as the passages just quoted. The point would be that in this type of parodic, *dandyesque* writing, the indiscernable force of the

---

Even if the dandy does not recognise himself in 'business men in whose eyes nature does not exist, except if it is useful to their business', this does not alter the fact that he affirms for his part the greatest contempt for all that in woman, in the countryside, in democracy and the people, in the shop, is suspect of referring to an *origin*. And in that, indifferent as he is to roots, he is a businessman, modern in the sense of capital, believing only in the circulation of intensities, no way preoccupied to 'find himself again in his being', as Hegel said of happiness, rather to lose himself in the strangest metamorphoses and the most perilous experiences. To lose himself, without giving anything, without giving himself: Jesuit without Jesus. (AE, 57).

libido is marked in the evasiveness – there can be no direct presentation of libido and death drive, no writing adequate to them. Throughout, *Economie libidinale* is written as closely as can be to theoretical argument, and it is this that allows me, up to a (limited) point, and still

> It is not true that the theoretical instance is purely and simply absent. It is, rather, very strongly diverted. It is infiltrated with something else. . . This book was written in scandalous fashion, and the scandal in it is that it is completely rhetorical, working entirely on the level of persuasion. (AJ, 12 [JG, 3-4])

somewhat parodically, to extract and restate theses here: but the infiltration of non-theoretical types of writing (obscenities, insults, bad-taste eroticism and so on) affects even what 'is' theoretical with marks of 'style'. This situation implies an acceptance of contradiction or at the very least a shameless duplicity. As one of the many comments on its own writing suggests, *Economie libidinale* cannot simply refuse the theoretical, and proclaim that it has moved 'beyond' into a new region called the libidinal (or whatever). Rather what it prescribes is 'that what one thinks be always assignable to a theoretical ensemble, to a system (semantic, formal, it matters little), and be the despair of such an assigning' (EL, 42).

The violence of this type of writing is obvious, and the book's reception suggests that it was largely successful in its scandalising aim: some more reasons for the scandal will appear in due course. Here we may simply note that the book in general is violent and in a sense advocates violence in thought, by the very celebration of intensity and force over theory and concept. This very 'Nietzschean' inspiration leaves it open to the same apprehension or misapprehension as Nietzsche's writing, and of this the book is well aware:

And we are plunged into the greatest anguish, for really, my dear sirs, radical-socialists of the concept, we are not simpletons, we are well aware of what profile can be seen on the horizon of thought as libido, the same scarecrow you get out of your pockets and wave above your fleshy ears every time an intensity goes past and we jump, crazy with joy and fear, into its whirl: the scarecrow of *fascism* – the same one you were waving in '68 in France, Germany, Italy. You don't have to be pushed very hard before you say it out loud: the idea-force is fascism. You'll always confuse *power [pouvoir]* and *potential [puissance]*, you'll always give the name of power-terror to the violence which threatens your power. (EL, 42-3)

And such accusations were indeed common in response to what *Economie libidinale* has to say about Marx.

In passing, you see the profound congruence that exists between this type of consideration of libido as process and what Marx calls force, labour force, as what underlies the whole system. In Marx it is this same energy which operates, but according to Eros, inasmuch as it too is subordinated to a constancy principle which within the framework of capitalism is the law of value, i.e. segmentation into units and the commutability of these units under an extremely simple category – equality of value (or quantities of energy, or quantities of work). (DP, 239)

We saw how the description of the theatre could be extended to questions of political representations or representational politics: so it is not surprising to find Lyotard seeking to extend libidinal analyses to such areas too. But this 'congruence' of Marx and Freud must be treated with care. Lyotard's relationship with Marxism is more complex and changing than that with Freud, and runs throughout his work. Not surprisingly, it is a relationship which varies considerably in intensity, and there is no sense in deciding that at one point Lyotard was 'a Marxist' and at another point stopped being one. Such judgements of inclusion and exclusion are eminently theatrical and 'erotic', and provide a dubious warmth of recognition at the cost of stifling thought. As we shall see later, *Le Différend* provides analyses of such mechanisms of inclusion and exclusion.

It is, however, undeniable that in this complex relationship, *Economie libidinale* marks something of a break, and this will detain us for a while – especially as much of what is advanced seems still quite relevant to the analysis of Marxism, in Britain at least. The section of *Economie libidinale* called 'The desire named Marx' is the most provocative of all: it led to the most violent reactions and lost Lyotard the most friends. It would be pointless to deplore the tone of this section of the book, as it would to idolize its provocations.

As we have seen, the parodic precautions which precede the section on Marx do not give rise to some pure (impossible) 'libidinal' writing, but to a libidinal reading, which treats Marx's text 'more like a work of art'. Lyotard first notes Marx's apparent inability to *complete,* unify, totalise his theoretical discourse: in the process of writing *Capital,* what was planned as a paragraph becomes a whole section; what was to have been a section becomes a whole chapter, and what should have been a chapter becomes a whole volume. (See too 'Un Marx non marxiste', DMF, 36-46, and specifically the table on p. 41.) There is what Lyotard calls a 'cancerization of theoretical discourse' (EL, 119), a perpetual running out of control of what was to have been a rational theoretical enterprise. Lyotard accounts for this by imagining a scenario in which Marx is 'a strange bisexual assemblage', simultaneously an old male theorist and an amorous young woman:

We are defending, dear comrades, the following thesis: little-girl Marx, offended by the perversity of the polymorphous body of capitalism, demands a great love-affair; the great attorney Karl Marx, delegated to the accusation of the perverts and the 'invention' of an acceptable lover (the proletariat), gets down to studying the dossier of the capitalist defendant. (EL, 119-20)

But it rapidly becomes clear that the attorney is as fascinated by the accused party as he is scandalized: and this fascination is the mark that the good unified body that he is supposed to derive dialectically from the perverse flows of capital cannot be so derived: 'The unification of Marx's body, which demands the putting-to-death of the polymorphous perversity of capital in the interests of the accomplishment of the desire for genital love, is not possible' (EL, 120). Just as Marx is unable to derive the whole (organic or inorganic) body of socialism (a whole body just as pre-capitalist forms are supposed to have been whole bodies), so he cannot unify his text into the 'artistic whole' he dreams of (letter to Engels of 31 July 1865, quoted EL, 120). The constant *deferral* of such a whole mimes a set-up of *jouissance*-as-delay which is none other than that of capitalism itself.

Why call such a delay *jouissance* rather than suffering? Is not the apparently interminable work of theory, undertaken in the difficult conditions of Marx's life, rather the price that has to be paid for eventual comprehesion, unity and reconciliation? Just as, in Marx's early writings at least, the proletariat must suffer like Christ for the redemption of humanity at large so, in such an objection, would Marx suffer as martyr witnessing and proclaiming that suffering.

But here, as in the case of Freud, what is wrong with such an objection is less the pathos it involves than a *petitio principii:* or the pathos is a result of begging the question. For the objection presupposes what is at stake – a body of capitalism to inflict suffering, a body of the proletariat to receive it, and a body of Marx to write it down.

And what if, precisely, it were this referential instance which were lacking for Marx's inspection, this body of Ratio, of the account to be rendered? What if what prolonged the research interminably were not, as 'psychoanalytic' or 'Nietzschean' triviality would not fail to say, the 'masochist' desire or 'bad conscience' of Karl Marx, but the vertigo of a terrible discovery (always hidden): that *there is nobody* to keep the accounts of suffering and *jouissance* and that that, too, is the dominance of money-capital? (EL, 123)

At this point in the argument Lyotard provides an important aside which should continue to defer the suspicion that 'desire' may become just another 'Great Zero'. For this would be the case, says Lyotard, if he were content to write a critique of such traces of 'ressentiment' as might be found in Marx, a critique which would *invert* values and proclaim the excellence of the movement of desire as against its fixation, of a precarious schizophrenic body as against the whole unified (in)organic body, of gratuity as against suffering-as-payment. Such a critique (of a type Lyotard thinks is still operating in the work of Deleuze and Guattari, and of Jean Baudrillard) retains a disjunctive (good/bad) model of thought,

Is it possible that any intensity is suffering only because we are religious, clerics of the Zero? Even saying that to oneself is perhaps a consolation.

What threatens us libidinal economists is building a new morality with this consolation, proclaiming and broadcasting that the libidinal band *is good*, that the circulation of affect *is joyful*, that anonymity and the incompossibility of figures *are great and free*, that all pain is reactionary and conceals the poison of a formation come from the great Zero. . . But it isn't an ethics, that or another, that we need. Perhaps we need an *ars vitae*, young man, but then one in which we should be the artists and not the propagators, the adventurers and not the theorists, the hypothesisers and not the censors. (EL, 20)

and carries on the work of exclusion which defines the theatre. Lyotard's analysis aims to be more complex; and just as the indiscernability of Eros and death-drive in Freud troubled any *simple* espousal or dismissal of the libido, so there is a split (but not dialectical) movement in Marx:

what Marx perceives as a failure, suffering (and maybe indeed lives through in *ressentiment)* is the mark on his work of a situation which is precisely the same as that of capital, and which gives rise to a strange success as much as to a frightful misery: the work cannot *form a body,* just as capital cannot form a body. And this absence of 'artistic' organic unity gives rise to two divergent movements always associated in a single vertigo: a movement of flight, of plunging into the body-less, and thus of continued invention, of expansive additions or affirmations of new pieces (utterances, but elsewhere music, techniques, ethics) to the insane patchwork – movement of tension. And a movement of institution of an organism, of an organisation and of organs of totalisation and unification – movement of reason. Both sorts of movements are there, potential effects in the *non-finito* of the work just as in that of capitalism. (EL, 125)

If Lyotard's purpose is not simply that of exalting one of these movements against the other, we may be at something of a loss to know what it is. The point is *not* to produce a *critique,* a theory of Marx's theory; *not* simply to show that Marx is still religious, alienated and so on; *not* to postulate a 'true atheism' against such religious residues – such an 'atheism' would simply be a new form of religion. The aim is, rather, to show intensities lodged in theory, to demonstrate that the cold serious discourse of political economy is also a set-up of libidinal economy. This requires perhaps endless caution if it is not to slip back into the forms it is attempting to disrupt. For example, Lyotard takes distance from Baudrillard by locating a trap set by rationality at the moment of its apparent defeat:

This perfectly simple trap consists in *answering the demand of vanquished theory*, and this demand is: 'put something in my place'. Now the important thing is the place, not the content of the theory. It is the place of theory which must be beaten. And that can only be done by displacement and flight. (EL, 129)

For despite claims to the contrary, Baudrillard still operates a critique, founded, as any critique must be for Lyotard, on the uncriticized postulation of a lost referent (to this extent Lyotard might be taken to advocate, not an anti-critique but an ultra-critique, and the massive return of a fundamentally Kantian-critical Idea of philosophy in the later work come as less of a surprise). In Baudrillard's case this lost referent is a primitive society of 'symbolic exchange', disruptive of political economy insofar as it is, in a sense, more honest about what is at stake in exchange (theorised by Baudrillard as castration). Baudrillard succeeds in avoiding Marx's dialectical location of *his* uncriticized referent (the proletariat) as the negation of the negation, by locating his supposedly subversive referent (hippy or marginal, for example) purely *positively* in modern society. But Lyotard (who is on occasion not very far from such enthusiasms himself (see for example DP, 46)) still finds this too theoretical, and for a very precise reason: 'We simply fear the consequences of this, of this small detail, of this "methodological" nuance: that the affirmative is delimited as a *region*' (EL, 132). *By its very position, any such region functions as a nature.* And no doubt the more so the more 'internal' to society it seems: for this is precisely the manoeuvre described above as constitutive of theatricality and representation, the 'mise en extériorité à l'intérieur'. And it is precisely this, this positing within the theatre of a non-theatrical space beyond the theatre, the description from within alienation, for example, of a non-alienated place beyond alienation, which Lyotard is attempting to avoid by means of the *indiscernibility* of Eros and the death-drive.

But the critical-theatrical set-up is constant in Marx, and cannot be limited to the writings of a 'young Marx' prior to the 'epistemological break' which would usher in science, as Althusser would have it. If the earlier texts stress a loss of immediacy in alienated mediation, later ones, supposedly written after the 'break', simply displace the theme of immediacy on to that of nature as the earth, the inorganic body of the land.

Lyotard quotes from the *Grundrisse* on pre-capitalist forms, on the natural

> . . . the earth [is] the original instrument of labour as well as its workshop and repository of raw materials. The individual relates simply to the objective conditions of labour as. . . the inorganic nature of his subjectivity, in which the latter realises itself. . . this relation to land and soil, to the earth, as the property of the labouring individual – who thus appears at the outset not merely as labouring individual, in this abstraction, but who has an *objective mode of existence* in his ownership of the land, an existence *presupposed* to his activity just like his skin, his sense-organs. . . – is instantly mediated by the naturally arisen, spontaneous, more or less historically developed and modified presence of the individual as *member of a commune* – his naturally arisen presence as member of a tribe etc. . . Just as the working subject appears naturally as an individual, as natural being – so does the first objective condition of his labour appear as nature, earth, as his inorganic body; he himself is not only the organic body, but also the subject of this inorganic nature. This condition is not his product but something he finds to hand – presupposed to him as a natural being apart from him. . . (Marx, *Grundrisse*, tr. Martin Nicolaus (Harmondsworth: Penguin Books, 1973), pp. 485, 488)

'givenness' of both the land and the communal body of labourers. Lyotard comments:

1. The body of the earth is termed *inorganic* only so as to be distinguished from the organic body of the worker himself; in fact it is a body organically linked to the organic body and is identical to it in all points in that, like the organic body, it is *given* and not produced; 2. the commune also forms part of this great (in)organic body, for it is as a member of the commune that the 'labouring' body (which does not in fact appear as such) can enter into a productive relation with the earth. And belonging to the commune is also *given* and not produced. The three instances, body proper, social body, body of the earth, are articulated together as so many pieces of a single machinery, which is *nature*. It is within this nature that 'production' is carried out, or rather, this 'production' is nature reproducing itself. (EL, 160)

It is this naturality which is lost in capitalism and which provides the only ground upon which Marx can base his critique. It cannot be said, as Poulantzas has suggested, that Marx simply uses a certain simplified presentation of pre-capitalist forms for the heuristic purpose of bringing out more starkly the specificity of capitalism. For in Marx, only such a radical split provides the need to explain anything, 'the discourse of political economy is engendered from the vacancy or gap it opens in the social subject' (EL, 162):

It is impossible to say that the invocation of the opposite in the form of a non-split society is only a facility of exposition in Marx – it commands his methodology (which is impossible, but that's another matter) and it commands his politics, which is very explicitly, and constantly, that of *abolishing the split* and establishing the great common full body of natural reproduction, i.e. communism. (EL, 163)

And this theme of a lost naturality informs even Marx's most 'scientific' analyses, brutally summarised by Lyotard as follows:

The whole 'critique' is articulated upon the following simple statements: profit hides surplus-value, surplus-value comes from the concealment of the use-value of labour-force by its exchange-value; or, from the concealment of its substantial, superabundant force by its property of being an exchangeable, self-sufficient commodity; thus capitalism must mistake the *origin* of its growth, and this mistake must be fatal to it. (EL, 175)

All of which can look very close to what Lyotard himself is trying to do: is not the description of libidinal force bound and de-intensified by the theatrical set-up precisely similar to Marx's description, in which the use-value *of labour-force* appears to undergo exactly the same sort of treatment at the hands of the capitalist set-up? And this would seem to return us to the 'profound congruence' noted between Marx and Freud. If this really is so similar, then we should have to conclude either that Lyotard's reading of Marx is completely misguided, or else that its conclusions can simply be re-applied to his own writing with similar results. It is clearly time to examine the suggested parallelism of Marx and Freud a little more closely, beyond the simple analogy of an external force being controlled by an ordering system.

An immediate difference can be noted: for Marx, what is supposed to give rise to events within the system is precisely this positive force of labour – it may be bound by the system, but it also necessarily produces periodic crises and will eventually bring the system down. 'The living force is the drive as force of events, capital its death as binding' (EL, 175). In Freud, on the contrary, it is the death-drive which is the source of events, and Eros, or the life-drives, which bind and produce the system. It would be simplistic to assume that this inversion were just the sign of an essential optimism in Marx and pessimism in Freud. According to Lyotard, the essential point is rather that in Marx the opposition of force and system is dialectical: the force is posited as *external* to the system, and therefore, again, as a *region* and therefore a *nature*. But in Freud there is no such dialectic (although the psychoanalytic treatment might consist in an attempt to construct one): the death-drives:

are not external to the regulated apparatus, rather they inhabit it, and this unthinkable cohabitation of the regulator and the deregulator in the same signs is, properly, the dissimulation or dissimilation by which every intense sign offers itself as a coded sign, and some coded (but non-assignable) sign conceals an intensity. Even if Freud himself made mistakes about this, for example in interpreting in *Civilisation and its Discontents* the death-drives as aggressivity, and thus re-establishing a sort of binarism of the drives, the fact remains that his invention of 1920 [in *Beyond the Pleasure Principle*] gives rise or occasion to a dissimulating monism: there is no equivalent of this in Marx, too Christian for that. (EL, 176)

Lyotard's siding with (a certain) Freud against Marx on this point is not just a question of preference. He argues, for example, that Marx's idea of a transcendence of force with respect to the system does not stand up to the current state of capitalism. Marx himself, in the *Grundrisse,* was aware that with the development of large-scale industry, *knowledge* tends to become an immediate force of production (this is a point to which Lyotard will return in *The Postmodern Condition* (CPM, 14 n 17 [PMC, 86-7 n 17])) and, increasingly, to relegate labour-force as such to a

---

To the degree that large industry develops, the creation of real wealth comes to depend less on labour time and on the amount of labour employed than on the power of the agencies set in motion during labour time, whose 'powerful effectiveness' is out of all proportion to the direct labour time spent on their production, but depends rather on the general state of science and on the progress of technology, or the application of this science to production. . . Labour no longer appears so much to be included within the production process. . . The worker. . . steps to the side of the production process instead of being its chief actor. . . As soon as labour in the direct form has ceased to be the great well-spring of wealth, labour time ceases and must cease to be its measure, and hence exchange value [must cease to be the measure] of use value. . . [Machines] are *organs of the human brain, created by the human hand;* the power of knowledge, objectified. The development of fixed capital indicates to what degree general social knowledge has become a *direct force of production.* . . (*Grundrisse*, pp. 704-6)

marginal position. And of course this has become increasingly the case. Marx attempts to salvage the situation *in extremis* by reading this possibility of a production without exploitation of the immediate labour-force (and therefore without a proletariat as such) as a new anonymous triumphant labour-force by a new emerging social subject.

But this attempt collapses: Marx needs to maintain that capital would be defeated by this new force because it would still need to try to measure its value in terms of labour-time – this 'moving contradiction' *(Grundrisse,* p. 706) would lead to the destruction of the system. But only Marx says that capital either does or needs to conceive of value in this way: maybe capital doesn't care at all about the *origin* of value, and is happy to measure it on the basis of an arbitrarily-chosen commodity, as Sraffa has argued. Once this is shown to be the case, then the fact that capital might indeed have had *originally* to draw on natural human energy proves nothing about its ability to survive indefinitely, and no more does it provide grounds for accusations and guilt. In this account, there is no ground for exploitation in the extraction of surplus value, insofar as that value is now seen to be drawn from nature by a system which is itself all but 'natural', and which can no longer be opposed as 'alienated' to a truer nature lost or to come (EL, 180-1).

Lyotard's purpose cannot then be to locate a transcendent place for his libido, to pretend to ground a critique in such a place. Whence the assertion that:

there is no external reference (even were it immanent [as in Baudrillard]) from which point the separation of what belongs to capital (or political economy) and what belongs to subversion (or libidinal economy) can always be carried out cleanly, a place where desire would be clearly legible, where its proper economy would not be scrambled. (EL, 133)

Again, libidinal economy is not to be opposed to political economy, and this apparently simple claim leads to surprising consequences: for if there is no *place* for desire other than the 'place' of capitalism, then it follows that 'all political economy is libidinal' (EL, 133-48), but also that 'there are no primitive societies' (EL, 148-55), and also that there is no alienation and so no redemption to be sought. The problem is not that of locating a place where desire flows (even a 'marginal' place) but of showing that desire flows even where Marx and even Baudrillard recognize only alienation and repression. If desire is not to be opposed to capitalism, it can be recognized *in* capitalism. Desire can invest work, for example, in its most 'alienated' forms, and it can invest the products of capitalism. Call this latter fetishism by all means, but 'where are you going to *criticize* fetishism from, when you know that one cannot criticize homosexuality or masochism without becoming a vulgar bastard of the moral order?' (EL, 135).

This insistence, which is perfectly consistent with all we have discussed so far, leads directly to some of the most 'scandalous' assertions of *Economie libidinale:* and, predictably enough given the essential place accorded to the death-drive in Lyotard's analyses, death reappears at this point. Lyotard anticipates the obvious objection that libidinal investment in capitalism is possible, but that, in extreme cases at least, it is nonetheless the result of power as constraint and domination. To the protest that, for the nineteenth-century English proletariat, the question was of such an investment or death, 'ça ou mourir', Lyotard replies that it is *always* a question of that or death, or rather of that *and* death:

Death is not an alternative to *that,* it is a part of it, it attests that there is *jouissance* in that, the unemployed English did not become workers in order to survive, they – hang on tight and spit on me – *enjoyed* [ils ont joui de] the hysterical, masochistic, I don't know what exhaustion of *hanging on* in the mines, the iron-works, the workshops, in hell, they enjoyed (being in) the mad destruction of their organic bodies, which was indeed imposed on them, they enjoyed the fact that it was imposed on them, they enjoyed the decomposition of their personal identity, the identity that a peasant tradition had constructed for them, enjoyed the dissolution of families and villages, and enjoyed the new monstrous *anonymity* of the suburbs and pubs morning and evening. (EL, 136)

On the basis of this passage, which says what it says without much need of commentary, Lyotard was generally accused of having moved over to the extreme Right, of writing an apologia of voluntary servitude, and so on. On two occasions he chose to respond to this type of accusation. The more detailed of these replies takes the form of a fictitious dialogue in *Les Transformateurs Duchamp* (TD, 21-6); the more concise, from which I shall quote at some length, in the unpublished section of *Au juste:*

I should like to make it clear that the general logic of the book was not, as was somewhat stupidly imputed to me, to look for the explanation of capital in a voluntary servitude or a desire for servitude on the part of the proletariat. On the contrary, what I wished to show in the passage which has been incriminated with remarkable regularity, was that the proletariat itself had been the point of fusion of the social metamorphosis called the birth of industrial capitalism. In the (essentially Marxist, but proletarian in general) political tradition, the proletariat is represented as a sort of constant subject which has to produce itself, reproduce itself and emancipate itself, i.e. to reinforce its stability and its constancy. What interested me, on the contrary, was showing (even if in an allusive way, and it was allusive since there was no precise textual or historical analysis) that the transformation of, for example, the expropriated English peasantry from the eighteenth century onwards, into an urban proletariat, belongs precisely to this general movement of metamorphosis. I believe I went so far as to say that wanting to 'save' the proletariat, or make it successful in its emancipation, could be simply (it hasn't always been so, but can be) to forget the extraordinary *puissance* which had manifested itself in the proletariat at its birth: in the acceptance (even if it was forced, but what isn't forced in these matters?) of this fantastic mutation in the mode of life, the mode of work, the way of talking, the relation to the family, to religion and anything you like. In this there was, not a desire for voluntary abasement, or I don't know what idiocies of that type, but on the contrary the recognition that, as they say, 'it took some doing' [*il fallait le faire*, literally, 'it had to be done']. (AJ, 194-5)

This is *not* the same as a Marxist recognition that such a transformation can have, in the ultimate movement of history, a positive effect within

> The Industrial Revolution. . . extreme intensity, if it was to be the revolution putting an end to the body, space, time and logic constituted in the neolithic age. And not only in the heads of bankers, manufacturers and engineers, but in the heads of workers, and their bodies. Describe their lot exclusively in terms of alienation, exploitation and misery, you present them as victims having merely suffered the whole process and having merely acquired credits against subsequent reparations (socialism). You miss and hide the same energy which will be spread in the arts and sciences, the jubilation and pain of discovering that one can *hold on* (live, work, think, be affected) where it was judged crazy. Something that Machiavelli reserved for the Prince, *virtù*. . . I'm talking of a mechanical ascesis. The proletariat, being submitted to it, contributed to modernity. It is inaccurate and stupid to make them a herd of cattle only able to enter the future backwards and beaten into it. (TD, 23-4)

the dialectic: simply 'we're dealing with a remarkable effect of *puissance*, and it's insufficient to represent it essentially in the form of a martyrology' (AJ, 196).

Refusing a certain piety which will continue to find these statements scandalous does not of course commit one to accepting their accuracy. It is, however, clear that such assertions depend on a refusal of a certain traditional position of the (Marxist) intellectual, studying the proletariat, full of commiseration for a suffering so constructed as to dissolve any *jouissance* into ideology and alienation still, or else postulating some pure good spontaneity and creativity of the proletariat which must be released from the deadening constraints of capitalism. (This latter point in fact led to Lyotard's break with Castoriadis's line within *Socialisme ou barbarie:* see EL, 142-5.) And along with critique, theory, alienation and the intellectual, it is inevitable that the notion of revolution be contested too: instead of wanting to 'start the Revolution again' with Castoriadis, Lyotard thinks a real escape from the impasse of historical materialism would have been made by

eliminat[ing] the idea of revolution, which has become and perhaps always was a little nothing idea, the idea of an overturning of positions in the sphere of political economy and therefore the idea of a maintenance of that sphere, or even, to be fairer to Castoriadis, the idea of an overturning of positions in *all* spheres; even this thought of a generalised overturning had to be pierced in its turn, for it was a wall again, the same wall at the end of the same *impasse* since where there is a thought of overturning, there is theory of alienation, nihilism and theorist-saviours, heads as depositaries of knowledge. (EL, 145)

The analyses of Marxism in *Economie libidinale* can easily read like a total dismissal. They certainly refuse the 'erotic' aspects of Marxism,

---

Totalitarianism is no more than the process of domination of the master ensemble over the enslaved ensemble. This process is not episodic, conjunctural, linked to the fortune of a given political party (the 'right') or a given social class (the 'bourgeoisie'): a left wing, united or not, even operating in the name of the proletariat, will carry out this same work of detection of threats, centralistion of information, diffusion of orders, elimination of events and of people and groups supposedly related to events. Given that the erotic dimension of the left's desire is more strongly marked than in any other group, one may even wonder whether it cannot wall up the circulation of energies more than any formation confident in the unificatory power of capital. (EL, 255)

giving rise to order and organisation, the party, 'an apparatus capitalising the desire for revolution' (EL, 126). But in the memoir for Pierre Souyri, quoted in the introduction, Lyotard states that in the wake of his own difficulty with Marxism, he became aware of 'a distant assertion, which escaped not only from refutation, but also from decrepitude, and retained all its authority over will and thought' (PS, 16-17). To discover that assertion re-emerging, we must wait until *Le Différend.*

One consequence of the premisses of libidinal economy as we have presented them so far is that in the final section of 'The desire named Marx', Lyotard should not be taken as saying that Sraffa is simply *right* about the economy and Marx simply *wrong.* But if what is at stake in what they say is to be scientific, then Sraffa manages a good deal better than Marx: Sraffa formulates 'a structural syntax of the language spoken by the exchanges of commodities' (EL, 186), whereas Marx is unable to close his theory precisely because he needs some reference to its outside, as labour-force, as nature.

Sraffa starts from the facts, as does Marx, but not the same facts: Marx's fact is, and remains from one end to the other of the career of the romantic attorney, the alienation of work to property, to capital, which is therefore not a first fact, but something which refers to a 'fact' still more archaic and hidden, the lost link-up of work and needs, by an immediate mediation, in a social nature or natural society: a nihilistic fact giving rise to *interpretation.* (EL, 183)

But this does not alter the fact that in terms of libidinal economy, Sraffa's model is one set-up among others, and should, in principle, be analyzable in terms of intensities and libido. In such a system, desire is no longer invested in a lost referent, but in value *as such,* onto the referral from one term to another within the system:

The discourse of theory is no less *jouissif* than any other; what it enjoys is situated in the very coldness of the model it constructs and which, *ex hypothesi,* is a model of *equilibrium* (static or dynamic equilibrium), or the *maximum of liaison* supposed to be in the object it is talking about, but above all really obtained in its own discursive arrangement. Speech without viscosity, fixed to itself by the screws of an infallible axiomatic, and so moving towards a body of language immobilised or immobilising itself, a body on the subject of which one could debate *ad infinitum* whether it is dead or alive, which is undecidable. (EL, 186-7)

Sraffa's model is not presented as the last word: it is explicitly limited to a hypothetical market 'in self-replacing state', and does not pretend to account for the possibility of expansion. The 'refinement' of Lyotard's libidinal analysis takes the next two sections of the book through complicated analyses of money and capital, of intensities and time, too complex to summarise here (though aspects of them will return when we present the analysis of exchange given in *Le Différend*). Rather, following on from the assertion just quoted that theory is analyzable in terms of libido, and that its specific *libidinal* set-up is nonetheless a result of its *discursive arrangement,* we shall move to the final section of the book, which turns its 'method' back upon itself, and also sketches analyses of a number of *dispositifs* which will be useful for the later work too.

What is this discourse? How is it legitimated? Where is it situated? What is its function? Who authorises you to talk in this way? Are you the owner of the great [libidinal] film? But how could you be, when it is ephemeral and offers nothing to hold or hold onto? Is your whole affair not pure imagination and rhetoric? Are you searching for the truth, do you claim to speak it, to have spoken it? Have you produced anything other than a new philosophy, one more system? More words? Have these words the pretension to change the world, at least? If not, what? Simply to note it down, miserable character! In truth, this is pure imaginary fabrication on your part, fulfilment of desire on the 'skin of language', as you would say, aestheticism, elitism. (EL, 287)

These questions, attributed to an imaginary adversary, lead into the final section of *Economie libidinale*. They are the questions of what Lyotard calls 'white terror', determined by reference to the truth, which, 'we know', is 'the arm of paranoia and power, the mark of unity-totality in the space of words, return and terror' (EL, 287). We should, says Lyotard, 'fight the white terror of truth with and for the red cruelty of singularities' (EL,

287). But this does not mean that such questions cannot be answered: or rather, that they cannot be *placed* in terms of the libidinal band.

Theory finds its *jouissance* in immobilisation: the libido invests the disjunctive bar itself, in its very disjunctive function. But insofar as *jouissance* means intensity, and in the fiction of the libidinal band, intensity implies rapid rotation of the bar, then we have somehow to think that the immobile disjunctive bar is *also* rotating at high speed, and thus

---

This type of argument can be made more simply by saying that any disjunction implies some synthesis of the dis-joined terms. Insofar as each term is defined or held in place by its relation to the other(s), then there is a necessary encroachment of each term on the other(s). Readers of Jacques Derrida will note the similarity of this approach to that which leads to the derivation of *différance*, and a similar perception will return at a crucial point in *Le Différend*.

---

rendering indiscernible the very disjunction it institutes. Such a combination of movement and immobility needs to be refined, however, and Lyotard attempts this by providing a preliminary analysis of a 'narrative-figurative' genre on the one hand, and an abstract genre on the other.

The 'narrative-figurative' genre takes us back to the theatre, to representation. Our preliminary description noted that in traditional theatre movement took place on the stage, and that, usually, the spectator was immobilised. But this common-sense description is in fact a total inversion of a libidinal analysis of the same set-up or *dispositif*. For in fact the specificity of the narrative-figurative genre is that it presents an 'organic body' which is none other than the organised 'scene' of realist painting, narrative or theatre, held in place by the frame. Insofar as this 'body' is organised, then it is, says Lyotard, *immobilised* and offered to the spectator as a *prey,* a victim. This immobilisation is a prerequisite of the spectator's *jouissance;* for the apparently immobile spectating body is allowed to move by the frame holding representation in place:

far from closing [the client's body] into a whole volume having its centre and its unity in itself, these movements [of affect] spread it out into heterogeneous, independent zones, open to autonomous incandescences: they are nothing other than... the partial drives. So there we have the set-up: a unified organic body

---

The sexual drive as a whole can be analysed into a certain number of partial drives: most of them can be easily attached to a determinate erogenous zone; others are, rather, defined by their aim. . .

The concept of partial drive is a corollary of that of a whole, an organisation. The analysis of a sexual organisation brings out the drives making it up. The opposition is also genetic, as Freudian theory supposes that the drives first function in an anarchic state and are organised subsequently. (Laplanche and Pontalis, *Vocabulaire de la psychanalyse* (Paris: PUF, 1967), p. 368)

promised to death through immobilisation (the victim), onto which is connected, under the name of client, and by the intermediary of an effaced misrecognized support, the Brownian motion of the partial drives. (EL, 290-91)

Abstract painting (and certain forms of 'modern' writing), alter this set-up: here there is no unification of a body-as-referent – no representation in any simple sense. In this case, says Lyotard, it is the 'client's' body which is immobilised, and the surface of the painting which 'moves', which is a polymorphous skin, tending to fix the spectator as *its* victim.

This is close to the theoretical set-up, says Lyotard. But not identical. Theory (in the strong, almost mathematical sense) is like abstract painting in that it too is 'abstract', it does not posit an organic totality as its referent: but it does posit such a totality *as the text itself,* in its discursive organisation. Like abstract painting, theory immobilizes and de-cathects the body of the 'client' (theory does not in principle aim to excite its reader): but it does not do this in order to liberate movement in its own organisation, because it frustrates movement there too, controlling it by strict rules (its system of axioms). And because the theoretical text is thus regulated, it can be *repeated* indefinitely (and this is of course a banal requirement of any theory if it is to be worth its name): the repetition of Eros: *jouissance* from fidelity in replication.

But this 'erotic' repetition is, again, *also* that of the death-drive; for theory tends towards the construction of a consistent organic body of its own only by imposing a requirement of *anonymity.* Theory is 'universal' only insofar as it is 'impersonal': theory 'passes through the destruction of the particular libidinal set-ups already formed on the body of the client and their dialysis into anonymity. The *forgetting* implied by the theoretical is already the amnesia proper to the Id.' (EL, 295-6). And this explains the apparent paradox of the simultaneously immobile and rapidly rotating bar of disjunction: theory depends on the disjunction of affects between text and 'client'; but in this disjoining, it makes of that very disjunction a possibility of repetition in anonymity, which is perhaps as close as we shall get to a definition of *jouissance.*

'As close as we shall get': not because *jouissance* is ineffable, but because it is rapidly becoming superfluous to what Lyotard is trying to do. The sketch of an analysis of three 'genres' in this final section of *Economie libidinale* is already pushing towards the notion of 'language-games', as used in *The Postmodern Condition,* and, beyond that, towards the notions of *regimes* of sentences and *genres* of discourse in *Le*

Différend. It seems clear, for example, that questions of libido can be removed from the description of these genres with little loss. As Lyotard notes in an essay written very shortly after *Economie libidinale,* these notions of energy and libido are a 'façon de parler' (RP, 130), a way of speaking, a turn of phrase. This unobtrusive and off-hand comment has enormous consequences for the whole project of a 'libidinal economy'. On the one hand, it implies that that energy, the libido and so on have no particular epistemological or ontological privilege, and on the other,

---

> But what is new is also something else, which is extremely serious: it says, there is no nature, no history, no Good Lord, no meaning received, given, revealed, discovered, there are chromatic, sonorous, linguistic energies (manner of speaking) which obey ordered constants only exceptionally, and which it is man's job (as it is that of any bit of matter), to play with in order to make perspectives, sets of relations. (RP, 129-30)

that energy and libido are always posited by language, by 'ways of speaking'. The curious result of this is that despite an obvious interpretation of the enormous difference in tone between *Economie libidinale* and *Le Différend,* despite the former's violent anti-theoreticism, it is in fact still *too* theoretical a book, as such still embroiled with the theatre, with representation and critique. Notwithstanding the subtlety and rigour of the attempt to account for theatricality and representation without reproducing them, despite the generalisation of 'theatrics' which should undermine the oppositions upon which the theatre depends, *Economie libidinale* does nonetheless rebuild the theatre, if only on the shifting ground of the libidinal band, which is no doubt still too ontological, still a *subject* despite all protestations to the contrary. Despite the insistence on the death-drive and on dissimulation, the libidinal band is still 'out there', transcendent, absence, Zero, inevitably proclaimed as 'good', as lost. The real problem of *Economie libidinale* is not that of its violence or its apparent break with theory, dialogue, the theatre, but the tenacity with which the theatre withstands such violence and even thrives on it.

This is certainly not to dismiss *Economie libidinale,* nor even to accept Lyotard's own rather deprecating comments on it in recent years. As I have attempted to show, much of what is advanced in that book can be saved from itself. The bare project of the book, that of describing and situating *dispositifs,* and that of seeking out the possibility of *singularities* and *events,* is never repudiated by Lyotard, and is in his view fundamental to the task of philosophy. The problem is no doubt linked to the book's anger against what it calls 'theory', which interferes with the attempt to situate theory as one genre among others. This anger is clearly to do

with Lyotard's increasing inability to identify with the discourse of
Marxism: once the anger has subsided, then the affirmative side of that

---

Having reached this point, we should like to be able to interrupt Lyotard for a
moment and say to him: Perhaps it was this truth of the militant which was
ill-founded; a desire made him take Marxist statements to be true, but perhaps
quite simply they were not true. . . From the observation that this truth was
only the expression of a desire, he moves on to the interpretation that the
desire expressed in this supposed 'truth' was the desire for truth. . . If Marxism
is not true, it is [for Lyotard] not because it is false, but because nothing is true.
(Vincent Descombes, *Le même et l'autre* (Paris: Minuit, 1979), p. 211)

inability, which *Economie libidinale* is all too eager to show, will become
the stronger.

We have seen that Lyotard relies on a certain reading of psychoanalysis
in order to formulate his 'libidinal economy'. But in view of the assertions
about theory on which such an economy rests, this reliance cannot simply
take the form of *applying a theory,* insofar as theory is the name of only
one, or a restricted set, of the *dispositifs* for which the economy is supposed to account. There is no good reason for assuming that psychoanalytic theory would be an exception to this ambition, and indeed it is the
object of more than one essay. In 'Freud selon Cézanne' (DP, 71-94), for
example, Lyotard shows how, alongside his massive and productive use
of theatrical models (Oedipus, Hamlet), Freud mobilises an entirely
traditional notion of the visual arts, 'theatrical' in the sense we have been
concerned to explicate and undermine:

The central intuition of this aesthetics is that the picture, just like the dream
'scene', *represents* an absent object or situation, that it opens a scenic space in
which, failing the things themselves, their representatives at least can be offered
to vision, and that it has the capacity to take in and place the products of desire
being accomplished. Like the dream, the pictorial object is thought of according
to the function of hallucinatory representation and lure. (DP, 73)

This implies that Freud is simply ignorant of the mutation in the practice
of painting going on around him, notably in the wake of Cézanne. If it is
true that such painting, 'far from favouring the putting-to-sleep of consciousness and the fulfilment of the unconscious desire of the lover of
painting, aims on the contrary to produce on the support sorts of analoga
of the unconscious space itself' (DP, 75), then the libidinal analysis of
this particular *dispositif* seems to allow at least part of psychoanalysis
to be situated as a particular *dispositif* in its turn. Or again, in 'Sur une
figure de discours' (DP, 135-56), Lyotard turns to the dispositif of the

psychoanalytical cure, at least as it is 'described, prescribed or dreamed' in Freud and Lacan (DP, 136), and attempts to show that it can be analysed in terms of a *dispositif* analogous to that set in place by Judaic religion,

In *modern* linguistic analysis, *I* is the one who speaks, *you* the one who listens to *I*, and can in turn speak, and say *I*. But in the Judaic position, *I* is the one who is seized by *your* speech; *you* is the one who 'speaks' ('first'), *I* the one to whom it is spoken. But you *does not reply*. . . the absolutely Judaic feature is that there is *no possible reversal* of this relation, that the positions of I and You cannot be exchanged. This absence of reversal adequately charcterises the position of the Jewish God. It excludes all *mediation* (Christ, Hegel), any *we* that would be I-and-you. (DP, 146-7) This type of analysis will return to inform the later work, allowing at once an insistence on *ethics*, and a suspicion of the self-evidence of dialogue and consensus.

with the unconscious in the place of Yahvé, the analyst as Moses and the patient as Israel. In slightly different ways, 'Figure forclose' (1968, published only in 1984), and 'Oedipe juif' (DMF, 167-88) pursue the same analogy.

Of more immediate importance here is the essay 'Apathie dans la théorie' (RP, 9-31), which immediately postdates *Economie libidinale* and continues the effort to analyse the theoretical dispositif and displace its claims to mastery. Lyotard returns in this text to *Beyond the Pleasure Principle,* in a slightly (but crucially) different way. Earlier uses of that text were motivated by an effort to extract from it the doctrine of desire as energy or libido: even if this extraction involved a deliberate interpretative violence, as we have noted, the text nonetheless served as a means by which to understand other *dispositifs* rather than as a *dispositif* in its turn. In this essay the stake is rather different, for Lyotard is now concerned to show that the essay *disrupts* the theoretical *dispositif*, rather than giving grounds for explaining it in terms of a particular modality of *jouissance,* for example. *Beyond the Pleasure Principle* now becomes a model of how writing might begin to cope with the task of unsettling theory, still described as 'terror'.

It is still the indiscernibility of life and death-drives which provides the starting-point, but now Lyotard is able to give a more precise idea of what such an 'undecidability' might be, by treating the psychoanalytic symptom as an utterer of *sentences:*

Let us take Dora's respiratory symptom. Is it due to the life-drives or the death-drives? Undecidable in [Freud's] final doctrine. If the symptom could talk, what would it say? First of all, certainly, 'I live', for the symptom is doing well, like a micro-organism resisting any 'external' aggression, including the aggression that can emanate from Dora's so-called 'organic body'. It would also say 'I kill', I kill it, the 'organic body' which I threaten with asphyxia and mutism. If it is objected that the reference of the discourse has changed from one statement to the next (hysterical micro-organism in the first, 'organic body' in the second), we will continue by saying: the respiratory symptom also says 'I am dying' or 'I live dead', in which case it is the death-drives which, referring to the micro-organism as unviable, nonetheless reveal in it a sort of monstrous regulation; and finally, 'I liven it up', it, the organism, by forcing it to increase its metabolism in order to respond to the challenge I'm throwing at it: does not Dora go to see Freud? Is the 'cure' not a reactivation of the exchanges of the 'body' with its *milieu?* In this case it is Eros which perturbs the body referred to, but with a view to more life, more differentiation. Thus we have *four* statements blocked together, such that it is undecidable whether the symptom comes from one or other principle by which the drives function. Sore throat, loss of the voice, hoarseness, asthma 'signify' both life and death. (RP, 20)

But here Lyotard is not concerned to claim anything like an ontological value for such an undecidability, but is rather interested in its effects on Freud's *discourse*. Freud constantly admits in *Beyond the Pleasure Principle* that he is not quite convinced by his own 'speculative' construction, and Lyotard diagnoses this as *itself* an effect of the undecidability of Eros and death-drives: Freud's 'scientific' desire (and his desire not to have to agree with Jung) lead him to stress that he is positing a dualism, but the undecidability noted by Lyotard means that such a dualism can never be established 'satisfactorily'. Freud's constant hesitations over the energetic level which the apparatus strives to attain (zero, minimum, 'at least constant') are an effect *in* Freud's discourse of the referent of that discourse: or rather, the mark that the referential function of that discourse is no longer completely ruled by 'scientific' principles. Further, Lyotard notes that Freud thinks that in view of the obscurity of this area of investigation, the best hypothesis is the 'loosest' [*lockerste*]: this quality of 'looseness' [*lockerheit*] being the very quality Freud had earlier in his career assigned to the psychical apparatus of the artist (RP, 22-3).

All of which is taken to mean that at this point at least, Freud is not writing theory:

Beyond the Pleasure Principle does not belong to the genre of scientific discourse. The third theory of the 'duality' of the drives escapes the theoretical and practical requirements of the genre of science. It is a *theory-fiction*. Its specific affect is *impassiveness* and not conviction. By impassiveness we must understand the impossibility of experiencing the yes and no of conviction. (RP, 24-5)

What moves Freud's writing is not then the aim of truth, but that of pursuing an idea as far as it will go, looking for something new rather than something true. Freud's discourse can thus be said to *parody* scientific language: it still has a referential function (referring to the economy of the drives), and its statements appear to obey the rules of denotation: but this reference (the death-drives, and therefore the duality of the drives as such) cannot be exhibited to observation, nor refuted by counter-example. This is not 'pure' fiction, and some of the text still obeys the rules of theory: but it is, like its object, an undecidable: 'as the same text both observes and does not observe the rules of the discourse of science, theory-fiction is dissimulated in theory, while it is the dissimilation of theory' (RP, 28).

It will have been noted that Lyotard still talks of 'affect' here, and contrasts the 'conviction' which is the traditional affect attached to scientific or theoretical discourse with the 'impassiveness' attached to Freud's. But this notion of affect is not at all the same thing as the notion of libido which informs *Economie libidinale,* which was purely quantitative. In fact the affect in question here is not at all Freudian in inspiration, although used to discuss Freud – it is much rather rhetorical (and it is no accident that this is the term we have seen Lyotard use in *Au juste* to qualify *Economie libidinale* itself): rhetorical in the sense of being concerned with persuasion, and more generally with *pathos* in the technical sense of the effect of a discourse on its addressee. Lyotard's analysis here is already almost entirely discursive and scarcely 'libidinal' at all. In short, the effect of *re-applying* the notion of the *dispositif* to the psychoanalytical discourse which had originally inspired it is to deprive that discourse of any foundational privilege. This is both encouraging, insofar as it suggests that the notion of *dispositif* is indeed generally applicable, even to the discourse which formulated it, and also disconcerting, insofar as one of the basic operators of that discourse (force, libido) no longer seems a necessary part of the analysis. It is in a text written one year later that Lyotard inserts the 'façon de parler' remark after a reference to energy: and if energy is a 'façon de parler', then it rapidly follows that, in a sense, there are *only* 'façons de parler'.

This 'linguistic turn' is confirmed in the final essay of *Rudiments païens.* Theory is no longer to be described in terms of libido, but in terms of language. The 'theatrical' residue which haunted *Economie libidinale* in spite of itself (because whatever its precautions, that book and the essays which go with it have to say that the libido or primary process are the *other* of language) is now largely dissipated. The emphasis moves towards a notion of parody which is very close to the 'theatrics' extolled in the earlier book, but without the now troublesome language of libido: the aim is still that of resisting theory without opposing it, but now the parody which ensues is argued purely in terms of language:

We accept here that [the theoretico-critical] genre, which has had such fortune in our culture, which assigns itself the objective of speaking the truth and dissipating illusions, is a particular case of the so-called literary genres, or, to be more precise, the arts of speaking. (RP, 233)

The danger here is obvious, and it is that the characterisation of theory or science or philosophy as somehow 'literary' or 'rhetorical' will dissolve essential differences into a newly and falsely homogeneous continuity. It is a commonplace criticism of recent French thought that its questioning of traditional oppositions (here of theory and fiction, truth and fable) ends up by 'making everything the same'. Nothing could be further from the truth: already in this closing essay, which in many ways remains tentative and programmatic, Lyotard begins the type of 'pragmatic' analysis which will lead eventually to *Le Différend:* this analysis does not at all aim to neutralise and destroy differences, but to provide precise characterisations of different discursive genres (including its own genre): this being the task of philosophy itself, according to Lyotard. If this later work is an 'improvement' on the positions of *Economie libidinale,* this will not primarily be because it is to be judged 'truer to the facts' – for this would be simply a judgement carried out according to one genre. The judgement of improvement (progress? – the question will return) will be, in a sense to be determined, rather an *ethical* one.

The notion of language involved in this 'linguistic turn' is, in the French context, a little odd, insofar as its major reference is not Saussure. To prepare the ground for such a notion, but also to disrupt the simple idea of a clean break in Lyotard's thought after *Economie libidinale,* the next chapter will turn back to earlier work, and specifically the rather daunting *Discours, figure.*

Patchwork 1

We cannot believe that deconstruction is a better insurance on intensities than construction. It is merely the negative of the negative, it remains in the same sphere, it nurtures the same terrorist pretension to truth, i.e. to the association of sign – here in its defeat, that's the only difference – and intensity, it demands the same surgical intervention on words, the same division and the same exclusions that the lover's demand demands of skin. (EL, 305)

All politics is a desire for Empire and empire. Every politician is a pimp.

The Empire is an indefinite expanse. What immobilises its *limes* for a moment is the running-out-of-breath of the flight forwards and the concern for exclusive appropriation.

Capital realises the Roman idea of the imperial expanse.

American presidents are Emperors, Washington is Rome, the USA is Italy, Europe is their Greece.

Certain 'nations' do not manage to become sedentarized in the Empire: they are placed in reserves, or on the confines, or are destroyed.

White skin arouses the desire of the resident aliens [*métèques*] as the inside calls for the outside: the skin hollows into interiority, simulating depth, and gives rise to prostitution.

Racism is the jealousy felt by the Imperial name for the names of the others, the nomad nations.

It is also the jealousy of each of these nations for its sisters; any jealousy can give rise to Empire. (MP, 18-20)

Nietzsche says: why have we become incredulous and wary? Because we were taught veracity and we have turned that requirement against the word which gave itself out as veracity itself, the revealed word. Similarly, one can say: why are national minorities rising in modern countries? Because we were taught nationality, and we have turned it against the minority which gave itself out as possessing the nation. Nations were born in the break up of the space of the Empire: but this break-up made many empires: for the provinces today, the national capital is like Rome was for the provinces of those times. On the French dimension, the royal or republican masters of Paris have been and are no less imperialistic with respect to the provinces than Rome with respect to its provinces or allies. The language used by Paris is suspected, detested (expected). Centralism is called into question, and with it the sociopolitical space proper to it, whose Euclidian features — isomorphy of all regions, neutrality of all directions, commutation of all figures according to laws of transformation, were already to be found in the Greek ideal and the Jacobin idea of citizenship.

What is being sketched out is a group (to be defined) of heterogeneous spaces, a great *patchwork* of singularities all of which are in a minority; the mirror in which they are supposed to recognize their unity in the form of the national image is breaking. Decadence of staging, as spectacular, that politics was. Europe comes down a notch in the definition of elementary political groups: while the masters try to unify it from above, the common people cut it up again from below. . . The decadence of the centre goes along with the decline of the idea of Empire. In this context, there Is more to be found on the side of the thinkers of multiplicities, like Thucydides and Machiavelli, than on the side of centralists of any persuasion. (RP, 145-6)

You come to live in a corner region. The Western empire here comes up against Its ultImate lImIt: further on is the reverse side of the Orient. But in latitude too, you are on the line of contact of the rich Northern hemisphere with the belt of poor Souths. All we have learned in politics, you and I, has been conceived of and practised according to the principles of unity, finality and identity. Europe will have fed and provided motive force, for a few centuries, and America after it, to the machine of central Empires, decorated with the sign of eagles. But here, Herbert, you are situated on its edge.

If from this uncertain zone in which you have just settled down there emanates a special warmth, don't go thinking that this is because the Empire neglects itself on its marches and allows the energies it puts to hard work in the centre escape into thin air. Its warmth comes from the fact that it is a border region where the so-called Imperial Empire, with its logic, spatiality, temporality with centralist pretensions, contradictions included, overlaps with the clouds of little centrifugal forces radiating in ephemeral fashion short stories in incongruent spaces. . . The chicanos are perhaps an antagonistic product of the capitalist empire, but you would be wrong to expect them to develop and resolve the contradiction you might suppose them to embody, by means of their struggles.

These struggles are in no way means to an end, they do not come under a different finality situated in the same field, but another field, where movements are centrifugal, time discontinuous and remarks paradoxical. The revolution, if you want to keep this word, in no way comes from a dialectic, for example the contradiction which by uniting overcapitalisation in the North and underemployment in the South would end up by making this contradiction burst out and would oblige men to resolve it by overthrowing the empire. The force of the swarthy resident aliens camping in your corner comes of their weakness: the heavy centralist phantasy does not have a total hold over their bodies, nor their minds. (RT, 116-19)

One can read Bloch in this way, and one can read Munzer in this way: like Tertullian, i.e. as leftists: nihilists established on an assured Elsewhere. But we 'revolutionaries' after 1968, says the fainted student, could not, any more than Bloch, 'Marxist' after 1956, be candid apologists, could not talk as though the secret of the right moment were in our power. What in fact exempts Bloch from sombre irony is humour, the impossibility of getting a foothold in the elsewhere and exploiting it theoretically and practically. The irony of *hos me* says: 'what is, is as though not being'; hope says: 'what is not, is as though being'; but the true brother of affirmative hope is the humour which denounces any flirting with irony, saying, 'indeed, *even* what is not, is as though being, and thus there is no nothing-ness and no "remainder", everything is or nothing is, say it as you will; the question is that of knowing if something can *happen*, if the relationship of forces can be twisted round, as hopes my sister hope, but nobody knows where and when this happens'.

Through hope, the less strong is made into the stronger (as in a particular figure of rhetoric, denounced by Aristotle), through humour, the less strong, wily enough not to demand more strength, confesses to a sort of 'passivity' (quite contrary to irony), it maintains 'the value of surprise: the minute [. . .], those little emblems that hardly break through', it allows itself to be surprised by 'some excess which nothing motivates externally', it confesses its un-power when it comes to determin-ing the favourable moment, the instant when this excess comes to break through day-to-dayness, its unpower when it comes to intensities. But this confession, which will still be nihilistic if it goes along with recrimination, is affirmative just as well, like hope itself, fully pulsional and in conformity with pulsional logic, since the humorous declaration of un-power is in itself already a trap, let's call it the *subter-fuge of weak strength*, a trap laid for powers, and whose spring is that these powers are jealous of weakness. (RP, 69-70)

The elimination of the *educable third party* belongs to the new perspective, as does the elimination of finality, truth and unity; and its maintenance belongs to the old perspective, in which we are also immersed. In the first case, there is no body to be organised or reorganised, but harassment. And here we should have to show, 1. that there are many other forms of harassment than bombs; and 2. in what harassment consists. We should see that it is always something like a *twisting round*, the ruse or machination by which the little ones, the 'weak' become for a moment stronger than the strong. *Make a weapon of illness*, said the Heidelberg socialist patients' collective. And the committee against the torture of political prisoners in the German Federal Republic: 'Become aware of this material strength which is weakness transformed into strength'.

This twisting belongs to a logic which is that of the sophists and rhetoricians of the first generation, not to the master-logician, to a time of opportunities, not that of the clock of world-history, to a space of minorities, with no centre. (RP, 153-4)

Discourse, Figure

Many of the premises of the 'libidinal economy' I have presented in the first chapter were initially worked out in Lyotard's long and rather formidable second book, *Discours, figure* (1971). For reasons which will become clearer as the discussion progresses, *Discours, figure* is not an easy book to discuss or even to present coherently: this chapter will not manage to summarise all its arguments, and will be quite severely selective. *Discours, figure* can, roughly, be said to fall into two parts, divided by a sort of applied analysis of what is called a 'Fragment of the "History" of Desire'. The second half of this work elaborates a sort of libidinal aesthetics on the basis of the type of reading of Freud I have discussed: and despite the considerable interest of that part of the book, it ultimately encounters the same problems sketched out with respect to *Economie libidinale*. Paradoxically, the first part of the book, which the second part aims to surpass, will retain us for longer: this first part relies on phenomenology rather than psychoanalysis; and if it will indeed appear that the grounds for criticising and ultimately rejecting the presuppositions of phenomenology are good, it will also be possible to see that it is nonetheless this first part of *Discours, figure* which looks forward most clearly to Lyotard's most recent work, and which also contains explicit grounds for critique of both structuralism in its classical forms, and the Hegelian dialectic which has haunted all contemporary French philosophers as a powerful discursive machine they would like to defeat. Careful consideration of this part of *Discours, figure* will also allow an approach to what is no doubt the fundamental drive in all of Lyotard's work, which is, as he puts it in *Discours, figure,* to 'rendre compte... du fait qu'il y a de l'événement', to account for the fact that there are events, or, more literally, that there is (some) event.

   Discours, figure begins with an apparently simple assertion that reading and seeing are not quite the same thing: phenomenologically, the experience of reading a text and looking at the world, or at a painting, are different sorts of experience. Certainly it is necessary to see the text one wishes to read, but this is a minimal visibility: in principle the phenomenal text is not seen as such, the 'materiality of the signifier' vanishes in the interests of an immediate intellection of the signified. Again in principle, insofar as I am reading, treating the book as text and not as an aesthetic object, I pay no attention to plastic values of the printed signs: I *recognize* those signs immediately and that is all that matters. It is of course possible to locate in this notion of the transparency of the signifier traces of idealism or, as Derrida formulates it much more rigorously, of 'logocentrism', but the fact remains that, whatever its *philosophical* validity, such a transparency is the most common *experience* of reading. The space of the text is barely spatial: it is *flat*, and the signs are linked according to a simple principle of horizontal contiguity. Against this, the visual space of the world is complex, multi-dimensional and *deep*, oriented around the spatiality of my own body held within it. Drawing extensively on the work of Merleau-Ponty, Lyotard stresses the richness and complication, or implication, of the body in the world: the visibility of the world is only made possible because my own seeing body is a visible thing in the world,

So what there is is not things identical to themselves which, afterwards, offer themselves to the seer, and it is not a seer, empty at first, who, afterwards, opens himself to them, but something we could scarcely get closer to except by feeling it with our gaze, things we could not dream of seeing 'naked' because the gaze itself envelops them, clothes them with its flesh. . . We say then that our body is a being with two leaves, on the one side a thing among things and on the other what sees and touches them; we say, because it is obvious, that it unites these two properties in itself, and its double belonging to the order of the 'object' and the order of the 'subject' unveils to us very unexpected relationships between the two orders. . . We place ourselves. . . in us *and* in things, in us *and* in the others, at the point where, by a sort of chiasmus, we become the others and we become the world. (Maurice Merleau-Ponty, *Le Visible et l'invisible* (Paris: Gallimard, 1964), pp. 173, 180-81, 212). On Merleau-Ponty and *Discours, figure*, see too Rodolphe Gasché's remarkable article, 'Deconstruction as Criticism', *Glyph* 6 (1979), 177-216.

the nexus of a 'chiasmus' crossing subject and object, in which the world is of the same 'flesh' as my body, and that body of the same 'objecthood' as the world it sees. And if it is felt that against this mutual belonging of body and world the experience of looking at a painting will approximate more closely to the experience of reading a text, then Lyotard insists on the plasticity of the painted surface, the rhythm of lines which solicit an answering rhythm in the body of the viewer, and the chromatic values which allow the flatness of the canvas to recede and open into the type of theatrical 'scene' we have already discussed.

This basic distinction between reading and seeing, established on the basis of phenomenological descriptions of experience, supports two series of terms used in *Discours, figure*. On the side of reading, terms such as flatness, surface, signification, opposition, systematicity, conceptuality, legality and the 'discourse' of the book's title: on the side of seeing, terms such as depth, *sens,* difference, instability, the body, desire and transgression, and the eponymous *figure*. The precise sense of some of these terms will become clearer as the discussion progresses: for the moment it is worth stressing the *simplicity* of this set-up, which seems to involve a critical opposition between 'good' things (*figure,* seeing and so on), and 'bad' things (discourse, reading and so on). Before correcting this impression of simplicity, which is indeed a false impression, it is worth noting that, however complex the twists Lyotard operates on these two series of terms, this initial critical moment is not negligible: the stubborn and apparently quite banal insistence that reading and seeing are not the same thing already disturbs a whole tradition of talking about literary texts in a language of visibility, from a certain *ut pictura poesis,* through the famous French critic Gustave Lanson's description of Balzac as 'the vigorous and faithful painter of one moment and part of French society' (*Histoire de la littérature française,* 14th edition (Paris: Hachette, 1917), p. 1004), to much more sophisticated approaches to texts, such as that of Jean Starobinski (see especially the introduction to *L'Oeil vivant* (Paris: Gallimard, 1961)); and disturbs too older and newer claims to 'read' visual phenomena (from world as book to the semiology of the image). However, Lyotard is not content to remain at this simple level, which would correspond to the position of *critique,* a position which, although ambivalently espoused in *Discours, figure* (and certainly not vituperated as in *Economie libidinale),* does not operate as the major organisational principle of the book as a whole: rather, in a sense very close to that elaborated by Derrida (as Gasché shows), the concern is not to *maintain* the apparent opposition between these two series, nor even to invert the traditional valorizations they imply, but to *deconstruct* them.

It is probably easiest to approach this deconstruction via Lyotard's discussion of structural linguistics, and specifically of Saussure, insofar as it is the structuralism inspired by Saussure's work which is the initial target of much of the insistence on phenomenological specificities in this first part of *Discours, figure.*

Like everybody else, Lyotard is interested in Saussure's famous claim about language being 'a system of differences without positive terms', and, also like everybody else, he is concerned about what becomes of *reference* in Saussure's doctrine, and what becomes of the *parole* which Saussure opposes to the system of *langue* and then largely leaves to one

side. Unlike almost everybody else, however, Lyotard has a close look
at Saussure's 'text' (the *Cours de linguistique générale* being assembled
of course from students' notes) and is not satisfied with general denunciations.

> [Saussure's] conception of structure leads him to absorb the whole of signification
> into cutting-up, i.e. into the system of intervals between the terms, or the system
> of *values*. And yet he does not give up having recourse at the very same time to
> an idea of signification which opposes it to value as vertical is opposed to hori-
> zontal or depth to surface. What could pass for a failing in a linguist determined
> to limit his study to the structure of language, that is, the temptation of introducing
> the thickness of the sign into the transparency of the system, is, however, much
> more than an error or a naivety; a fact which one could term transcendental is
> betrayed here, namely that all discourse constitutes its object in depth; when
> this discourse is that of the linguist and he takes signification as his object, he
> spontaneously thematises it as something thick, he is led to posit signification
> as a sign. In reality this depth is an effect of object-positioning due to the current
> discourse: which holds signification at a distance and posits that it is a sign just
> as it does any object. (DF, 93 4)

This passage (which also gives an idea of the difficulty of much of *Discours, figure)* expounds the core of the book's discussion of structuralism,
and will be worth explicating in some detail.

The first part of the passage depends on the recognition that Saussure
tends, in one whole aspect of his thought, to derive linguistic meaning
entirely from *value,* from the *place* of a given term in the system of
langue: this is in the spirit of the famous 'differences without positive
terms' remark, and Lyotard quotes further from the manuscript sources
on which the edition of the *Course in General Linguistics* is based (see
Robert Godel, *Les sources manuscrites du Cours de linguistique générale*
(Geneva: Droz et Minard, 1967)) to make the point clearly:

> The meaning *[sens]* of a term depends on the presence or the absence of a
> neighbouring term. From the system, we arrive at the idea of value, not that of
> meaning. The system leads to the term. Then it will be seen that signification is
> determined by what surrounds [the term]. The word does not exist without a
> signified and a signifier: but the signified is only the summary of linguistic value
> and presupposes the play of the terms among themselves (...). What is in the
> word is only ever determined by the concourse of what exists around it, associa-
> tively and syntagmatically. (Godel, 237-40; quoted DF, 97)

The notion of value, which is most familiar at the level of the phoneme
(as all the books say, the phonemes of /cat/ are determined by the difference of that sequence to /bat/, /cut/, /cap/, and so on), is here extended

to the level of semantics: and this tendency in Saussure is emphasised in followers of his doctrine such as Jakobson: open the dictionary to discover the meaning of the word 'horse', and you find an exemplification of what Saussure says. On the one hand, the dictionary provides other words which can be substituted for 'horse', and on the other, provides examples of exemplary sentences in which the meaning of the word is determined by its immediate context with minimum equivocity. First, the 'associative' links, secondly, the syntagmatic ones: the signified of the signifier 'horse' is in fact simply the virtual set of constraints which hold that signifier in its place in the system: it would rapidly follow from this that, strictly speaking, there is no signified as such, no 'positive term' at all (DF, 99-100). But if this is so, why is there nonetheless a certain hesitation in Saussure, and, especially, why such an attachment to the notion of the signified? It is not sufficient for such an attachment to be impatiently denounced as a residual idealism, and for the signifier to be chosen as the easy guarantor of 'materialism' – if only because, as Derrida has shown and as Lyotard is well aware in *Discours, figure,* once the signified is called into question, it is no longer strictly speaking possible to speak of the signifier as such either, insofar as signifier can only mean what signifies a signified. Lyotard's answer to this problem is suggested in the passage we are attempting to explicate, and depends on the assertion, not that Saussure simply 'bracketed out' the referent and the reality of *parole,* but that it is precisely an ambiguous attachment to the situation of *parole* which accounts for the attachment to the notion of the signified, and that this notion of the signified in fact depends on a confusion of that signified with the very referent from which it is supposed to be sternly cut, or, more precisely, on a confusion of the operation of *signification* with the operation of *designation.*

Lyotard approaches the question via a discussion of *negativity,* and, on the basis of the initial distinction between reading and seeing, argues that although there is indeed a negativity involved in seeing, this negativity is of a type different from the negativity which inhabits the system of *langue:* these two distinct types of negativity will become linked to designation on the one hand, and to signification on the other:

Negativity is a position which rules over two heterogeneous experiences. There is a negation implied in the visible: distance, the constitutive spacing of space, negation experienced in variability. The experience of this mobility which engenders extension, thickness, figure, is a privileged object of description for the phenomenologist, it is the constitutive seeing that Husserl attempts to rediscover beneath its collapse into formed vision, it is the permanent genesis of objective space and body fomenting beneath them in the flesh according to Merleau-Ponty. Saying that it is *beneath* can mean that it is unconscious, but this unconsciousness belongs to the transcendental order... No doubt painting is what brings us as close as possible to the transcendental activity, if it is true that this activity is indeed a force of disjunction rather than a force of synthesis. What the painting shows is the world in the process of being made... From this point of view, the painting is the strangest of objects when it fulfils the function given it by modern painting: it is an object in which is shown the engendering of objects, transcendental activity itself.

The negation which works in the system of language appears to be of a different sort, as does its unconsciousness... [The unconsciousness of seeing] refers to a phenomenology, [that of language] to an archaeology. In the first of these, it is the very act which is unconscious of itself and forgets itself in the naive natural fascination of the object it has in view; for the second, unconsciousness belongs to the order of the virtual, it precedes and surrounds the act because it is what makes the act possible, it invests it and remains unknown to it because the act erases it by its presence. Actual unconsciousness is this shadow which light is for itself, the anonymity of seeing which sees the thing and does not see itself; virtual unconsciousness inhabits, not the nucleus of the act, but its surroundings... (DF, 27-30)

But if this distinction appears to remain at the 'simple' level of the distinction between reading and seeing, then things become more complicated as Lyotard strives to show that, even if these two orders of the negative are heterogeneous, something like a 'seeing' does nonetheless inhabit language, not in the naive way assumed by Lanson, but strangely and, perhaps for essential reasons, ungraspably. This 'seeing' involves the question of designation as opposed to signification, and will be approached via the question of *deixis*. Although we are still here moving

---

Placing speech in existence comes down to placing existence in speech. Now every linguistic system has special words for this purpose, deictics. . . *Here, now, I, you, this* receive no *signification* from the fact of their position in the system of *langue*, they only operate by *designating* an object, a referent, in the spatio-temporal field in which the current discourse is being proffered. Terms of pure designation, taking their value only with respect to the linguistic present, indices which from the heart of the system of *langue* signal towards its outside, the sensory field in which the speaker and listener coexist. (DMF, 86)

within the purview of structural linguistics, this question also engages with the second object I said would be under attack in *Discours, figure,* namely the Hegelian dialectic.

I cannot here attempt to summarise the detail of Lyotard's reading of the opening chapter of Hegel's *Phenomenology of Spirit:* the essential point is the following. Hegel, on Lyotard's reading, attempts to show that immediate 'sense-certainty' breaks down when obliged to express itself in language. Its 'here' and 'now' provide no linguistic certainty: 'now' will sometimes be day and sometimes night, 'here' sometimes a house and sometimes a tree, and so on. But such contradictions occur only insofar as sense-certainty is forced to confront the obligation of linguistic expression: Hegel also recognises that contra*diction* is not contra*sensation,* and attempts to analyse that certainty in terms of a sort of pre-linguistic signification based on *indication,* which will lead us finally to *designation* as such while rooting that designation in the phenomenological order of seeing. But in finding a dialectic at the heart of sense-certainty, Hegel's pretension is still that of discovering a sort of infra-language which will lead from the apparent immediacy of sensation to the mediations of the concept. He attempts to do this by showing that even gestural indication is in fact never immediate at all, that any 'here' cannot ever simply be indicated in itself, but depends on situation with respect to other 'heres', any 'now' on situation with respect to other 'nows': 'Thus the gesture [of indication] will be a dialectic of gestures, the place a dialectic of places, and situating will involve a laconic introduction of the other into the same and [therefore] its mediation' (DF, 37).

Against this movement, Lyotard argues that such simple mediation is impossible, precisely because of the distinction already made between the two sorts of negativity. It is indeed true that the determination of 'here' depends on negative relations with indicators such as 'in front', 'behind', 'left', 'right' and so on, but the negativity involved here is not that of the linguistic or conceptual system, but that of the body in space:

the place indicated, the *here,* is grasped in a *sensory field,* as the focus of that field to be sure, but not in such a manner that its surroundings are eliminated as is the case in the choices operated by a speaker; they remain there in the uncertain and undeniable, curvilinear presence of what sits on the edges of vision, as a reference absolutely necessary to the indication of place, as Hegel understands it, but a reference the nature of which marks a complete break with the nature of a linguistic operation: the latter refers to a discontinuous inventory, whereas sight refers to a topological space; the linguistic operation is subject to the rule of the spoken sequence which requires the unicity of the actual and the elimination of the virtual, whereas sight determines a sensory field ruled by the quasi-actuality of the virtual and the quasi-virtuality of the given. Hegel is quite right to say that there is negativity *[du négatif]* in the sensory, that it is natural to doubt, that animals are cleverer than the sensualists when they despair of the reality of things sufficiently to eat them; but this destruction which is there in the field of the sensory is not the invariant negativity which makes of language the means of understanding one another. (DF, 38)

This refusal of the Hegelian mediation does not, however, lead to a simple reinforcement of the apparent opposition between the 'reading' series and the 'seeing' series from which we began, but to the attempt to produce a non-dialectical complication of those two series, and eventually a deconstruction. Discussing the originality of indication with respect to the language-system, Lyotard is obliged to use words such as 'here', 'now' and so on: if this necessary expedient is *not* to lead him back into Hegel's totalising gesture, then he will have to establish that in some sense such words do not in fact belong to the language-system as formulated by Saussure, or at least that the calculation of their 'value' cannot be achieved simply along the lines of the calculation of the value of 'horse'. This stress on the oddness of such terms, which linguistics knows as 'deictics', is thus vital to the enterprise of *Discours, figure*. Here is Lyotard's first formulation of their difference:

the interest and enigma of these words which...wait for their 'content' on their actualisation in a discursive act, is precisely that they open language onto an experience which language cannot stock in its inventory since it is the experience of a *hic et nunc,* of an ego, i.e. precisely of sense-certainty. Every other word remains potentially loaded with its significations in the virtual table of *langue,* even when no-one pronounces it; it is not my discourse which creates the content of the word, and its position in the sentence only actualises one of the meanings attached to it. Whereas in truth the meaning of an indicator [i.e. a deictic] is not, it can only *exist:* we can give no definition of *I,* of *here* while still remaining in the semantic field in which they are placed, without carrying out on them a metalinguistic operation which is equivalent to a change of level, as in the grammarian's definition: '*I* is the first person pronoun', which consists in transferring the term onto the level of its syntactic function and consequently in grasping it at a level quite different from the lexical level on which I am placed when I define, for example, the whale as an aquatic mammal. (DF, 39)

And this is, finally, where we can return to the problem over signification and designation announced earlier with respect to Saussure. For what is specific to these deictic terms is that their 'signification' cannot in fact be separated from their designation, except in the immediate spatio-temporal situation of their utterance as part of an act of *parole*. Although Lyotard does not put it in quite this way, we might say that the deictic is the place of a certain collapse of the distinction between *langue* and *parole* on the one hand, and on the other, of the distinction between signified and referent. Deictics are indubitably part of language, and yet they do not strictly speaking signify: rather they open the 'flat' negativity of the language-system onto the 'deep' negativity of the sensory field.

In the remarkable critique by Jacques Derrida of the first *Logical Investigation*
[by Husserl] (*La Voix et le phénomène* (Paris: PUF, 1967) [tr. *Speech and
Phenomena* (Evanston: Northwestern University Press, 1973)]), it does not
appear that Husserl's analysis of indication is attacked in the right place. It is
certain that the idea of an 'indicated signification' is inconceivable and contrary
to the principle of the ideality of meaning, as Derrida notes; but first of all Husserl
himself abandons this idea. . . and secondly it is impossible to draw from it a
justification for bringing the deictic signifier back to the status of any other
signifier in the system, which all in all is not very far from what Husserl does.
Rather one must. . . refer its use to a supposed exteriority, here that of the
speaker himself: without this dimension of designation, no deictic is conceivable.
In other words, the deictic is not a simple value inside the system, but an
element which from the inside refers to the outside; it is not thinkable *in* the
system, but *through* it. A difference of the greatest importance, which does
not imply any return to the 'metaphysics of presence', as Derrida might fear.
(DF, 115-16 n 18)

It will be remembered that this negativity was described as 'transcendental', to do with the constitution of objects. Engendered through the
negativity of distance, objects display only one of their faces, and hide
others. To use Merleau-Ponty's example, it is impossible to see all six
faces of a cube simultaneously. And were the perceiving eye immobile,
it would be unable to constitute the cube as such at all: the eye moves,
and the cube is the result of a synthesis of its successive perceptions of
the object, which is thus in the same voluminous space as the eye and
the body of the perceiver. Again, this movement is quite different from
the 'mobility' of the speaker among the semantic sub-sets of the language,
gathering the elements needed for articulation into discourse, working
according to Jakobson's principles of selection and combination. And
this different movement is marked in language in deictics, which will
provide a first theoretical anchoring point for the notion of the *figure*.

And this also allows us to return to the passage about Saussure we are
attempting to explicate. We saw that Lyotard suggested an ambivalence
in Saussure's account of signification: on the one hand, the tendency to
absorb it into the notion of value, into the system of differences; on the
other, an attachment to the notion of the *sign*, of signifier hiding and
revealing its signified: it will be remembered that Lyotard linked this
latter tendency to a 'transcendental' fact, to the constitution of objects.
For Lyotard, this question of the transcendental and the constitution of
the object as revealing/hiding has much more to do with the sensory
than the linguistic. Any object is constituted as deep, concealing another

side: Saussure famously likens the sign to a piece of paper and the signifier and signified to its recto and verso. In order to describe the sign in this sort of way, Saussure, said so often to bracket out the referent, is *taking the sign itself as his referent.* The referent, pointed out in a specific act of *parole* by deixis, allows, as we have seen, an irruption into the flat space of the system of the deep space of perception. The depth Saussure is thereby led to attribute to the sign is thus not specific to the sign, but is a property of the act of reference operated by his own discourse, as an act of *parole,* on the object 'sign' or 'language'. In other words, language is not made up of signs, but insofar as it designates objects, presents those objects as signs, with a manifest side and a hidden side: the linguist's language happens to constitute an object called 'language' or 'sign', and thus becomes embroiled in the transcendental negativity of distance, depth and movement which it also tries to evacuate from that object by simultaneously theorising signification as value.

It will be said that the illusion of the signified, tenacious, ingrained by centuries of idealist realism, takes its motif from a transfer of the relation of designation onto that of signification, in a sort of 90° rotation which brings the designatum onto the signified and makes the latter get confused with the object. Thus is grounded the sort of double of the world which Platonic mythics calls 'thinkable', intelligible, but which Platonic dialectics, at the beginning of the *Parmenides,* for example, quickly shows to be, precisely, unthinkable in its relation to the signifier. It is because the same status is attributed to the signified as to the designatum, because it is placed at the end of a modifiable distance which separates it from the signifier, because one makes of it an essence thought exactly on the model of the entity of the thing, in short because one has transferred into the heart of the table of language a 'perspective' which is impossible there, i.e. the perspective according to which what is aimed at or intentionalised is offered to the speaking subject – because of this that in the end signification can seem both to manifest and to hide a signified, to signify it according to this relationship of depth, of figure on ground which belongs to our experience of the visible. What is true is the immediate presence of the signified, which is nothing other than the potential operations enveloping the signifier when it appears in the spoken sequence: *there is no signified,* except by an effect of mirage. (DF, 100)

Precisely. Except that the solution is too simple and 'positivist' (Ibid.). Lyotard's aim is not to denounce an illusion and destroy an 'error': or at least not in this way, which cannot account for the tenacity of the error. As our original text on Saussure said, the tendency to hang on to this view of signification in spite of the more 'rigorous' analysis in terms of value is not simply a mistake, but reveals a truth; namely that the referent or designatum of *any* discourse, whatever its scientific pretensions, positions its designatum 'at a distance', and obscures the clarity which is the normal experience of language use. 'The linguist is condemned to the fate of all speakers: we cannot speak without tracing this distance between our discourse and its object' (DF, 103): simply, the object of the linguist's discourse is language itself, which provokes that discourse to trace that same distance in the very discourse which argues against it.

This complex imbrication of our two types of negativity cannot be neatly dialecticised in terms of knowledge, but sits uneasily on the account of language which provides the basis for structuralism. On this account, attempts to talk about texts in terms of vision, or of visual phenomena in terms of reading, fail to to justice to this complex situation, but resolve it arbitrarily in favour of one negativity or another. Lyotard's notion of the *figure* will attempt to provide a better account of what is at stake.

A text is what does not allow itself to be moved. The intervals which separate its elements, letters, words, sentences, which punctuate them, are the projection onto the sensory support, the page, the stone, of the intervals which separate the distinctive and significant terms in the table of *langue*. And yet language is also a deep thing, it must also be possible to make it the object of operations of fiction; and the proof can be found in the very work of establishing the language; that proof is that the linguist, at the very moment of establishing the place of terms in the plane of structure, which has no thickness, makes use of a procedure, commutation, which nonetheless demands depth. But there are other pieces of evidence which bear witness to the fact that a text must not only be able to be read according to its signification, which comes under linguistic space, but *seen* according to its configuration, which is supported by the sensory-imaginary space in which it is inscribed. Fiction, which is what makes figure out of text, consists entirely in a play on intervals; the figure is a deformation which imposes a different form onto the disposition of the linguistic unities. This form is not reducible to the constraints of structure. (DF, 61)

Analysis of the deictic and the process of designation has allowed us to trouble the apparently simple opposition of the series of seeing and reading, and led to the awareness that the very discourse of linguistics, even if it attempts to discuss signification purely in terms of value, in fact depends on the 'deep' space of designation or reference in order to constitute the 'flat' structural space of its object. This complication in the relationship of the two negativities, which refuses dialectical sublation into a higher-level 'knowledge', suggests that the two spaces in question cannot in any simple sense be mutually exclusive, and this is what Lyotard is approaching in the above passage via the notion of *form*. For various reasons, 'form' has become a difficult word to use in the context of Anglo-American literary theory, either being assimilated to 'structure' (whereas Lyotard opposes the two), or recalling notions of 'organic form' (with which Lyotard's conception has little in common – if anything, 'form' in Lyotard's sense would be what *disrupts* 'organic form'). For example, structural analysis of folk-tales or myths may establish a structure for these objects: this structure, as worked out by a Lévi-Strauss, functions as a sort of matrix from which several versions of tale or myth can be generated. Lyotard is not very interested in this type of set-up, where the structure is quite loose and where the form is therefore not perceived as the result of a violence operating on structural constraints, but as an exploitation of the 'play' allowed by those constraints. The two negativities here apparently coexist quite peaceably (DF, 61-2): Lyotard is more interested in cases where the form involves disruption of structural rules at quite basic and constraining levels, rather than merely operating as 'stylistic variants' within the broad units prescribed by the structural analysis – and he finds such cases in what he calls 'radical poetry', and specifically in Mallarmé's text, 'Un coup de dés jamais n'abolira le hasard'.

At first, Mallarmé's poetics would appear to exemplify a Saussurean insistence on the 'arbitrary nature of the sign', and even take it to the point of 'abolishing' object or referent altogether: 'Mallarmé's "elimination" is the deepening of the spacing of reference as an unbridgeable distance separating Word and thing and guaranteeing the former its ideal import' (DF, 63). But this 'death-work' operated by literature on the world is not simply the abolition of the world, or at least the visible form of the words of Mallarmé's work will still in some sense show the recreated world: 'Un coup de dés' will attempt to use its typography to present what Mallarmé calls a 'notion' in the sensory space of the object. If the first aspect of Mallarmé's work suggests that chance, 'le hasard', can indeed be abolished by a radical separation of language from reference, the second suggests that this chance will *never* be abolished (and this is what the 'title' of the work states): and in the famous later statement from the poem, 'rien n'aura eu lieu que le lieu', nothing will have taken place but the place, comes an awareness that the language of the text is spatial, inseparable from the depth and chance of its other (DF, 63-4). The curious typographical disposition of the work introduces into the page a plastic element, depending not on the regulated spacing of text in the normal sense, but on the visual, gestural experience of the body in space:

What then is this space of the 'Coup de dés'? A logical space, because words are written in it; a sensory space, because what is between the terms is as important as the terms (...); imaginary, because the figure of these intervals is ruled only by the fiction carried by the discourse... When word becomes thing, this is not in order to copy a visible thing, but to make visible an invisible, lost 'thing': it takes the form of the imaginary it is talking about... The book-object contains two objects: an object of signification (made of signifieds linked together according to the rules of syntax) – this is an 'ideal' object, which says: 'there is no notion (no signified) outside the sensory world'. We *understand* this object. And then, an object of *signifiance,* made up of graphic and plastic signifiers (gaps, typographical variations, use of the double page, distribution of signs across this surface), made in fact of writing disturbed by considerations of sensibility (of 'sensuality'). The first object allows the second to be understood, the second shows the first. (DF, 69, 71)

Mallarmé's poem presents, in Lyotard's terms, a discourse worked on by the *figure,* and he summarises the types of figure discovered in the text as follows:

From these elementary considerations, we can already distinguish three types of figure at work in the 'Coup de dés': the image, which is the figure placed in the order of language, but on the plane of the signified (comparison, metaphor); the form, a sort of figure which also has its place in language, but which works on the linguistic signifier, and is not signified in the discourse; the sensory figure, which is a configuration distributing the linguistic signifiers (here graphic signifiers) according to demands which are not those of discourse strictly speaking, but those of a rhythm (here a visual rhythm). These figures are thus arrayed from the pure signified to the plastic signifier, via the linguistic signifier, they form a chain or a relay between the intelligible discursive order and the sensory spatiotemporal order, they prove the presence of forms able to cross the barriers separating the intelligible world and the sensory world, forms independent of the milieu they inform. (DF, 71)

In this analysis, we have moved from a claim that the depth of reference pierces the flat space of the linguistic system, and that this is most clear in the case of deictics, that this necessary incursion of the transcendental, object-constituting distance of negativity complicates the simple or virtual negativity of the *langue,* and explains an ambiguous attachment on the part of Saussure to an account of signification in terms of signs rather than values – from this to an assertion that a certain form of artistic practice can in some sense reveal or bear witness to this through its manifestation of 'figures' which do a certain violence to the invariant spacings of the *langue.* These figures are the result of the impossibility of maintaining the separation we initially approached through the phenomenological difference between reading and seeing, and constitute what Lyotard calls a 'deconstruction' of the opposition between them. These figures introduce all sorts of complications into the discourse which talks about them: insofar as they are a disruption of discourse, then they will, to put it simply, be difficult to talk about. Moreover, they cannot in principle become an object of *knowledge*, insofar as, in Lyotard's account at least, knowledge presupposes precisely the neat separation of its own discourse from its object of knowledge. The figure disrupts this arrangement with a violence, *as an event*, which Lyotard does not hesitate to link to *truth* and not to knowledge.

> Utopia is that truth never appears where it is expected. That means a lot of things, including at least the two following which will serve us as guides. First, truth shows itself as an aberration when measured by signification and knowledge. It jars [*elle détonne*]. Jarring in discourse deconstructs its order. Truth in no way passes through a discourse of signification, its impossible *topos* cannot be located by the coordinates of the geography of knowledge, but it makes itself felt on the surface of discourse by effects, and this presence of meaning is called expression. Only not every expression is truth. (DF, 17)

And in fact the presentation so far has tended to remain all too simply in the domain of knowledge, and come close to suggesting that the figure is no more than the reintroduction of reference into Saussure. If this were the case, then the enterprise of *Discours, figure* would be reducible to those recent attempts to argue for reference (and thereby, it is thought, all the seriousness of 'the real' and eventually, perhaps, 'the political') by playing Frege against Saussure. But there is already a discussion of

> The most accessible account of these issues is no doubt Christopher Norris, 'Sense, reference and logic: a critique of post-structuralist theory', in *The Contest of Faculties: Philosophy and theory after deconstruction* (London: Methuen, 1985), pp. 47-69: see Norris's note 3 (p. 232) for further references. I cannot here go into Norris's own confusions about 'post-structuralism'.

Frege and the doctrine of sense and reference in *Discours, figure* which in fact shows a profound congruence between Saussure and Frege, despite the latter's undeniable and important stress on reference, insofar as both in principle want to maintain the separation which is here in question, and which is most evident in Frege in the relegation of 'literature' to the domain of the individual 'image' in an enclosed subjectivity, as opposed to the objective exteriority of reference and truth-value which would be that of science (DF, 105-16). To escape from such limitations, we need to stress that what is meant by *figure* is not just reference, designation, the depth of corporeal space, and this will prepare for the abandonment of the phenomenological stress which has marked this first part of the book:

Signification does not exhaust meaning, but nor do signification and designation combined. We cannot remain with the alternative of these two spaces between which the discourse slips – the space of the system and that of the subject. There is another space, the figural. We must suppose it to be buried, it does not allow itself to be seen, nor thought, it is indicated laterally, fugitively at the heart of discourses and perceptions, as what disturbs them. (DF, 135)

In other words, our presentation so far has been partial: we have tended to assume that the figural involves the incursion of visual or perceptual space into the space of discourse, and thus uncritically accepted a rudimentary phenomenological grasp of the nature of the former. But the figural can also disrupt visual or perceptual space too, and demonstrating that this is so is a vital move in the deconstructive project of *Discours, figure.*

Lyotard was certainly not concerned to reclaim the naive self-evidence of sense-certainty against Hegel: and he is also suspicious of the phenomenological assumption of a normal, proper body 'at home' in the world. He notes, for example, that it is abstract to think of perception in isolation from emotion, and criticizes Merleau-Ponty for precisely such an abstraction (DF, 137 n 3), but emotion could not simply be added into the description without disturbing it, for emotion would be impossible 'if our bodily hold on the world were not uncertain in its basis, if the possibility of a non-world were not given at the same time as its "certainty"' (DF, 137). The problem with this phenomenological description is that, just like the linguistic order to which it has thus far been opposed, it tends to think its specific negativity in terms of *op-position:* the figural space, which will work against the perceptual just as much as against the linguistic, will work according to *difference.* Again there is a danger of confusion here, insofar as difference was presented as precisely the principle of the linguistic system, according to Saussure's most well-known dictum. But the doctrine of value, as taken up and refined by Saussure's followers, and notably Jakobson, tends to resolve any apparent fluidity of difference into the more rigid ordering of opposition, and indeed this move is also explicitly made by Saussure himself, in an obscure passage probably most often overlooked by those of us who largely take his doctrine on trust from secondary sources. Consider for example this passage taken by Godel from the notes of Saussure's 1910-11 lectures:

In a state of *langue,* there are only differences (. . .). When we arrive at the terms themselves, which result from the relation between signified and signifier, we shall be able to talk of opposition (. . .). Because the differences condition each other mutually, we shall have something which can look like positive terms, by the placing opposite each other of such and such a difference of idea with such and such a difference of sign. At this point we shall be able to talk about opposition, because of this positive element of combination (Godel, p. 92; quoted DF, 142)

Here difference (which begins to sound very like Derrida's *différance)*

> What is written *différance* will be the movement of play which 'produces', by what is not simply an activity, these differences, these effects of difference. This does not mean that the *différance* which produces differences is before them, in a simple and in itself immodified in-different present. *Différance* is the non-full, non-simple, structured and differing/deferring origin of differences. The name 'origin' therefore no longer fits it. (J. Derrida, 'La différance' in *Marges – de la philosophie* (Paris: Minuit, 1972), pp. 3-29 (p. 12))

can never be grasped as such: the only differences perceptible in the linguistic system are in fact already oppositions. Difference is always already regulated into opposition in the *langue:* insofar as 'poetic language' disrupts such regulated oppositions, then it seems reasonable to refer it to difference as against opposition, and as this disruption was earlier placed under the notion of the figure, then difference in this non-oppositional form appears to be a characteristic we can attach to the figural space.

It is also difference which Lyotard finds, linked to what we have so far called loosely 'emotion', disrupting the at-homeness of the body in the world: the characterisation of difference is crucial, and I cannot do better than quote *Discours, figure* at great length here

This possibility [of 'a non-world', of emotion] is not merely a theoretical power of suspension of the worldly thesis, but this power of épochè (so long as it is not only reduced to a discursive denegation, which we understand will always easily be turned round as the involuntary symptom of an affirmation) itself issues from

> This question of 'denegation' as formulated by Freud is also discussed at some length by Lyotard, who includes a re-translation of Freud's 1925 article, 'Die Verneinung' ['Negation', PFL, 11, 437-42] in *Discours, figure*. (DF, 131-4)

a properly corporeal power of abolition, of untying the links kept up by body and world, and we have an experience (if we may use this word, given that this is a break in experience), a normal experience of this 'inexperience' in the facts of orgasm and sleep. It will be said that this inexperience requires experience, that it has, so to speak, edges by which it touches that which is presentation, that even if there is not retention of presence in orgasm or deep sleep, they can only ever be, not only thought, but 'lived' through difference, in opposition to states of holding onto the world, and of Dasein.

There is no reason to say the opposite; but this difference must be distinguished from the opposition said to be the secret of signification in the order of language, and above all it must be distinguished from the depth of negation included in the experience the subject has of the sign. We shall see that difference is neither the flat negation which holds apart the elements of a (linguistic) system, nor that profound denegation which opens the referential or representative field as over against discourse, and that if it is event, lapsus or orgasm which come to mind as examples with which to begin to sketch the field of difference, this is not by chance, but is because in all these 'cases', contrary to what happens in signification or designation, *the gap is not that of two terms* placed in the same plane, inscribed on the same support, and, possibly, reversible given certain operational conditions, but on the contrary is *the 'relation' of two 'states' which are heterogeneous yet juxtaposed in an irreversible anachrony.* Hegel was right to say that the spirit is quick to scar over its wounds: the fact is that there is no wound for language. And Merleau-Ponty is not wrong to absorb every relation of body to world into an originary faith, since both have to be there together, held by that faith, or else they are neither of them there. And yet we can detect effects of difference right in the discursive order and right in the perceptive order, without even invoking silence and darkness, i.e. the voiding *[le néant]* of these two orders. It suffices that there be in the heart of these orders abolitions irreducible to the gaps of opposition or to the depth of designation, insane events, i.e. operations or effects of operations requiring an 'order' which cannot come under the negativities we have identified, *precisely because it is inscribed in those negativities only negatively,* of an order one is for this reason tempted to assume is positive. (DF, 138-9)

Let us leave for a moment the nature of this 'positivity' emerging from negativity. We have seen, in a preliminary way, how discourse can be invaded by the figure, in the analysis of the Mallarmé text. What about the space of perception? The first move here can seem surprising, and requires explanation. Having apparently opposed the depth of perceptive space to the flatness of the language-system, having underlined the incommensurability of the experiences of perception and of reading or hearing language, Lyotard begins his discussion of the way the figure disrupts the space of perception by *assimilating* that space to the space of the text, from which he seemed previously so keen to distinguish it. But this is not an inconsistency: at this point in the argument, the apparent opposition between the two spaces and their specific negativities has been to some extent called into question – we have dwelt at some length on how the 'depth' of perception in fact, via designation and the deictic, inhabits the very space which is supposed to exclude it: the first move of the discussion of the effect of the figural on the space of perception argues that the space of language, of the opposition, of the system, also inhabits the space of perception, via the notion of *attention:* 'attention writes space, traces in it lines and triangles; for it, colours are like phonemes, units which work by opposition and not by motivation' (DF, 155). Attention already marks an incursion of the organisational negativity – hitherto associated with discourse – into perception.

As Lyotard makes clear, it would be to do an injustice to the efforts of a phenomenologist such as Merleau-Ponty to assume that he simply accepted this sort of organisation unquestioningly: the effort of Merleau-Ponty's descriptions is precisely to reach a level beyond such secondary rationalisation or equalisation. The phenomenologist stresses the mobility of the eye, the ability of sight to synthesise the here and the elsewhere, to perceive a 'figure' only on a 'ground', to recognise that the visible only ever offers itself containing elements of invisibility, the hidden face of objects which was previously put to good use against the simplifications of structural linguistics. But at this further level of reflection (or *surréflexion*), it is precisely this aspect of perception, linked to the mobility of the

---

In other words, we glimpse the necessity of an operation other than reflexive conversion, more fundamental than it, of a sort of *super-reflexion* which would also take account of itself and the changes it introduces into the spectacle, which would not, then, lose sight of the raw thing and raw perception, and which, finally, would not efface them, would not cut, by a hypothesis of non-existence, the organic links of perception and the thing perceived, and would give itself, on the contrary, the task of reflecting on the transcendence of the world as transcendence, to talk of it not according to the law of word-meanings inherent to the given language, but by an effort, perhaps a difficult effort, to use them to express, beyond themselves, our mute contact with things, when they are not yet things said. (*Le Visible et l'invisible,* p. 61)

eye, which has to be called into question, for it is just that mobility which allows the space of vision to be organised into recognisable objects, into figures on grounds, and thereby represses the possibility of difference. Immobilising the eye again allows the formulation of that difference at the heart of perceptual space, in the notion of peripheral vision:

Spatial difference is still more paradoxical than the gap which 'gives' the invisibility of the other side of the thing in the gestaltist articulation, it is also more rudimentary, it is the ungraspable distance between the periphery of the visual field and its focus. This gap gives much more than the here and the elsewhere, than the recto and the verso, it gives the qualitative discontinuity of the two spaces in their simultaneity, the curved, crepuscular, evanescent, lateral space of the first peripheral contact with something and the stabilised, constant, central rectangular space of the grasp in the foveal zone. This grasp is a taking, a prehension, a taking possession, it is of the order of the hunting, working, linguistic grasp; the first contact, the entry of something into the edge of the field, that's a visual alterity, an invisibility of the visible; and yet not simply the back of what is grasped face-on in the centre. This fragile, oblique tact gives the visual event which comes even before the sketch. (DF, 158)

This peripheral vision is inevitably lost in any attempt to *examine* it: it is not just the blur that could be deliberately produced on an out-of-focus lens, which blur could then be carefully considered by focal vision: peripheral vision is curved, but this curvature can only be dismissed as confusion, or as something to be brought into focus, on the basis of an unexamined acceptance of the idea that 'real' visual space is organised according to the laws of Euclidean geometry. Such a position again insists on opposition between focal organisation and lateral confusion, and assumes that in principle and ideally the lateral can always be focalised: this assumption survives in the phenomenological insistence on the mobility of the eye. But as Lyotard points out:

In so-called diffuse vision, the periphery is not merely blurred, it is other, and any attempt to *grasp* it loses it. Here is difference within the visible. In the recto/ verso couple there is a possible reversion or equalisation of the terms, one is on the way to language via stereometry and geometry. In the diffuse/punctual couple, there is qualitative modification and irreversible loss, at the same time as a retention of the lateral in the focal. No possible equalisation. It is not a question of the opposition of two terms, but of a difference of *qualia* which implies their irreversible inequality at the same time as their juxtaposition. It is striking that in order to reveal this one must stop not only the movement of the word between terms, but also that of the eye between things or their faces. There is thus something false even in the movement of the eye: it lends itself to the construction of the knowable, it represses the truthful. The truthful is the unbalanced configuration of space before any construction: it demands that the movement of the eye be deconstructed, in an immobility which is not a state of mobility. (DF, 159)

Something of this paradoxical immobility can, says Lyotard, be found in the work of Cézanne, immobile for hours in front of the Sainte-Victoire, until not only colours and values shift as 'impressions', but the whole homogeneity of space begins to shift: this shifting is the event which even the phenomenological description can only jettison in the construction of coherent form; and this event is that of the irruption of the figural, of

---

Merleau-Ponty wants to move from the I to the One [*on*, the impersonal pronoun] . . . Preconceptual system as much as one likes, but like every system, able to account not for the fact that there are events (in the visual field or elsewhere), but precisely for the fact that the event (donation) is absorbed, received, perceived, integrated into a world (or a history, etc.) The enigma of the event will remain entire even if one tries to descend to the level of the One. It is not the search for the condition (impersonal or not) of the given which immobilises Cézanne before his mountain, it is that of donation. Phenomenology cannot reach donation because, faithful to the Western philosophical tradition, it is still a reflection on *knowledge*, and the function of such a reflection is to absorb the event, to recuperate the Other into the Same. (DF, 21)

difference, into oppositional organisation, of the truth into the calm field of knowledge.

It still remains to make more precise the irruption of difference into discourse: for although Lyotard chooses to end this first section of *Discours, figure* with the discussion of visual space I have just summarized, there runs throughout the book an insistent awareness of a danger of simply valorising the apparent 'other' of discourse, and of identifying the figure too simply with the visual, however modified the description of that field. Although the manoeuvres of the argument should in principle have guaranteed against the possibility of such a reading, which merely re-affirms the opposition which served as a starting-point but which has long since been called into question, it is perhaps a useful precaution to return to discourse, especially as the Mallarmé example, on which we have so far relied for an idea of the irruption of the figural into the discursive, is in many ways only preliminary, and still uses a relatively straightforward notion of vision to make its point. The care required with the re-presentation of Lyotard's argument is not here merely a basic academic requirement, but itself bears witness to difference as against opposition ('as against' is misleading: the relationship between difference and opposition is itself one of difference, not opposition):*Discours, figure* is itself something of a collection of events and disruptions, and this is part of its difficulty.

Jakobson, following Saussure's notion of value at the level of the phoneme, makes a clear statement of the way in which linguistics makes differences into oppositions: 'All the differences existing between the phonemes of a given language can be brought down to binary, simple and indecomposable oppositions between distinctive features. It is therefore possible to break down the phonemes of any language into distinctive features which are themselves indivisible' (quoted DF, 142-3). And this principle can no doubt be extended to the levels of morphemes and lexical items too. The question is by now familiar: difference as such cannot be *recognized* – simple non-coincidence in the sounds of a language is, in an important sense, imperceptible: which phonemes enter into opposition is decided by an appeal to 'higher' levels of organisation, and opposition determined retroactively, as it were, on the basis of whether a given variation 'makes a difference' at that higher level. A similar point could be made about, for example, the structural analysis of narrative. Lyotard argues that even generative grammar, despite the fact that it does not obviously work with the same sorts of opposition, still tends to reinforce this 'positive', oppositional re-writing of what started out as just difference: Chomsky's 're-write rules' appear to leave no place for difference as such at all. And yet here too a certain persistence of difference can be located, in the notion of ungrammaticality: if a sentence does not obey the rules prescribed by the generative-transform-ational grammar, or breaks the regulated spacing of terms as seen in structural linguistics, without thereby becoming senseless, then, simply enough, the 'sense' involved must be of an order different to that of the grammar or structural model. Lyotard calls such examples by the name 'poetic language', which 'is to ordinary language as difference is to opposition' (DF, 144). Lyotard is prepared to go to great pedagogical lengths to illustrate this by a simple example, and I shall follow him in his discussion of it – here the French can be translated fairly literally into English without aberrations occurring.

'I print you / I swim you / I music you' (H. Pichette, *Les Epiphanies* (Paris: K, 1948), p. 40; quoted DF, 144: I have modified the second line to retain the grammatical effect of the French 'je te rame': the literal 'I row you' does not work). Lyotard notes that the degree of deviance or difference (the equivalence is his) increases through these three statements: taking the most extreme, 'I music you', we can compare it with a 'grammatical' sentence such as 'I know you'. This enters the system of language by its virtual opposition with statements such as 'I know him', 'You know me', and so on: these terms are virtually present, in an absence of the order of Freud's preconscious. The sentence 'I know you' is not an event in the system of language (though of course a particular use of it in a particular situation could be something of an event), it is simply a possibility which would be predicted by a generative grammar and simply accounted for in a regular way by a structural model. 'I music you', on the other hand, does not work in this way: it is not separated from more 'probable' terms in this sentence by regulated separations, it is not clear that there *are* any virtual elements around 'music' in this context:

The occultation which accompanies the statement 'I music you' is no longer the effacement of the system in the chiaroscuro (or the preconscious) thanks to which 'I know you' is held up in full light. The withdrawal of the absent elements does not create virtuality, but violence. *Music* is a term actualised by transgression, its presence bears witness to the fact that under the ground here there is, not a system, but forces, an energetics which disrupts the ordering of the system. When you make a verb with a noun, there is event: the system of rules of the language not only cannot account for this new usage, but is opposed to it, resists it, and between it and the statement the relationship which is established is that of conflict. (DF, 145)

This then is the figure, and the difference it traces: back to the language of force already seen (more virulently) at work in *Economie libidinale.* It will come as no surprise that this force and its disruptive effect are seen as the trace of a work which will soon be linked to the dream-work, to the primary process and the death-drive. This, then, is what structuralism in all its forms represses, and that repression can now be described as the accomplishment of its own desire.

Let us, however, leave these psychoanalytical themes hanging a little longer, and retain for the moment the philosophical deduction of difference to which they will give a content which I shall later attempt to call into question. Here we can return to the second object of attack, the Hegelian dialectic, which has gone along with structuralism throughout this discussion. Earlier, that dialectic was criticized on the basis of a phenomenology of perception which has since been cast into doubt. It will be remembered that the doubt was directed against the tendency of that phenomenology to make the body too simply 'at home' in the world, and the initial move of *Discours, figure* was to use such a phenomenology to oppose to the system of structural linguistics certain claims which can all loosely be gathered under the notion of the 'subject' as the subject of experience. Now, says Lyotard, that opposition must be questioned: the subject, apparently the ground for a critique of the system, is still left in the order of a world, and that order makes of the world something like a written text in the simple sense of an order of invariant spaces allowing recognition and knowledge. The 'at-homeness' is that of the subject in the system, and this 'at homeness' is eventually guaranteed by dialectical mediation between these two poles: and such a dialectical mediation depends, precisely, on opposition and the repression of the radical sense of difference being elaborated in *Discours, figure*. To question this dialectic, Lyotard appeals to a remark made by Marx in the *Critique of Hegel's Doctrine of the State*. In the context of a discussion of the role of the Estates in the State, Hegel makes the following general statement: 'It is one of the most important discoveries of logic that a specific moment which by standing in an opposition, has the position of an extreme, ceases to be such and is a moment in an organic whole by being at the same time a mean' (Quoted by Marx, *Early Writings,* tr. Rodney Livingstone and Gregor Benton (Harmondsworth: Penguin Books, 1975), p. 134, and in DF, 138). After detailed discussion of the concrete issue in question, Marx moves on to attack this general logical set-up, and denounces the 'confusion that results from the definition of extremes which assume the roles both of extremes and of mediating factors. They are Janus-heads facing both ways, with one character from the front and another from behind' (Marx, 154; DF, 138). Marx goes on:

It is remarkable that Hegel could have reduced this absurd process of mediation to its abstract, logical and hence ultimate undistorted form, while at the same time enthroning it as the *speculative mystery* of logic, as the scheme of reason, the rational mode of deduction *par excellence.* Real extremes cannot be mediated precisely because they are real extremes. Nor do they require mediation, for their natures are wholly opposed. They have nothing in common with one another, they have no need for one another, they complement one another. The one does not bear within its womb a longing, a need, an anticipation of the other. (Marx, 155)

And to the possible objection that 'extremes meet', that North and South Poles or male and female sex mutually attract each other, Marx retorts:

both the North and South Poles are *poles;* they are identical in *essence.* Similarly, both the *male* and *female* sex belong to one species and have one essence, the essence of man. North and South are the opposite determinations of a *single* essence; the distinct sides of one *essence at the highest point of its development.* They are the essence in a state of *differentiation.* They are what they are *only* as a *distinct* determination, and moreover as *this* distinct determination of an essence. The true, real extremes would be a pole as opposed to a non-pole, a human as opposed to a *non-human* sex. The differentiation in this case [i.e. *'extremes meet'*] is *one of existence,* in the former situation ['the true real extremes'] it is *one of essence, of two essences.* (Marx, 155-6: the interpolations are by the translators of the volume)

What retains Lyotard's attention in this passage is Marx's attempt to think a relationship which would not fall into a system of oppositions, that is, 'if it is true that thinking and placing the object in such a system are the same thing, the possibility of thinking a relationship without thinking it' (DF, 139). Hegel's method inscribes sexual difference within the horizon of a totality by making the sexes complementary opposites: picking up on Marx's idea of a non-human sex, Lyotard heads straight for the unconscious – what a Hegelian reading of sexual difference represses is, in his reading, the event and the violence of castration, which it recuperates with a view to a totality of the species reproduced via procreation. But this view is that of consciousness and rationalisation:

On the other scene, the sexes are not complementary. The truth of sex does not reside in Freud's often-repeated remark that there is basically only one, masculine, sexuality: even if it is true that the girl discovers her sexuality only late and by comparison, and that boys and girls perceive the female sex as absence, such a *position* is not yet that of sexuality, i.e. that of a system in which one passes from masculine to feminine by negation, it is not the position in the order proper to desire. This order is marked in that the noting of this absence greatly exceeds the noting of an absence, but gives rise to the strangest, wildest representations, at the same time as it gives rise to the most unexpected effects. When, supplied with the North Pole, one discovers the South Pole, one is not seized by the violence of an irreparable event which requires all the force of the imaginary to fill by representations, and all the disorder of affect to displace onto other representers; rather the opposite: such a discovery is that of a complement, it is a recognition, but the entry of the subject into desire via castration is always something like its death. The No of the non-human, inhuman *(unmenschlich)* sex indicates difference, another position (scene) which deposes that of consciousness, of discourse and reality.

In summarising this first section of *Discours, figure,* I have held off the psychoanalytic moment for as long as possible: this is because the general schemas of argumentation which inform this part of the book are largely independent of psychoanalysis. But also, as I shall now argue, the move into psychoanalysis which we shall now follow ends up by compromising some of the rigour of the thought which led to it: put briefly, I shall try to show that, against his best intentions, Lyotard ends up by transforming the relationship between difference and opposition, which the logic of the book so far requires to be a relationship of difference, back into one of opposition (and possibly this determination is already implicit in the earlier recourse to the distinction between 'ordinary' and 'poetic' language). This is not at all to dismiss the rest of *Discours, figure,* which contains analyses too rich and complex to summarize in great detail here. In attempting to do justice to this part of the book I shall concentrate on two important moments: the first a critique of Lacan, contained in a chapter on Freud's conception of the dream-work; the second a formulation of the specificity of the work of art as *critical.*

Lyotard's insistence on dream as essentially dream-*work* is justified by a well-known addition of Freud's to *The Interpretation of Dreams.*

Freud says that many analysts are guilty of a confusion in that they look for the essence of the dream in its latent content. This is a mistake, in that this latent content or statement of the dream is of exactly the same order as conscious thought: what is specific to the dream is not the thought but the work which makes of that thought a specific form: 'The dream is at bottom nothing other than a particular form of our thought, made possible by the conditions of the state of sleep. It is the *dream-work* which constructs this form, and it alone is essential to the dream, the explanation of its particularity' (PFL, 4, 649 n 2). We should, says Lyotard, take this difference between thought and work seriously, and specify what sort of difference it is: the relationship between work and thought is not that of one discourse to another, their distance is not that of the negativity of designation and the constitution of objects discussed above, not even that informing the relationship between the linguist's metalanguage and the language which is the object of that metalanguage. No more is it the relationship between a text and its translation into another language: the dream-work does not operate a transcription of the dream-thought, but a *transformation,* producing an object which is essentially different from the thought from which it began. Clearly this relationship is germane to the notion of difference as formulated above with reference to Marx.

Insistence on this difference will lead to the disagreement with Lacan: Lyotard states bluntly, 'the dream is not a discourse because the Traumarbeit is quite different from the operations of speech', and opposes this to Lacan and to 'the current penchant for stuffing the whole of semiology into linguistics' (DF, 251). And insofar as Lacan's major claim is that the truth of Freud's discovery can be the better grasped with the insights of structuralist linguistics, the disagreement appears inevitable.

Lyotard's critique centres on Lacan's link of the two 'central' aspects of the dream-work, condensation and displacement, to the tropes of metaphor and metonymy, respectively, and specifically to the notions of metaphor and metonymy elaborated by Jakobson in his famous article 'Two aspects of language and two types of aphasic disturbances'. Jakobson's distinction is consistent with the 'rigorous' strand of Saussurean linguistics which tends to describe signification entirely in terms of value, and to describe that value as a result of the convergence of paradigmatic and syntagmatic axes: on the one hand by what terms might be substituted for the term in question, and on the other, the terms around it in the actualized chain of speech or writing. In terms of the paradigmatic axis, the speaker operates a *selection;* in terms of the syntagm, a *combination.* Further, the 'vertical' axis of the paradigm encourages Jakobson to link it to the trope of metaphor (substitution on the basis of similarity), and the 'horizontal' axis of the syntagm is almost automatically linked to metonymy (sequence, one thing then another, and so on). Jakobson uses this distinction to describe his 'two forms of aphasic disturbance', depending on whether the problem affects the selective or combinatory functions of language. He goes on to associate the series paradigm-selection-metaphor to the genre of poetry (in which the other aspect is not of course absent, but, according to Jakobson, subordinate), and the syntagm-combination-metonymy series to prose: and further, metaphor to the schools of romanticism and symbolism, metonymy to realism (think of the careful 'one thing after another' descriptions of the classical realist novel). So far, Jakobson has limited his claims to the domain of articulated language: where they can certainly be contested (as they have been by Gérard Genette, for example: see 'La Rhétorique restreinte', in *Figures III* (Paris: Seuil, 1972), pp. 21-40), but where they are certainly legitimate in principle. But at the end of his article, Jakobson claims that his two categories can be extended to all symbolic processes, and invokes Freud and dreams... where the association is unexpected: here condensation and displacement are *both* linked to metonymy (condensation more specifically being seen as a synecdoche by Jakobson), and metaphor reserved for 'identification' and symbolism. Lacan, who draws heavily on Jakobson, links condensation to metaphor and displacement to metonymy: Lyotard notes that the French translator of Jakobson drew this discrepancy to Jakobson's attention, and Jakobson explained it by suggesting that Freud's notion of condensation was imprecise enough to allow both interpretations.

Lyotard is having none of it. What if the imprecision were in fact due to the illegitimate application to a particular domain of categories which belong to another? What if the problem lay in a desire to find in the dreamwork operations of language, come what may? In other words, what if this desire led to 'metaphor' and 'metonymy' themselves being taken in a 'metaphorical' sense without this supplementary operation being recognized or admitted? Now it may be thought that this is an odd accusation for Lyotard to make, or at least that it rests on the stage of preliminary opposition between discourse and figure which we have seen to be progressively complicated earlier in the book. And Lyotard indeed says of this metaphorical use of 'metaphor' and 'metonymy' that given the dream's recalcitrance when it comes to talking, Lacan and Jakobson 'make discourse dream' (DF, 253), and it could reasonably be supposed that the project of *Discours, figure* is to show that discourse does indeed 'dream'. Indeed: 'only it will have to be agreed that the "language" of the unconscious does not have its model in articulated discourse, which is spoken in a language, as we know; but rather that the dream is the height of disarticulate, deconstructed discourse, of which too no language, even normal language, is truly exempt' (DF, 253: this also – momentarily – complicates Lyotard's own previous use of the opposition between 'poetic' and 'normal' language). A certain rigour can be demanded even where the object of the discourse is the unconscious, and Lyotard's reading endeavours to show that this is lacking in Lacan.

Lacan defines metaphor simply as 'one word for another', and contests the Surrealist idea that the 'creative spark' of metaphor springs from the bringing together of two disparate images or words:

> The creative spark of the metaphor does not spring from the presentation of two images, that is, of two signifiers equally actualized. It flashes between two signifiers one of which has taken the place of the other in the signifying chain, the occulted signifier remaining present through its (metonymic) connection with the rest of the chain. (*Ecrits: A Selection*, tr. A. Sheridan-Smith (London: Tavistock, 1977), p. 157; quoted DF, 254)

Lyotard suggests that the most interesting thing about this definition is that it omits what is essential for a poetic or 'creative' metaphor, namely that such a metaphor is *not* authorised by usage, by the code of *langue:* in a normal case of paradigmatic selection, one term is of course actualised, but there is no particular 'occulted' signifier to 'remain present' – rather, as we have seen, the other terms available in the paradigm are simply 'virtualised'. Metaphor as trope, on the other hand, demands that the selection actualised do violence to the normal paradigm of substitutive possibilities, as we saw in the relatively trivial 'I music you' example. To this extent Lyotard is defending the surrealists against Lacan. The 'creative spark' comes of the irruption of the figural in the discourse, not in discourse following its normal rules of selection and combination.

Now for the link claimed by Lacan between metaphor and condensation. He writes,

> *Verdichtung,* or 'condensation', is the structure of the superimposition of the signifiers, which metaphor takes as its field, and whose name, condensing in itself the word *Dichtung,* shows how the mechanism is connatural with poetry to the point that it envelops the traditional function of poetry. (*Ecrits,* 160)

Can this link be maintained, given Lacan's definition of metaphor? Lyotard looks to Lacan's subsequent 'algorithm' of the metaphorical structure for guidance. That famous and enigmatic formula reads as follows:

$$f\left(\frac{S'}{S}\right) S \cong S\,(+)\,s$$

and Lyotard provides the following gloss:

> The metaphorical function of the signifier is congruent with the emergence of signification. The metaphorical function is noted $\frac{S'}{S}$), the emergence of signification S (+) s. 'The sign + placed between ( ) here manifests the crossing of the bar – and the constant value of this crossing for the emergence of signification.' This bar (−) is, in Lacan's algebra, what separates the signifier and the signified, it is the mark of 'non-sense'. Crossed (+) by metaphor, it re-establishes a contact between signifier and signified and consequently establishes meaning. As for the notation of the metaphor itself $\frac{S'}{S}$, it satisfies the definition of metaphor given by Lacan: S' is the stated term which occults the signifier S.... If I am not mistaken about the 'crossing of the bar', metaphor is for J. Lacan the trope by which the signified is alleged. Metaphor 'is placed at the precise point at which sense is produced in non-sense'. (DF, 256)

Lacan's equation is based on an elaboration of his version of Saussure's notion of the sign, which Lacan rewrites as $\frac{S}{s}$, 'which is read as the signifier over the signified, "over" corresponding to the bar separating the two stages' (*Ecrits*, 149), and Lyotard points out that this reading involves a certain forcing of Saussure, whose own schema places the

---

Four principal features distinguish the algorithm:

1. The disappearance of a certain parallelism between the terms inscribed on either side of the bar, since one must read not only, as Lacan indicates, 'signifier over signified', but 'big S' on 'little s' (which is, moreover, written in italics).

2. The disappearance of Saussure's oval [surrounding the two parts of the sign], which is never absent and which symbolises, as is well known, the structural unity of the sign.

3. The substitution, for the Saussurean formula of two *faces* of the sign, of the designation of two *stages* of the algorithm.

4. Finally, the stress placed on the bar which separates S from s. (Jean-Luc Nancy and Philippe Lacoue-Labarthe, *Le Titre de la lettre (une lecture de Lacan)* (Paris: Galilée, 1973), p. 39). Reflecting on this series of shifts a little later, the authors comment: 'Nothing in fact authorises this deviation [*détournement*, hijacking] if not, already, a certain use of Freud, a certain manner of projecting more or less explicitly into Saussurean linguistics, to disrupt its functioning, a whole conceptual apparatus stemming from psychoanalysis. . . the second part of the text ([‘The Agency of] the Letter in the Unconscious’) opens precisely with the "linguistic" reading of Freud's text, which repeats word for word, for a certain time at least, the Freudian reading of linguistics the condition of which it however was. . . In what logic is one in fact to articulate that Freud is to be read according to Saussure, himself read according to Freud?' (p. 87): in his 1973 seminar, Lacan himself says that this book (except for its final 30

pages) 'is a model of good reading, to the point that I can say that I regret having never obtained anything equivalent from those close to me' (*Le Séminaire, Livre XX, Encore* (Paris: Seuil, 1975), p. 62) – it is all the more regrettable that *Le Titre de la lettre* has not been translated into English.

signified over the signifier, and whose 'bar', 'so far from being that of repression or of the censorship, has so little consistency that it will tend to disappear at the same time as, in the later lectures, the notion of value will supplant that of signification' (DF, 257). Lacan is confusing this notion of signification-as-value (which is also that of Jakobson), and what Lyotard calls *sens,* which is linked to difference and the figure:

When an [English] speaker says 'night is falling', the statement does not bar the signification, which is absolutely transparent for the [English] hearer. The indissociability of signifier and signified, which Saussure never fails to emphasise and Lacan to keep quiet about, is the complementary property of this transparency. On the other hand the statement can secrete thickness through its *sens,* but most often it will be necessary to have recourse to contextual factors (if, for example, the sentence is spoken with reference to Hitler's coming to power) in order to interpret this meaning. (DF, 257)

So although it claims the authority of structural linguistics, Lacan's explanation of the metaphor in fact escapes the domain of signification strictly speaking and works in the domain of *sens:* to this extent it cannot be compatible with Saussure's doctrine of the sign, nor with Jakobson's doctrine of metaphor. Lacan's metaphor presupposes a depth which is not in principle present in Saussure or Jakobson; and if it is found that Jakobson's account also involves a depth, then this is due to a confusion too, between properly linguistic categories and *rhetoric.*

————————————

Compare Paul de Man's comment: 'One of the most striking characteristics of literary semiology as it is practised today, in France and elsewhere, is the use of grammatical (especially syntactic) structures conjointly with rhetorical structures, without apparent awareness of a possible discrepancy between them. . . One can ask whether this reduction of figure to grammar is legitimate' (*Allegories of Reading: Figural language in Rousseau, Nietzsche, Rilke, and Proust* (New Haven and London: Yale University Press, 1979), pp. 6-7) – despite all apparent differences, De Man and Lyotard are curiously similar around the question of such a discrepancy.

Lyotard explains this introduction of depth into Lacan's model, under cover of a structural linguistics thus misread, as a result of Lacan's preoccupation with the question of the *subject.* This becomes clearer once we interrogate Lacan's link of metaphor and condensation, which is the point of his presentation here. In order to explain how condensation is metaphorical, Lacan says that this is because the subject is only ever metaphorically present in discourse: 'we accede to meaning only through the double twist of metaphor when we have the one and only key: the S and s of the Saussurian algorithm are not on the same level, and man only deludes himself when he believes his true place is at their axis, which is nowhere' (*Ecrits,* 166). When he says 'signified', continues Lyotard, Lacan is thinking 'subject':

The whole theory of metaphor is a theory of the metaphor of the *subject:* the subject only apprehends itself via metaphor, i.e. in missing itself, precisely because it is signified by a signifier. And the signifier is the Other. The bar between S and s expresses this expressive repression. (DF, 257)

So Lacan's notion of the 'metaphorical structure' is strictly speaking incompatible with the structural linguistics which it quotes as its base. This would be inconsequential enough, if it is true that Lacan's major preoccupation here is to account for Freud's doctrine of condensation. And as this does indeed seem to involve questions of depth, of two 'levels' (latent thought and manifest content) separated and constituted by the dream-work, then it might appear that the critique of Lacan for his use and abuse of structural linguistics is not strictly pertinent. But the point is not to establish pedantically that Lacan misrepresents Saussure, but to lead to a questioning of his fundamental tenet that 'the unconscious is structured like a language': this questioning also needs to stress that what Lacan says about condensation is incompatible with what is said about it by Freud (whom Lacan is so concerned to 'spell out', so as to 'situate the development of psychoanalysis according to its first guidelines, which were fundamental and never revoked' (*Ecrits,* 161-2)).

For Freud, condensation is a *compression,* which forces the dream-thought into a smaller space, by omission and overdetermination. Lyotard wants to argue that this operation is *fundamentally* non-linguistic and supports this claim by looking at Freud's description of condensation when it takes language as its object: Freud writes:

The work of condensation in dreams is seen at its clearest when it handles words and names. It is true in general that words are frequently treated in dreams as though they were things, and for that reason they are apt to be combined in just the same way as are presentations of things. (PFL, 4, p. 403, quoted DF, 259)

Lyotard suggests that such a treatment of language is immediately and obviously different from what *Jakobson* says of metaphor in his generalisation of the notion of substitution: 'Substitution was for Jakobson a *constitutive* operation of discourse; condensation for Freud is a *destitutive* transformation of discourse' (DF, 259). What of Lacan? For Lyotard, he is as far from Freud as is Jakobson: for Lacan relegates the dream-work's treating words as things to the 'considerations of figurability' which he sees as a secondary operation : the logic of Lacan's argument is that the use of *speech* in a dream is not of vital importance, because the dream-work does indeed treat speech as just one among many elements of representation, but that dream is nonetheless fundamentally 'a form of writing rather than of mime' (*Ecrits,* p. 161), and therefore follows the laws of the signifier. For Lacan, the 'considerations of figurability' are secondary considerations *within* the domain of these laws, and this leads him to refuse any notion of a general 'figurative semiology', which he assumes would have to be on the same level as a notion of 'natural expression' (Ibid.). The proof of this for Lacan lies in the problem dreams have in representing *logical* relations such as causality and contradiction. The nature of this 'proof' is obscure, for it would appear that such a

> Let us say, then, that the dream is like the parlour-game in which one is supposed to get the spectators to guess some well known saying or variant of it solely by dumb-show. That the dream uses speech makes no difference since for the unconscious it is only one among several elements of the representation. It is precisely the fact that both the game and the dream run up against a lack of taxematic material for the representation of such logical articulations as causality, contradiction, hypothesis, etc., that proves they are a form of writing rather than of mime. The subtle processes that the dream is seen to use to represent these logical articulations, in a much less artificial way than games usually employ, are the object of a special study in Freud in which we see once more confirmed that the dream-work follows the laws of the signifier. (*Ecrits,* 161)

problem could be invoked to support Lyotard's idea that dreams precisely do *not* follow the 'laws of the signifier'. Freud's own discussion of the matter is hesitant, beginning with the assertion that logical relations may well be found in the dream-*thoughts,* but are not part of the dream-*work* as such (4, 422-3), and he duly draws an analogy with the plastic arts in this respect (Ibid.). But he goes on to make of this a 'provisional' statement of the issue (4, 424), and proceeds to find that dreams can nonetheless 'take account of some of the logical relations between their dream-thoughts' (Ibid.), and suggests that, for example, logical connection can be represented in the dream by simultaneity in time, by producing an 'introductory' dream to correspond to a dependent clause and a main dream to correspond to a principal clause, and so on. Much of this discussion seems to anticipate on the role of the fourth and final element of the dream-work, secondary revision, which is reponsible for a sort of 'first interpretation' of the dream before any waking interpretation (4, 631), and to which the tendency for some appearance of clarity and logical order in dreams can be attributed. Insofar as secondary revision is akin to waking thought, then its push towards logical relations is not surprising: but would hardly suffice to make of this element any sort of proof that the dream-work as a whole, and condensation and displacement in particular, 'obey the laws of the signifier' as Lacan would have it. Lacan's argument seems to reduce the importance of the 'considerations of figurability' by insisting on an element which is linked to secondary revision, with the aim of showing that condensation and displacement in the dream-work are not essentially different from metaphor and metonymy in discourse. Lyotard is prepared, provisionally at least, to concede that there is indeed one aspect of the means of representation which can be assimilated to the 'systems of writing' of hieroglyphs and rebuses, but points out that Lacan completely omits to mention another aspect which would be more troubling for his argument: namely that the 'considerations of figurability' lead to the replacement of signified by *designatum* in a way much more amenable to analysis via Lyotard's notion of the figural than via Lacan's stress on the signifier: Freud quotes examples from Silberer (4, 460-61) to illustrate this point, which disrupts the system of the signifier just as the consideration of designation previously disrupted the system of *langue*.

The 'concession' made to the notion of 'writing', as Lacan uses it, is clearly vital: but surely the 'secondary revision' (which is part of the dream-work, and which, according to Freud, should not be thought of as coming along *after* the other three elements, but as present from the start) confirms Lacan's point? If Lyotard were simply concerned to *expel*

At this point it is impossible to avoid considering the relationship between this secondary revision of the content of dreams and the remaining factors of the dream-work. Are we to suppose that what happens is that in the first instance the dream-constructing factors — the tendency towards condensation, the necessity for evading the censorship, and considerations of representability by the psychical means open to dreams — put together a provisional dream-content out of the material provided, and that this content is subsequently re-cast so as to conform so far as possible to the demands of a second agency? This is scarcely probable. We must assume that from the very first the demands of this second factor constitute one of the conditions which the dream must satisfy and that this condition, like those laid down by condensation, the censorship imposed by resistance, and representability, operates simultaneously in a conducive and selective sense upon the mass of material present in the dream-thoughts. (PFL, 4, 640-1) 'discourse' and extol 'figure', then this would be true: but if, as must be repeated, the aim is to show an originary *complication* of discourse and figure, then the argument remains open for a while yet, and requires a further consideration of what Freud says of secondary revision.

Freud states that secondary revision is to the content of dreams what preconscious thinking is to perception – it demands order, and attempts to make what is perceived conform to expectations and probability: this activity takes place in the interests of intelligibility, but not always of truth: 'In our efforts at making an intelligible pattern of the sense-impressions that are offered to us, we often fall into the strangest errors or even falsify the truth about the material before us' (4, 641). Secondary revision, similarly, 'approaches the content of dreams with a demand that it must be intelligible, [...] subjects it to a first interpretation, and [...] consequently produces a complete misunderstanding of it' (4, 642). And this is why it is possible for Freud to say that the demands of secondary revision 'have the least cogent influence on dreams' (4, 641). Secondary revision can produce elements of apparent clarity and coherence, but these are misleading. In order to give an illustration of this effect of secondary revision on dreams, Freud invokes a famous comparison which brings us back to Lyotard's earlier apparent concession on the question of writing and the rebus:

If I look around for something with which to compare the final form assumed by a dream as it appears after normal thought has made its contribution, I can think of nothing better than the enigmatic inscriptions with which the *Fliegende Blätter* has for so long entertained its readers. They are intended to make the reader believe that a certain sentence – for the sake of contrast, a sentence in dialect and as scurrilous as possible – is a Latin inscription. For this purpose the letters contained in the words are torn out of their combination into syllables and arranged in a new order. Here and there a genuine Latin word appears; at other points we seem to see abbreviations of Latin words before us; and at still other points in the inscription we may allow ourselves to be deceived into overlooking the senselessness of isolated letters by parts of the inscription seeming to be defaced or showing lacunae. If we are to avoid being taken in by the joke, we must disregard everything that makes it seem like an inscription, look firmly at the letters, pay no attention to their ostensible arrangement, and so combine them into words belonging to our own mother tongue. (4, 643).

Lyotard takes this analogy very seriously, because here his difference with Lacan will quite possibly be clarified or shown to be false. He is aware that, at first sight, secondary revision appears to pose a serious threat to his thesis: for here the dream-work is clearly in collusion with the order of discourse, of rational thought, which Lyotard is concerned to argue it in some sense undoes or deconstructs. But this collusion is ambivalent and originary, and in Lyotard's view confirms the impossibility of assimilating the operations of the dream-work and those of the linguistic order.

The investigation of the 'enigmatic inscriptions' discovers that most of them consist of the type of pseudo-Latin inscription described by Freud, with an illustration to which the inscription in some way refers. If these are to be compared, as Freud suggests, to the dream after the intervention of secondary revision, then the dream-thoughts would correspond to the solution of the enigma (the 'Latin' re-read as a statement in German dialect), the manifest content to the (usually) apparently meaningless inscription, and the image to the considerations of figurability; the whole being put together by an activity analogous to secondary revision.

The transformation of the latent thought into the manifest content is complex. The language of the solution-text is transposed into the appearance of another language, and this transformation depends on a phonematic analysis and reconstitution of that text. Read out loud, the 'Latin' text is roughly homophonous with the sentence in German dialect. The re-written version of that sentence is only *pseudo*-Latin: Lyotard calls this a 'pseudo-graph'. It aims to provoke the suspicion that the resulting inscription does have a meaning in Latin (and very occasionally it does: this would correspond to those dreams which appear ordered and coherent and in no obvious need of interpretation – which are, as Freud insists, the most misleading). Even when the Latin is intelligible, the meaning is not the same as that of the 'solution', but 'heterosemic'. Lyotard then proposes, jokingly, to call the inscription a 'heterosemic homophonic pseudo-graph'. (DF, 267)

The relation between this inscription and the image of the *Rätselhafte Inschrift* also needs to be considered. These inscriptions do not fall outside the space of the image, as with the rest of the text of the *Fliegende Blätter* (and notably the 'Solution in next issue' printed under the examples reproduced in *Discours, Figure*): the text mimics engraved letters which are situated in the same space as the image:

By this simple placing of the inscription, we move from the linguistic space, the space of *reading*, which is the space where one *hears/understands* [entend], to the visual space, that of painting, where one *looks*. (DF, 267)

The argument is by now familiar: the text becomes enigmatic, and frustrates understanding, by being placed in the *depth* of the visual, where it is *seen* rather than, or before, being read: 'the read belongs to the system of spacings which constitutes the code of language; the seen requires opening, transcendence, showing-hiding. The enigma signals to the eye, and this is why the dream gives its preference to visual images' (DF, 268). This enigma is not that of some 'pure' vision or figure, but of the *line*, which can close into the formal identity of the letter, or open into the deep space of the visual.

It is this ambiguity of reading and seeing which Lyotard links to the secondary revision, and it gives rise to the pseudo-coherence of the manifest dream, its pseudo-legibility and pseudo-intelligibility. This 'pseudo-' is the mark of the insistence of discourse in figure: the secondary revision promises meaning and coherence, it is already a sort of interpretation, says Freud (PFL, 4, 642), but it also blocks that interpretation and maintains the figural depth in the discursive presentation. This complication is originary, according to Lyotard: the 'clear' text of the latent thoughts is always-already 'distorted' by the figural, in a mixture characteristic of dream, daydream and phantasy, in which the order of desire and the order of discourse (the law) are engaged in a primal conflict.

The dream-work is not a language; it is the effect on language of the force exerted by the figural (as image or form). This force transgresses the law; it prevents understanding, it allows seeing: this is the ambivalence of the censorship. But this mixture is primary, it is found not only in the order of the dream, but in that of the 'originary' phantasy itself: discourse and figure at once, speech lost in a hallucinatory scenography, initial violence. (DF, 270)

Can we say that this insistence refutes Lacan? Lacan himself clearly thought not. In the introduction to the 1970 selection of his *Ecrits*, Lacan writes the following:

'The dream does not think. . .', writes a professor very pertinent in all the proofs he gives of this. The dream is more like a crumpled inscription. But when did I say anything that objects to this? . . .

Beyond the fact that this author could not even put forward the facts from which he argues without taking as established what I articulate of the dream, namely that it requires a textual support, what I properly call the agency of the letter before all grammatology, where can he get the idea that I say that the dream thinks? A question I pose without having re-read myself.

On the other hand he discovers that what I inscribe as an effect of the signifier does not correspond to the signified delimited by linguistics, but well and truly to the subject.

I applaud this discovery all the more because at the date at which his remarks appeared, I had for ages been hammering out for whoever wants to hear that the signifier (and it is in this that I distinguish it from the sign) is what represents a subject for another signifier. (*Ecrits*, ed. 'Points', p. 11)

And earlier in this presentation, Lacan suggests that his insistence on discourse in no way commits him to an acceptance of the laws of linguistics. This comes down to the idea that Lyotard is in fact *confirming* Lacan's doctrine. And it may well be that Lacan's writing exemplifies the sort of language Lyotard suggests has to be invoked if the dream is indeed to be thought of as being structured like a language ('a "heavy" language, a language which works, which hides, which shows, metaphorically no doubt, but with a metaphor now understood after the fashion of a work [of art]' (DF, 260)): the fact would remain that that language would be unable to account for itself in terms of the doctrine it puts forward – Lacan's 'practice' of exploiting the figural in the discursive would thus be inherently mystified and mystificatory, and no doubt this would go some way towards explaining the effects of authoritarianism so often noted of Lacan. Lyotard's argument against this is not that the discursive and the figural can be neatly separated and kept in their respective places, but that their imbrication is not simply a confusion, nor something to be exploited from a position of mastery. (For an excellent account of the Lyotard/Lacan confrontation, see Peter Dews, 'The Letter and the Line: Discourse and its other in Lyotard', *Diacritics,* 14:3 (1984), 40-9.)

Lyotard's argument around the figural depends on a notion of transgression: put simply, the figure transgresses the law of discourse, refuses to respect the invariant spacing and rules of substitution which define the system of *langue:* Jakobson is wrong to assimilate (creative) metaphor and paradigmatic substitution to this extent. The drive of Lyotard's use of Freud is to assimilate this transgressive activity to desire seen in terms of the primary process, in much the same terms as those we have seen elaborated in *Economie Libidinale.* So far we have tended to depend on a notion of *visibility* (linked to the operation of designation) to support the category of the figural as disruptive of the 'flat' space of discourse, or of 'difference' to disrupt the 'discursive' organisation of perception in terms of attention and focus. But this notion of the visual, however conceived, is scarcely enough to support the invocation of desire – and could still rely on essentially phenomenological descriptions, and this is still true of the argument against Lacan, at least in the way I have presented it. The movement of the argument must return briefly towards the visual, the figure, to make more precise the necessity of the link of the figural and desire. For better and for worse, it is to the idea of transgression that Lyotard appeals to make this link (DF, 271).

The approach to the figural via phenomenology argued for an introduction of the negativity of referential 'depth', 'variability' and so on into the 'flat' negativity and invariance of discourse. Desire, understood in terms of the primary process, cannot be conceptualised in these terms, insofar as it is as disruptive of that second negativity as of the first: whence the attempt to conceive of it as *positive,* announced above. If, stressing the importance of the 'considerations of figurability' in the dream-work, we assimilate this aspect to the depth of reference, then we run the risk of forgetting the disorder of the visual aspect of dreams, its own distortion and mobility. Taking the depth of the perceptual visual field as norm for the hallucinatory visual field quickly leads back to the phenomenological reality of the body in the world and ignores the 'suspension' of that reality in sleep:

In the dream and the neurotic symptom, these properties of the worldly figure disappear. So that when Freud teaches us that one of the essential operations of the dream is figuration, let us beware: our duty is to infer that we have left the order of language, but also to suppose that we are no longer in referential or worldly distance either, if it is true that this figure is no more *bound* to the constraints of designation (among which are to be found both variability of view-point and unilaterality of the visible), than it is to those of language. We are indeed dealing with a representation, but the rules of the scenic space are no longer those of sensory space. Not only is the author's text censored out [*caviardé*], overprinted, scrambled, but so are the faces of the actors, the place where they are, their clothes, their identity; as for the scenery, it changes in the middle of the action, without warning. And the action itself has no unity (DF, 276-7).

The transgressions operated by the figural on the space of waking percep-tion can be further specified in order of complexity. First the *figure-image:* this is still in the order of the visible, and is still held in depth: but it disturbs the recognition from an ordered viewpoint of the object it out-lines, by allowing more than one object to occupy the same space, or the same object to occupy different positions simultaneously. Up to a point, this is still within the bounds of phenomenology, but presents simultaneously what the phenomenology of perception allows only suc-cessively: Lyotard provides a Picasso drawing, and many of the works of analytic Cubism could be invoked here too. This is the visual space of the dream.

Next in order of complexity: the *figure-form.* This is no longer at the level of the visible *theme* of the scene, but at that of its unseen *scheme:* for example the Euclidian geometry which organises the space of perspec-tival painting, or the *Gestalt* which distributes a given configuration in terms of figure and ground – in the theatrical metaphors used earlier in the discussion of *Economie libidinale,* the *machinery* or scenography. The transgression of this by the *figure-form* is the disruption of the 'bonne forme', the good form still accessible at the level of the figure-image: harder to exemplify too. But if this good form is Apollonian, then the figure-form is Dionysiac, indifferent to any overall composition of unity: Lyotard suggests the example of Jackson Pollock's 'action painting', presenting no hallucinated object of desire, but the movement of desire itself, giving rise to no recognisable figure at all.

Finally and most mysteriously, Lyotard postulates the figure-matrix. This is *essentially* invisible (and not merely conventionally so, as was the figure-form). There are many possibilities of confusion here, beyond the essential 'confusion' which this name attempts to evoke. On the one hand, it appears that this figure-matrix names simply transgression itself, the transgressivity of transgression, 'difference itself' (DF, 278). As such, it cannot be presented in discourse nor as image or form: 'it does not allow the minimal putting into *opposition* demanded by its spoken expression, or the minimal putting into image or form presupposed by its plastic expression. Discourse, image and form miss it equally, as it resides in the three spaces together' (Ibid.). On the other hand, and perhaps more justifiably in view of the term 'matrix' in the name, Lyotard suggests that this is the 'originary' phantasy, and in a sentence which sits awkwardly in the text at this point, says, 'The works of a man are only ever the offspring of this matrix; it can perhaps be half-glimpsed through their supcrimposition, in depth' (DF, 278-9). These two types of description are certainly not equivalent, and I am not sure that they are strictly speaking compatible. Within the logic of *Discours, figure* as discussed so far, the derivation of the *figure-matrix* is coherent and necessary. The resistance to any formulation of this 'matrix' as an origin is also a rigorous consequence of the doctrine of difference, as is the refusal of any systematization of the figure-matrix in a discourse. At this level, there are obvious affinities between Lyotard's enterprise and that of Derrida. But even if a reading of Freud is a useful stage in the derivation, nothing suggests that the result of that derivation must retain concepts such as 'unconscious' or even 'desire' as part of its essential definition. This is not to deny that questions of the 'singularity' of an individual's work are important: but nothing has so far shown that *Discours, figure* is at a stage to address these, nor even that the question of an 'originary phantasy' is the appropriate way to do so.

With these provisos in mind, it is still possible to follow the critique of phenomenology which the appeal to psychoanalysis has allowed to begin, and to radicalise the notion of the figure elaborated so far. And, according to the oscillating movement of *Discours, figure* itself, this will return us to discourse, and the effects of the figural on it.

Previously, we saw that discourse was not in fact exclusive of figure, but we tended to link the irruption of the latter in the former in terms of the visibility and phenomenology of the body in space which the reading of Freud has questioned. Now that the figural has been elaborated further, and produced the triad image/form/matrix (whatever reservations have been left unresolved around the last of these terms), it seems possible to look for a more complex articulation of that triad with the three terms associated with discourse, namely signifier/signified/*designatum*. It seems immediately as though the third term of the discursive series can be linked with the first of the figural series: the reference of the discourse is, in principle, a recognizable object of that discourse. This possible articulation would also apparently allow more sense to be made of the appeal to desire: for the distance at which the visible, recognizable object is held, the negativity of designation, can be taken to suggest that the object is *lost* from any possession as it reveals itself only to hide its other side in its constitution as sign.

This general link of designatum and figure-image must be complicated, however: it is not clear what it would mean to talk about the 'visibility' of an imaginary or fictitious referent, for example. Lyotard is concerned, not to make of the 'real' referent the standard or normal case and the fictional or imaginary the deviation from it (as would be the case for Frege), but to suggest that 'reality' is in fact secondary with respect to the imaginary: 'Reality is only ever a sector of the imaginary field which we have accepted to renounce, from which we have accepted to decathect our phantasies of desire. This sector is bordered on all its edges by the imaginary field in which desire-fulfilments by phantasy continue perpetually' (DF, 284). And in the struggle between this reality and phantasy, it is the latter which is the more powerful and suggests the fragility of the first; which implies that the 'visibility' in question here is precisely not that of 'the real world': at any rate, the opposition of real and imaginary is not the one to trouble the articulation we are looking for.

Whether real or imaginary, it would still seem that the figure-image, via its complicity with designation, allows the visible to enter discourse. The phenomenological perspective on which Lyotard has relied depends on such a recognition, which stresses the opacity of the figural in discourse, its troubling of the rules of the *langue,* its power to contest the 'arbitrary' nature of the sign by working directly on the reader's body, rhythmically and affectively.

This type of analysis reveals the phenomenologist's dream, which is to reconcile language and the world, the speaking body and the perceiving body, to deny the 'arbitrary' sign which cuts the system of *langue* from contact with its (lost) referents. Phenomenological analyses of the figure pick out a notion of 'expressivity' through which the word is supposed to place us in an accord with what it designates, and which would be the achievement of poetry. The problem encountered here is simply that such an analysis makes of language a *nature,* a world in which the body is essentially at home as it is supposed to be at home in the world of perception. And this manoeuvre simultaneously makes of nature a language or a speaker, the source of figures: according to this view, which Lyotard finds exemplified in the French aesthetician Mikel Dufrenne, Being speaks to me through the word. This is not essentially different from what Lyotard found at the beginning of Hegel's *Phenomenology:* the visible made discursive. What it creates here is a poetics of reconciliation, of the 'bonne forme', of harmony and balance, of Apollo rather than Dionysos. It is by contesting this attempt to reconcile discourse and figure that Lyotard will elaborate his notion of the work of art as *critical* (and therefore potentially political).

The immediate implication for the articulation of discourse and figure, however, is that this articulation cannot simply be said to take place between the designatum and the figure-image. Lyotard attempts to show this by analysing the structure of the rebus, another of Freud's comparison-points for the dream-work: the rebus is more complicated that the 'enigmatic inscriptions' discussed earlier, for here text and image are imbricated in a way which disrupts both. Again, this is a long and patient analysis which I can scarcely hope to summarise adequately: suffice it to say that in the rebus the 'figural' is not only present in the recognizable *image,* but also in the *form.* One example given by Lyotard is a drawing of a nose surrounded in a circle by insects: certainly the image of the nose has to be recognized, and the insects, with more difficulty, have to be named as bees: but this latter recognition takes place retrospectively under pressure of the 'solution', which depends on the position of the images being taken into account: the solution, 'Un essaim d'abeilles' (a swarm of bees), deriving by homophony from 'Un nez ceint d'abeilles' (a nose ringed by bees), where the element 'ceint' depends entirely on the positioning of the images, at the level of the figure-form.

As with the enigmatic inscriptions from the *Fliegende Blätter,* there are limits to the analogy, which is primarily heuristic: insofar as the composition of the rebus is determined by the need to find a (discursive) solution, then there are limits to the exploitation of the figure – the spatial distribution of the images has to be easily describable, for example, if it is to be pertinent to the solution. But the rebus has the advantage over the inscription that properly discursive elements can be included as part of the image: in another example, a letter E made up of images of roofs is followed by another E made up of eyes and a T made up of rats, giving the solution: 'Aide-toi et Dieu t'aidera' (Help yourself and God will help you), by homophony from 'é de toits, é d'yeux, t de rats'.

The rebus is composed with a view to a temporary frustration of an understanding it nonetheless promises and eventually delivers. By contrast, Freud insists that the dream-work is precisely *not* carried out with a view to being understood: the secondary process controls the primary process much less in dreams than in the rebus. The poem, for it is here that Lyotard will search primarily for his 'critical' work of art, is no doubt on the side of the rebus in some respects, insofar as its production of 'images' is not undertaken with a view to hallucinatory satisfaction of desire, nor to preserve sleep. On the other hand, the figures it produces are not strictly speaking 'images' at all: the poem shows the figural intimately inhabiting the discursive without destroying it, and this is the whole problem to be accounted for.

And this means a first separation of the 'poem-work' from the 'dream-work', and an approach to the value of the 'critical':

Even more than the dream, poetry is interesting not for its content, but for its work. This work does not consist in *externalising,* in images, forms in which the poet's desire, or ours, is accomplished once and for all, but in *reversing* the relation of desire to figure, in offering the former, not images in which it will be fulfilled and lost, but forms (here poetic forms) by which it will be reflected as a game, as unbound energy, as process of condensation and displacement, as primary process. Discourse is not poetic because it seduces us, but because, beyond this, it lets us see the *operations* of seduction and the unconscious: lure and truth together; ends and means of desire. Our poetic pleasure can thus greatly exceed the limits fixed by our phantasies and we can do this strange thing: learn how to love. The pleasure of the game reverses the game of pleasure. (DF, 322)

This possibility of a critical function has in fact already begun with the dream seen *from a waking state:* the memory of dream-images is just as likely to disgust as to satisfy. From the vantage-point of consciousness, the dream can only appear disordered and irritating:

This irritation signifies that the same operations which accomplish desire and therefore make it escape from the preconscious in sleep, would to the contrary have the function of signalling desire to us when we are not asleep. For then the subject has passed over to the side of the preconscious (or of the ego), to the other side of his desire: the reversal in the function of the deconstruction corresponds to this reversal in the place of the subject. (DF, 323)

The threatening disorder of desire seen from this position can, however, also denounce what is taken to be 'order', open the order of discourse to its other: and thus be 'critical' (but in Lyotard's sense of 'deconstructive') of discourse as the repression of desire. But, crucially, this critical function depends not on a call for desire to be fulfilled come what may: 'it must also be the *non-fulfilment* of the phantasmatics from which these figures proceed', otherwise it could be no more than 'a vulgar alienated-alinenating expression' (DF, 324). No doubt it is all too easy to read the

Phantasy cannot be liberated since phantasy contains within itself its prohibiton [*interdit*], i.e. the fact that it is a *mise-en-scène* stemming from the interdiction of desire. . . If the artist is someone who *expresses* his phantasies, if the relation is that of expression, the work interests only himself or people who have a complementary phantasmatics and thus recognise themselves in it. An art of this type will necessarily be repetitive: this is the case with Giacometti. I believe that the true relation between art and phantasy is not direct, the artist does not produce, outside, systems of internal figures, but is someone who struggles to deliver *in* the phantasy, *in* the matrix of figures whose place and heir he is, what is properly primary process and not repetition, 'writing'. (DMF, 236 [DW, 74]) Both in this essay, and more fully in *Discours, figure* itself, Lyotard tracks in the work of Klee a progression from a 'bad' expressive relation to phantasy to a 'good' critical one (DF, 224-39; the 'good' side is here already formulated in terms of 'the invisible to be made visible', which return in the later work).

Lyotard of *Discours, figure* or *Economie libidinale* as simply suggesting that desire is good, its discursive repression bad, and that desire should be liberated in all its anarchic potentiality. *Discours, figure* suggests that this is not the case: we are always in fact faced with a negotiation of desire and repression, discourse and figure: the difficult question which will remain to be addressed in Lyotard's later work is that of *how to judge* what is here called the 'critical function' of what is here called 'desire' – and this question of judgement, with its aesthetico-political dimensions, will remain through the apparent later repudiation of the major manifest themes of these earlier works.

The figure cannot, then, be limited to the 'image', the visual, the domain of the phenomenological description. The rebus also works at the level of the figure-form, and so does poetry. The following lines from E. E. Cummings are, in Lyotard's terms, inhabited by the figural, which cannot be described in terms of the image:

there is a here and
that here was a
town (and the town is

so aged the ocean
wanders the streets are so
ancient the houses enter the

people are so feeble the feeble go to
sleep if the people sit down)... (Quoted, DF, 319-20)

The figure-matrix remains as a problem: I noted above that its definition appeared to pull in two directions at once – on the one hand towards a type of *a priori* which could reasonably be compared with Derrida's *différance;* on the other towards a sort of idiomaticity of an individual poet, generating particular figures from the matrix of the originary phantasy. This second aspect is troublesome and needs to be made more specific: the obvious danger is that such an insistence would make of reading a quest for symptoms of that phantasy, and confuse the critical and the clinical. Lyotard takes explicit trouble to avoid such a confusion, but in so doing runs the risk of exceeding the delimitation of the 'figure' itself.

A long and detailed analysis of Freud's famous account of the phantasy 'A Child is Being Beaten' (1919) tracks the figure-matrix through verbal and image forms, towards increasingly complex territory: the versatility of the phantasy denies simple verbal or hallucinatory recognition and seems indeed to disrupt image and form (DF, 327-47). The affective charge of the phantasy is no less ambiguous. How are we to describe the phantasy's self-identity, in the face of such a dispersion (which it takes Lyotard 20 closely-written pages to unpack)? This identity must be formal, given the large diversity of content the phantasy can allow: how is this formality to be described? This indeed seems difficult, if the matrix is supposed to be in some sense essentially transgression: surely the very notion of form implies the very type of recognizable relations and intervals characteristic of the opposition the matrix is supposed to transgress in difference?

Here again, it must be remembered that the outcome of this search for the figural cannot be something pure: the 'purely figural' is a contradiction in terms. Even at this level of enquiry, the figure-matrix will be a tension of the 'discursive' and the 'figural': and this tension of their difference will bring us to the death-drive. The tension is, happily enough, at the heart of the 'Child is Being Beaten' phantasy, in the very notion of beating. Beating involves a rhythm of contact and separation between two surfaces, and this rhythm is erogenous. Drawing on the work of the psychoanalyst Serge Leclaire (*Psychanalyser* (Paris: Seuil, 1968)), Lyotard locates *jouissance* in the *difference* between tension and discharge, in the spacing of the contact in this case. But this purely temporal difference is not in itself enough, insofar as *jouissance* depends on the greatest possible inequality between energetic levels in tension and discharge: and this prompts Lyotard's separation from Leclaire's use of the term 'letter' to describe this effect, insofar as the letter would imply too calculable and oppositional a determination of that difference and that energetics. On the other hand, the 'difference' necessary to this description cannot be absolute: for absolute difference would be death, with which the 'petite mort' of *jouissance* has traditional affinities, but with which it is not identical. We must be dealing with what Derrida would call an 'economy of difference'.

Lyotard attempts to make this clearer by appealing to Freud's often-reformulated two principles of psychic functioning: in their earliest version, the constancy-principle and the inertia-principle. The first of these attempts to keep energy low or at least constant, which it is said to do by *binding* it: this 'binding' would be compatible with Leclaire's notion of the letter, and would, according to Lyotard, allow for the possibility of the determination of energy into signification and recognizable representation. The second principle attempts quite simply to evacuate all tension from the system. In Freud's earlier work, the 'pleasure-principle' appears to be linked to the drive to inertia, to discharge; but in *Beyond the Pleasure Principle,* the pleasure-principle apparently moves over to Eros, to binding of energy into more and more complex unities: and now, the 'Nirvana-principle' which seeks to return to a state of zero tension, is linked to the death-drive. But the relationship is complicated by Freud's apparent hypothesis that the pleasure-principle in fact serves the death-drive. Lyotard here finds the way of specifying the problem of the figure-matrix as form and transgression, on 'the razor's edge' between constancy and Nirvana, in the state of tension between tension and discharge, life and death, life-death. The figural is not simply the death of discourse, but discourse never quite successfully binds the figural either: desire is never quite literalised, the death-drive is what is never quite brought back to presence, the force that repeats the *fort* in the fort/da game. There is indeed binding in the unconscious, but never the formalisation of the signifier: the unconscious can only be 'recognized' in the failure of recognition produced by the 'unbinding' of the death-drive; it is only 'itself' in what constantly separates it from itself: and it is the death-drive which is to be found as the principle of figurality.

Despite the ambivalence we have noted around the figure-matrix, there is nothing in this description to justify a 'clinical' use of the above analysis. Lyotard certainly does not want to say that the poetic (critical) text is an 'expression' of the phantasy, seduction, wish-fulfilment. Taking his distance from some of Freud's own analyses of art, Lyotard stresses some of Freud's more general points, and notably that the 'truth' of art depends upon its *not* presenting itself as truth and salvation (this would be what distinguishes it from religion): the form of the work blocks the discharge of desire in fulfilment upon the content. This implies a critique of a number of psychoanalytic theories of art, and notably those which would postulate some harmonious reconciliation of primary and secondary processes, of the Apollonian and the Dionysiac. Such a reconciliation is precisely the function of the phantasy, providing a possibility of satisfaction to fill the empty space left by the withdrawal of the object (the mother): if the work of art is to be 'critical' in Lyotard's sense, it must operate differently:

The function of 'poetic' work (in general: it can be cinematographic, pictural. . .) is to reverse the nature of the relationship between Eros-logos and the death-drive. What is reversed is not the relationship between two objects in a given space: the drive's vicissitude is quite capable of and familiar with such a simple reversal; for example when it replaces X beats Y with Y beats X. Very far from tearing the (verbal or figurative) representatives from their appurtenance to the order of the drive, this reversal is the attestation of that appurtenance. The poetic reversal indeed bears on 'form' and 'content'; but we can now replace these approximative terms with pertinent concepts: whereas the phantasy fills the space of dispossession, the work dispossesses the space of accomplishment. The phantasy makes opposition out of difference; the poetic makes difference again out of *this* opposition. (DF, 360)

In the discussion of the dream-work, we saw that secondary revision held a curious place: both superadded to the 'real work' of the dream, a late attempt to prepare the dream for some sort of reception by consciousness, and yet always-already at work, in at the beginning. We might take this ambivalent status of secondary revision as a guide to the assertions of *Discours, figure:* any pure difference, in the form of some absolute mobility of the primary process, is always already compromised with binding and stasis, Eros and Logos. The figure is always already bound up with the discursive, and only this could account for the existence of a book such as *Discours, figure.* This is not to reduce the argument of the book to a dialectic: the battle of discourse and figure is never, even in principle, resolved either way. The 'critical function' of the work is not that of delivering up the primary process (this would itself be an illusion of the secondary process (DF, 23)), but of resisting its absorption into the secondary, from within the secondary. Conscious thought is all for secondary revision, and is disconcerted by its failure to bind and order. To the extent that 'truth' irrupts in the event of that failure, then it is not surprising that *Discours, figure* should itself scarcely form a harmonious totality, or that my own account of it should have caused me so much difficulty, and required so much secondary revision itself. Lyotard addresses the question in the opening pages of *Discours, figure:*

A good book, in order to let the truth be in its aberration, would be a book in which linguistic time (the time in which signification develops, the time of reading) would itself be deconstructed; a book that the reader could take up at any point and in any order, a book for grazing. (. . .) This book is not a good book, it still stands in signification, it is not an artist's book, deconstruction does not operate in it directly, it is *signified.* It is still a book of philosophy thereby. Certainly the signification is fragmentary, there are lacunae and, I hope, rebuses. Nevertheless that only makes for an uncertain, intermediate object, which I should like to be able to call, in order to excuse it, an inter-world, like Klee, or a transitional object, like Winnicott; but which it is not really, because this status only belongs to the figural things of game, painting, and because here again we don't allow the figure to go into words according to its own game, but we want words to *say* the preeminence of figure, we want to *signify* the other of signification. (DF, 19)

It is not hard, as so often in *Discours, figure,* to recognize an affinity here with Derrida's call for a 'double writing': and this, finally, brings us back to the reservations stressed earlier about the psychoanalytical dimensions of Lyotard's book. In discussing the derivation of the matrix-figure, I suggested that one aspect of it came close to Derrida's *différance,* and another, precisely through the insistence on the phantasy, inevitably returned, despite protestations, to some features of a clinical psychoanalysis in its relation to works of art: the insistence on the terms of psychoanalysis cannot but re-introduce the very notion of the *subject* criticised with relation both to phenomenology and to Lacan. It does not seem necessary to consider the psychoanalytic elaboration of primary and secondary processes, of Eros and the death-drive, as more than *approaches* to the question of difference, which in its 'formality', has no essential link with anything psychical. This possibility, which is certainly implicit in *Discours, figure,* but masked by some of its attachment to Freud (and possibly by its anger at Lacan) 'surfaces' at least once very explicitly: stressing the 'opacity' of the phantasy and its irreducibility to figure-image or figure-form, Lyotard writes:

Analysing, we therefore finally meet with a thickness, an opacity. I shall suppose the figural to be there, deconstructing not only discourse, but the figure as recognizable image or good form. And under the figural, difference, not simply the trace, simply presence-absence, indifferently discourse or figure, but the primary process, the principle of disorder, the push to *jouissance;* not any interval separating two terms in the same order, but an absolute breaking of balance between an order and a non-order. Excavating this depth of the *pseudarchè,* we shall perhaps get our hands on the truth of difference, already felt in the sensory order, in the order of the visual field, but where it is only metaphor: the pseudarchaic field is its proper field, the one it needs to try to install itself. (DF, 328)

The refusal of the trace as the element of the same from which discourse and figure could be differentiated, the 'absolute breaking of balance' and

---

When J. Derrida talks of the trace, and. . . when he talks of archi-writing, the error, I think, is that of not dissociating what is letter and what is [l]ine. It's obvious that the line does not function like the letter. For the letter is made up of a set of distinctive features, and if it can bear meaning, this is because, just like speech, it offers the receiver easily recognisable elements, in a binary logic. This is not true of the line. . . . One can in no way say that the line traced by Klee's pencil on a piece of paper is loaded with effects of meaning in the same way as the letters he writes under that line, which say simply: Salto mortale, for example. Absolutely not. (DFM, 228-9) [Derrida would of course reply that the difference between line and letter is itself a trace]

the desire (however jokily put) to grasp the truth of difference suggest that a price has to be paid for the discursive attempt to champion the figural. Can an 'absolute breaking of balance' (or even a notion of transgression) be strictly compatible with an attempt to think difference rather than opposition? Can psychoanalysis in fact allow difference to be thought in this way? If, indeed, 'there is no absolutely Other' (DF, 11), then what is (pure) 'non-order'? Even if the psychoanalytic part of Lyotard's book knows this, and argues it, it appears that a term such as 'unconscious' brings with it a mass of sedimentations not easily removed. The argument of *Discours, figure* appears to me to be more powerful than the psychoanalytic ground it seeks: we have seen how *Economie libidinale* goes some way toward challenging that ground, and how it is partially destroyed in the attempt. *Economie libidinale* led to the need to go beyond the language of desire and the libido and to adopt the language of 'façons de parler': this is what is taken up in *Le Différend* – but is already suggested in *Discours, figure* itself. 'Sense is present as absence of signification; and yet signification takes hold of it (and it can, one can say everything), it is exiled on the edges of the new speech act' (DF, 19): this enigmatic sentence already states one of the major themes of the later book.

Patchwork 2

The latin term *disjectio* more or less covers the sense of *dissemination* and deconstruction. Neither the former nor the latter is sufficient to obtain 'some measureless dislocation' [Derrida, *Marges*, p. xxii]. Proof (here is an argument): the definition of deconstructive strategy: 'A *reversal* of the classical opposition [between terms such as speech/writing, presence/absence, etc.] and a general *displacement* of the system.' This double operation, presented as the 'only condition' capable of giving deconstruction 'the means to *intervene* in the field of oppositions it criticizes and which is also a field of non-discursive forces' [Ibid., p. 392], could, taken literally, be just as well (here is a refutation) a definition of the work of the speculative dialectic itself. (D, 284)

One writes before knowing what there is to say and how to say it, to find out if possible. Philosophical writing is in advance over what it ought to be. Like a child, it is premature, inconsistant. We begin again, it is not trustworthy, in order to reach thought, over there, at the end. But thought is here, mixed up with non-thought, trying to unscramble the bad speech of childhood. (PE, 160-1)

Buren turns his back on realism, like everything that thinks. It will always be true that to think is to suspend the predicate of reality. . . To think is to have ideas, and ideas go beyond what is given. . . Reality is what is presupposed; suspending reality means examining the presupposed, discovering operators where there used to be data. (FV, 28)

Realism, whose only definition is that it intends to avoid the question of reality implicated in that of art, always stands somewhere between academicism and kitsch. When power assumes the name of a party, realism and its neoclassical complement triumph over the experimental avant-garde by slandering and banning it – that is, provided the 'correct' images, the 'correct' narratives, the 'correct' forms which the party requests, selects, and propagates can find a public to desire them as the appropriate remedy for the anxiety and depression that public experiences. (PE, 21 [PMC, 75])

Here, then, lies the *différend:* modern aesthetics is an aesthetic of the sublime, but a nostalgic one; it allows the unpresentable to be alleged only as an absent content, but the form, because of its recognizable consistency, continues to offer to the reader or viewer matter for consolation and pleasure. But these sentiments do not form the true sublime sentiment, which is an intrinsic combination of pleasure and pain: the pleasure that reason should excede any presentation, the pain that imagination or sensibility should not be equal to the concept.

The postmodern would be that which in the modern alleges the unpresentable in presentation itself; what refuses itself the consolation of good forms, the consensus of a taste which would allow us to feel together the nostalgia for the impossible. A postmodern artist or writer is in the situation of a philosopher: the text he writes, the work he accomplishes are not in principle governed by already-established rules, and they cannot be judged according to a determinant judgement, by application of known categories to this text or this work. The artist and writer thus work without rules, in order to establish the rules of what *will have been done.* Whence the fact that work and text have the properties of the event, whence too the fact that they arrive to late for their author or, what comes to the same thing, that their *mise en oeuvre* always begins too soon. Postmodern would have to be understood according to the paradox of the future *(post)* perfect *(modo).*

It seems to me that the essay (Montaigne) is postmodern, and the fragment (the Atheneum) modern. (PE, 32-3 [PMC, 81])

So long as art presents that there is (some) unpresentable, it belongs to romantic, sublime aesthetics, it mixes the suffering of not being able to find the plastic (or literary) expression of the absolute with the glory of conceiving and wanting it. . .

. . . the essential fact of post-modernity, the incorporation of the sublime in the beautiful, the synthesis of the infinite and the finite in the figure of experimentation.

The division of the beautiful and the sublime has become outdated. . .

The disproportion does not consist in the incommensurability of Ideas with the data of experience, it is in the inexorable erosion of experience under the effect of the ideas realised in axiomatics and operational apparatus. The sublime of immanence replaces the sublime of transcendence. (AE, 124, 149, 153)

Obviously the only interesting thing for the philosopher is to think what he can't manage to think: without that, I wonder what the hell he'd be doing. . . When you're trying to think something in philosophy, you don't care less about the addressee, you don't give a damn. Someone comes along and says, 'I don't understand a word of what you say, of what you write': and I reply, 'I don't give a damn. That's not the problem. I don't feel responsible towards you. You're not my judge in this matter. . .'. There's no contempt, it's not at all a problem of contempt. (RG, 63-4)

It is reasonable to suppose the 'sensus communis' which grounds the sentimental 'we' of art. It would be crazy to demonstrate it. (AV, 59)

Le Différend

Narrative

Given the apparent strength of the 'façons de parler' remark in *Rudiments païens,* and the continuing preoccupation with the event, it seems reasonable for Lyotard to centre his research more specifically on the problem of locating what becomes of the event in various 'façons de parler' – or, as will increasingly be the case, on the respect accorded by the various 'façon de parler' to the event which a 'façon de parler' *is.* For a while, this research centres on the particular 'façon de parler' of *narrative.*

Attention to narrative (of course a privileged object of analysis for structuralism from the 1960's) is not however entirely new to Lyotard's work, and there is a long analysis from the 'libidinal' period, involving a very particular narrative, and already raising questions around the question of the referent and the event which will persist right into *Le Différend.* The narrative in question is that provided by the Renault motor company to the press following the death of Pierre Overney during a demonstration outside their Billancourt factory in 1972. Perhaps because of the emotive charge of the incident, Lyotard's analysis is patient and cool, drawing on the resources of what *Economie libidinale* would no doubt characterise as one of the most theoretical of theoretical *genres,* that of the structural analysis of narrative as practised by Gérard Genette.

This is in fact the essay to which we have already referred in the opening discussion of theatricality – in which traditional historiography was criticized for its pretension to break down the walls of the theatre in order to seize and present, beyond representation, the reality of the referent. In this case the reality in question is as stark as possible: the violent death of Pierre Overney: in taking on history in such an example (and later, in the wake of Adorno, Auschwitz will provide an even more pressing test case), Lyotard is giving himself a more telling, because more difficult, challenge. How can he sustain the claim that, like any story-teller, the historian 'produces' rather than 'reflects' a referent?

Clearly he cannot, in such an extreme form (and it will be remembered that *Economie libidinale* warned us about the implications of too easily adopted a metaphorics of production): as Lyotard points out, the simple espousal of 'production' over 'reflection' is a simple reversal of the type to be suspected:

> To say *production* is certainly to signal towards an *economics* of narration: only this economics, most often borrowed from Marxism, is received in all credence and substituted without examination for the reference which was supposed to be lacking in 'artistic' narrative activity. The support which the story lacked is immediately slipped onto the narrative instance, as its productive accomplice [*suppôt*]. And the activity of story-telling is described as though it were productive in the sense that wire-extrusion or die-casting or mixing plaster or jointing are metamorphoses into products of elements of production: sweet repose in the lap of the industrial model, and its machine. (DP, 181-2)

The objection to this reversal is, familiarly by now, that it fails to displace the terms in question: Lyotard goes on to show that such a model of production is partial, and argues, as in *Economie libidinale,* that production in this industrial sense is secondary and derived with respect to

---

In truth, *social production is solely desiring production itself in determined conditions.* We say that the social field is immediately shot through with desire, that it is the historically determined product of desire, and that the libido has no need of any mediation nor sublimation, no psychic operation, no transformation, in order to invest the forces and relations of production. (G. Deleuze and F. Guattari, *Capitalisme et schizophrénie: L'Anti-Oedipe* (Paris: Minuit, 1972), p. 36). It is not clear to me that Deleuze and Guattari in fact manage to delimit a libido prior to these investments: their refusal of the 'idealism' of an account of the unconscious as a theatre (in Freud), leads to a substitute idealism of the unconscious as a factory (Ibid., p. 31). This is what Lyotard is attempting to escape.

libidinal production or desire. And just as this more general production contains, so it is claimed, the resources necessary to disrupt the familiar process of industrial production (Lyotard is already calling such resources 'the power of simulacra' (DP, 183)), so this generalized level of production can, certainly, give rise to familiar totalising narrative (hi)stories, but can also, when narrative is in the hands of Proust or Joyce (but also Sterne or Rabelais) disrupt such 'organic bodies' by, for example, upsetting neat linear development.

This unsettling function brings us closer to what Lyotard might at this stage mean by the event. He is not for a moment contesting that in this case the event is the death of Pierre Overney. But in this analysis we can no longer simply accept the traditional view that the event 'comes first' in an unquestioned 'real' world, nor, in the simple reversal-model, that it is purely 'produced' by the narrating agency. In the libidinal analysis of 1973, we must rather attempt to begin with no such presupposition:

We shall therefore begin by presupposing neither reference nor support for the narrative instance. This instance produces itself of itself [se produit elle-même] in one go, 'each time', and engenders with itself the distribution of the functions which, after hundreds of others and especially G. Genette, we call narrative and

---

If [narrative] theorists agree on anything it is this: that the theory of narrative requires a distinction between what I shall call 'story' – a sequence of actions or events, conceived as independent of their manifestation in discourse – and what I shall call 'discourse', the discursive presentation or narration of events.

In Russian Formalism this is the distinction between fabula and sjuzhet: the story as a series of events and the story as reported in the narrative. Other theorists propose different formulations, whose terms are often confusing: récit, for example, is sometimes fabula, as in Bremond, and sometimes sjuzhet, as in Barthes. But there is always a basic distinction between a sequence of events, and a discourse that orders and presents events. Genette, for instance, distinguishes the sequence of events, histoire, from the presentation of events in discourse, récit, and also from a third level, narration, which is the enunciation of narrative; but from the way in which Genette uses his categories Mieke Bal argues, rightly I believe, that 'in the end Genette distinguishes only two levels, those of Russian Formalism'. (J. Culler, 'Story and Discourse in Narrative Analysis', in The Pursuit of Signs: Semiotics, Literature, Deconstruction (London and Henley, Routledge and Kegan Paul, 1981, pp. 169-87 (pp. 169-70)). Lyotard's analysis goes on to question this opposition which Culler thinks narrative analysis cannot do without.

---

story. We do not analyse the story along the axis: real history → narration → narrative, but not along the axis narrative → narration → referential history either. Rather we should imagine the synchrony or total achrony of the story, the narration and the narrative. It is on the basis of the complex bloc that they form that emerge the axes in question and possibilities of articulated diachronisation... The function of a narrative of the regulatory type, as is the Renault communiqué, is precisely to produce a common temporal instantiation and a common measure of duration for these three orders. But Sterne, or Diderot in Jacques le fataliste, or Proust disjoin this unity, and attest joyfully and painfully to its being out of date, and proliferate incompossible temporal instances. (DP, 184-5)

It would follow that the event being sought is not to be found simply on the side of referentiality, in the 'real', but in the disruption, still thought of here in terms of tension and energy, of a restrictive narrative temporality. The 'tensivity' is nonetheless associated with the death of Overney, which it is the function of the Renault narrative to absorb:

This event does not have to be taken into account by virtue of being 'real', attestable outside the theatrical volume engendered by narration. Nor is it worthy of consideration because it is 'sensational', likely to engender many a metamorphosis on the 'social body'... these effects are clearly not without their importance, but they are legible only on the surface of the 'social body' and considering them uncritically will not fail to plunge us back into the ('sociological') naivety of belief in this social body, and thus in its preexistence, and thus in a reference assignable to the death of Pierre Overeny. If this death is an event, this is *above all* as a tensor or intense passage, and this tensor requires not the three-dimensional Euclidean space of the theatrical volume and the organized social body, but the n-dimensional, neutral and unpredictable space of the libidinal film engendered by the tensor-event itself in its amnesiac singularity. (DP, 185)

In other words, says Lyotard, Overney's death is an 'event' not because of its causes and effects, but because of it senselessness or *inanity:* despite the efforts of the Renault company's narrative, and even of the demonstration's organisers, Overney's death is an event insofar as it refuses to be absorbed into the *order* of a classical narrative, brought to book in a narrative *account,* its tension exchanged for other tensions.

The attempt to separate the event from any simple question of reference (and the consequent need to elaborate that question in more complex fashion) is confirmed in a later passage of this analysis, where Lyotard interrogates Genette's categories of mode and *distance:*

If the libidinal economist says, like the poetician, that there is no mimesis, this is not because discourse cannot make itself the mime of what is not discourse (i.e. the event), he thinks on the contrary that discourse can become an intense event, and that the intense event participates, precisely, in that property which classical rationalism generally reserves for discourse – self-sufficiency or irrelativity. But if he does not admit the category of mimesis, nor therefore the classifications of narrative distances on the showing/telling polarity, this is because he does not accept what is assumed in Genette as much as it is in Plato, namely that there *is* a reality, here called 'story', by whose standard one could measure the deformation the narrative imposes upon it. (DP, 206-7)

Lyotard's aim, as we have already seen in discussing *Economie libidinale,* is consistently to work *prior* to such a set-up, which is obliged to presuppose subject and object and a distance between them. 'Reality' and 'the referent' have, then, to be thought of as supervening on this prior condition which I have consistently suggested need not be thought of in terms of the libido. In this essay, Lyotard suggests that a reality would be describable as 'the consensus of all the libidinal regions about an intensity': but precisely this (the operation of an equilibration of charges and investments) is the object of Lyotard's consistent suspicion (it is no

accident that the word 'consensus' reappears as a crux of the later disagreement with Habermas). In the language of 1973, such a consensus
implies the elimination of differential intensity on the libidinal band (the
link with Freud's constancy-principle is again obvious), and, thereby, a
necessary occultation of the event in the construction of a reality:

One can only arrive at a consensus about an intensity by *splitting* it, a little as
Marx explains that the object he (very unfortunately) calls 'use' (here it would
be, precisely, non-use) can only become a commodity by doubling up into an
exchange-value. Overney's death recounted must become exchangeable; its
inanity, its 'at a loss' cannot be admitted by the consensus. Narrative eliminates
the loss, conserves all that is (re)producibility of a place of instanciation for the
event, of a temple or a theatre, an organic social body. The terrible irrelativity
of Overney's death both forbids its being forgotten and does not allow it to be
recalled and localised, for the unconscious libidinal band is, for lack of filters, a
receptacle for everything and a memory of nothing. (DP, 206-7)

The aim of the Renault narrative is precisely to promote such a consensus
(as is the aim of the story told by Overney's comrades), to produce a
memory of the event by providing 'filters': in the Renault story, death
becomes the price paid for the demonstrators' wounding of the social
body in a mythical scene of fault and necessary reparation.

This relatively 'early' analysis suggests, beyond its 'libidinal' claims, that
narrative is indeed a good place to look for a possible elaboration of the
event: not simply in the obvious sense that narratives recount or represent events, but that such recounting or representing is a particular way
of dealing with the event, of neutralising what is here still thought of as
a quantitative charge. On the other hand, it is also claimed that narrative
can in some sense *be* an event.

  Following the 'linguistic turn' in Lyotard's thought which I have linked
for expository convenience to the 'façons de parler' remark in *Rudiments
païens,* Lyotard tends to think for a while that narrative is not only one
set-up for dealing with the event, but perhaps the fundamental one, and
that narratives can be located behind apparently non-narrative *dispositifs:*
where the challenge of *Economie libidinale* came to be that of describing
the apparent other of libidinal analysis (theory) as itself libidinal, this
change of emphasis attempts to redescribe that theoretical genre as in
fact a narrative genre. The most well-known instance of this type of
argument is of course *The Postmodern Condition,* but its most powerful
statement is probably to be found in the 'dialogue', *Instructions païennes,*
one of the enigmatic cluster of texts published in 1977 (the same year

as *Rudiments païens* and of a more obviously narrative text, *Récits tremblants:* another narrative fiction, *Le Mur du pacifique,* appeared in its first version in 1976, and as a book in 1979). Precisely because of the claims it makes for the centrality of narrative (though also, relatedly, because of its local link to the context of the French legislative elections of 1977 and to the discussion around the so-called 'nouveaux philosophes'), this book up to a point resists theoretical summary: in its different way, this is, like *Economie libidinale,* an attempt to contest the position of theory non-theoretically, by showing that theory is (also) non-theoretical. The new tone of the analysis is suggested early on by the 'instructor' figure of the dialogue:

> Don't forget that he who is speaking at this moment and who in general designates himself by the word 'me', me, then, who as it happens am speaking, am only going, in drawing your attention to some points of *petite politique* and present history, to tell you a story, precisely, and unfold my little narrative. I urge you, as a preliminary instruction, not to wonder whether it is more or less true than another, but rather to consider that it exists; that it proceeds, weakly or strongly – I'm no judge of that – from a story-telling potential which is almost invincible in everyone. . . My narrative is not universal history being recounted through my mouth. And I do not lay claim to the profession of theoretician, which is that of saving the world by reminding it of its lost meaning. (IP, 17-18)

And a further comment will specify that in any case:

> It is my opinion that theories are themselves narratives, but dissimulated narratives; that one should not allow oneself to be taken in by their pretension to omnitemporality; that the merit of having produced a narration previously, even if it was in the form of an unshakeable system, never acquits one of the task of starting again now; and that one is not right to be coherent and immutable, i.e. equal to oneself, but that one is right to want to be equal to the story-telling potential one believes one can hear presently in what others are saying and doing. (IP, 28-9)

And this generalization of narrative also encounters anew and answers somewhat differently the vexed question of reference and reality: and answers it with disconcerting simplicity – now it is claimed that *the reference of narrative is always simply another narrative.* (This value of the disconcerting is assigned a positive political value in the context of the 1977 elections: here the best to be hoped is that people ('le commun') will exceed with their narrative inventivity the programmed narratives of Left and Right alike (IP, 9-10).)

This 'solution' to the problem of reference is a point of contention in the dialogue, and again violent death provides the test-case: against the scandalized interlocutor's invocation of 'the Commune, Cronstadt, Budapest in '56... and the dead', the reply is simply that

The dead are not dead so long as the living have not recorded their death in narratives. Death is a matter for archives. One is dead when one is narrated and no longer anything but narrated. (IP, 19)

What of the shells which killed those who died?

Shells do not speak, but they are references of the narratives which prepare them and comment on them, and they are also an extra bit of persuasion administered to incredulous addressees by narrators determined to convince. (IP, 19-20)

Reality is never given, but always situated by particular narratives *as* referents: just as story-teller and addressee do not precede the story told but are positioned by it. This motif, elaborated and complicated, will remain through all the later work.

The analysis of the Renault narrative scarcely presented any grounds for its suspicion of equilibrating narrative and for its defence of intensity (intensity as value could hardly be given grounds). *Instructions païennes* provides greater precision on both of these questions, and in both cases the sign of that precision is 'justice': this new and increasingly important motif in Lyotard's thought is grafted onto the earlier notion of the 'pagan' which insists in the title of both *Rudiments* and *Instructions,* and which was prepared by the discussion of pagan 'theatrics' borrowed by *Economie libidinale* from Pierre Klossowski, and associated with the notion of impiety. The very reason for the issuing of these 'Pagan instructions' is that 'we want...justice' (IP, 10), and the object of the instructions

---

... popular, properly pagan, 'peasant' in the sense of pagan (and not the other way around). The people of the *pagus* (who are not the people of the village) are people who only tell a story to the extent that it has been told, and who are themselves told in what they tell... *Pagus* was said of the region of limits on the edges of boroughs. *Pagus* gives *pays* [country]. It is not the *Heim* or the *home*, the habitat, the shelter, but the environs [*parages*], the countryside [*contrées*], which are not necessarily uncultivated, the horizons of strolls during which one sees the country a bit. (AJ, 74-5 [JG, 38]; cf. IP, 42-3)

is 'justice in impiety' (the defence and elaboration of this paradoxical conception is one of the major imports of the recent work). The link of these terms is tightened insofar as it is argued that piety (which we might gloss as the uncritical recitation of any canonical narrative) necessarily gives rise to injustice, but that not all impiety is just: these two claims marking Lyotard's difference with the Left, but also with the liberalism of which he will, later, so often be accused by the Left: 'The liberals can be quite impious, but they're not very just at all, and those on the left want justice, but at the cost of an extreme piety' (IP, 11).

The baldness of the claim that piety and injustice are implicated in each other can be linked, in the local context of this text, to the increasing importance of Soviet dissidence (the brief phenomenon of the 'nouveaux philosophes' and the recent concern of French thinkers with, broadly speaking, questions of ethics can also be linked to this) and notably to the impact of Solzhenitsyn's *Gulag Archipelago*. Lyotard simply notes as an effect of this that the majority of French intellectuals (traditionally never far from the C.P.) are now refusing to recite the Marxist narrative, because they feel it gives rise to serious effects of injustice wherever the attempt is made to carry it through. Solzhenitsyn's book is taken to show that the Stalinist narrative has maintained its status only by preventing its privileged referent or *narré* (the proletariat) from becoming narrators in their turn, confining them to the posts of addressee and referent. *The Gulag Archipelago* bears witness to the 'almost invincible' narrative potential which remains and which filters out from the camps in the form of 'little narratives' which cannot be fitted into the general narrative of Stalinism. The effect of the diffusion of such little stories is to undermine the ability of the general narrative to impose its credibility on the addressees supposed to recount it in its turn.

Lyotard is careful not to accord Solzhenitsyn's book causal status in the story he is telling in *Instructions païennes* (IP, 25-6): but the effect is that any simple oppositional model of a good narrative (Marxism) and a bad narrative (capitalism) can no longer seriously be sustained, or can only be sustained at the price of ever more piety. And once the opposition of just two major narratives is disturbed, then a multiplicity of more-or-less antagonistic narratives can circulate without necessarily re-amalgamating into two great blocks of opponents. A certain dispersion of political action in the West since 1968 can of course also be linked to this general schema.

It is important, and characteristic of all of Lyotard's thought, that such a break-up of large-scale narratives (the 'grand' or 'meta-narratives' of *The Postmodern Condition)* is not the object of lamentation but of affirmation – that intellectuals assign the increasing lack of respect for such narratives to a disenchantment or depression (of an increasingly alienated subject in monopoly capitalism, for example), is simply a 'pure projection of the disappointment they feel in their need to believe in a major narrative' (IP, 30). Lyotard will want to celebrate and promote such little narratives which resist totalisation into any universal history:

It is not at all a question of [civil societies as networks of narratives] standing heroically against States in a sort of death-defiance. . . If uncertain and ephemeral networks of narratives can gnaw away at the great instituted narrative apparatuses, it's by multiplying somewhat lateral skirmishes as was done [in France] in the last decade by women who had had abortions, by prisoners, by conscripts, by prostitutes, by students, by peasants. (IP, 34-5)

To the objection that this is equivalent to celebrating 'n'importe quoi' and that firing out stories is not an end in itself, Lyotard responds by invoking the 'finalité sans fin', the 'purposivenenss without purpose' of Kant's 3rd *Critique* (in this text Lyotard rejects the first two *Critiques* as infected with 'the illness of knowledge and the rule' (IP, 36)), thus inaugurating a reference which in many ways dominates the later work, and which will require elucidation.

We might accept readily enough Lyotard's stress on the importance of 'popular' narrative, and even his claim that clouds of such narratives,

A decisive perspective has just been opened: that history is made of clouds of narratives, narratives reported, invented, heard and played out; that the people does not exist as a subject, that it is a heap of billions of little futile and serious stories, which sometimes get attracted into constituting large narratives, sometimes disperse into fanciful wanderings, but which in general just about hold together, forming what's called the culture of a civil society. (IP, 39)

rather than one big narrative, constitutes 'history', and still wonder why we should think of theory or science as a concealed narrative. If theory is a discourse which claims in some sense to speak for its object or referent, how are we to know that it really does so? Because of a pre-supposed or explicit theory of that theory, which determines the rules according to which its statements are acceptable: how do we know that these rules are right and legitimate? Because of a further discourse of legitimation, precisely: and here we rejoin Lyotard at *The Postmodern Condition*. The form of the argument here is that as a discourse bound to the truth of its referent cannot presuppose the validity of its own access to that truth (which would amount to not respecting the referent at all, but merely its own internal discursive organisation), then it needs to have recourse to a different type of discourse to provide it with a grounding. In *The Postmodern Condition* Lyotard determines this different type of discourse as narrative discourse, and formulates the problem as follows:

Scientific knowledge cannot know and make known that it is the true knowledge without resorting to the other, narrative, kind of knowledge, which from its point of view is no knowledge at all. Without such recourse it would be in the position of presupposing its own validity and would be stooping to what it condemns: begging the question, proceeding on prejudice. (CPM, 51 [PMC, 29])

And working with the broad and simplifying categories characteristic of *The Postmodern Condition,* Lyotard suggests a change from a sort of classical and premodern science which produced narratives seeking for legitimation in an origin or ground, a first principle or a transcendental authority, to 'modern' forms of legitimation, which jettison such an appeal and recognize that the rules of the discourse of the truth are legitimate to the extent that they are the object of a consensus on the part of those using that discourse: this broadly democratic or autonomous (rather than transcendental) type of legitimation allows for the possibility that the discussion of experts can lead to an improvement in the rules for speaking the truth, and that this improvement can be projected into a future under the sign of progress. The so-called 'Grand Narratives' of legitimation appear only at this point, and are oriented teleologically by some idea or ideal to be attained, rather than retrospectively by some origin to be revived or unearthed.

These narratives are opposed by Lyotard to two other types of narrative: on the one hand the so-called 'traditional' narrative of a so-called 'primitive' society, which appears to appeal to a traditional past in order to legitimate a broad sweep of 'knowledge', but in fact legitimates itself in the present of the recitiation of that narrative, and on the other the 'little

---

What I am getting at is a pragmatics of popular narratives that is, so to speak, intrinsic to them. . . The narrative 'posts' (sender addressee, hero) are so organized that the right to occupy the post of sender receives the following double grounding: it is based upon the fact of having occupied the post of addressee, and of having been recounted oneself, by virtue of the name one bears, by a previous narrative — in other words, having been positioned as the diegetic reference of other narrative events. The knowledge transmitted by these narrations is in no way limited to the functions of enunciation; it determines in a single stroke what one must say in order to be heard, what one must listen to in order to speak, and what role one must play (on the scene of diegetic reality) to be the object of a narrative. (CPM, 39-40 [PMC, 20-21])

narratives' of postmodern science which apparently need no legitimation beyond the fact that they are interesting, their 'interest' being defined in terms of their breaking with the given consensus in the scentific community at the time. This would, so the story goes, prevent their cohering into anything like a Grand Narrative, and this would be the mark of their post-modernity.

We no longer have recourse to the grand narratives – we can resort neither to the dialectic of Spirit nor even to the emancipation of humanity as a validation for postmodern scientific discourse. But. . . the little narrative remains the quintessential form of imaginative invention, most particularly in science. (CPM, 98 [PMC, 60])

Narrative is doing a lot of work in this description. In what is no doubt a laudable attempt to question the pretension of discourses of knowledge to transcribe a message delivered by reality in the form of facts, and simultaneously to resist the temptation, once this pretension collapses, to allow the criterion of efficiency or performativity to act as a legitimation, given the decline of the traditional Grand Narratives, Lyotard here certainly relies too heavily on the assumption that narrative is the 'other' of scientific or theoretical claims. It is all too easy to suspect some nostalgic investment in the traditional form of narrative here represented by his favourite Cashinahua Indians (see too AJ, 63-6 [JG, 32-3], LD, 219-23, PE, 56-9 and 73-5), and it is hard to see why it would follow from the idea that contemporary science, in some of its branches at least, values inventiveness or creativity, that such inventiveness should essentially (rather than sociologically) take the form of story-telling. Further, making paralogy or dissensus rather than consensus the aim or telos of discussion can all too easily suggest that Lyotard is himself proposing a sort of Grand

The second assumption [made by Habermas] is that the goal of dialogue is consensus. But as I have shown in the analysis of the pragmatics of science, consensus is only a particular state of discussion, not its end. Its end, on the contrary, is paralogy. (CPM, 106 [PMC, 65-6])

Narrative leading to a dispersion or diaspora as a desired state beyond current illusions. Such a conception is unthinkable in quite a strong sense, I think, and it could be shown that it relies on a misreading of *The Postmodern Condition*.

In Derrida's discussion of Levinas, a footnote opposes Levinas's thinking about violence to that of Eric Weil, but could almost have been describing in advance the disagreement between Lyotard and Habermas. For Levinas, in Derrida's formulation, 'The "end of history" is not absolute Logic, absolute coherence of the Logos with itself in itself, is not agreement in the absolute system, but Peace in separation, the diaspora of absolutes' (*L'Ecriture et la différence*, 171 n 1). It is not immediately easy to read Lyotard as not suggesting the same:

but a generous reading of *The Postmodern Condition,* influenced by some of Lyotard's later work, would be able to argue that such a diaspora or dissensus is precisely unthinkable as an end of history, and is, on the contrary, *present now,* in a difficult sense which would have to be elaborated via Kant's description of the Idea of Reason, complicated by Derrida's account of the trace.

But although I would argue that this is a misreading, the importance accorded to narrative by the book perhaps makes such a misreading inevitable, and suggests the need to elaborate more carefully the ideas already noted in the earlier work, which would stress a multiplicity of 'façons de parler' and resist the temptation to subsume so much of this multiplicity under the heading of 'narrative'.

It is not correct to accord the narrative genre an absolute privilege over the other genres of discourse in the analysis of human phenomena, or linguistic (ideological) phenomena in particular, and still less in the philosophical approach. Some of my earlier reflexions may have succumbed to this 'transcendental appearance'. (PE, 45)

Rhetoric and Pragmatics

This importance accorded to narrative seems to be an intermediate step in the generalising of the notion of the *dispositif.* Once the libidinal language is recognized as essentially that (a language), and can in principle become one more *dispositif* rather than a general ground of explanation for all *dispositifs,* then a general field of 'façons de parler' is opened up, which might be described in terms of a generalised rhetoric. If all language is in some sense thus rhetorical, it is hard not to accord some privilege to uses of language which might in some sense be said to be aware of their own rhetorical nature (this will be a fundamental principle of the thought of Paul de Man, for example). The other side of such a privilege will be an attempt to demonstrate the nature of the mystification affecting uses of language which do not recognise that fundamental rhetoricity; uses which have traditionally gone under such names as 'theory', 'history', 'science', 'philosophy'.

This type of argument, perhaps first clearly stated in the closing chapter of *Rudiments Païens,* leads to the type of 'pragmatic' analysis used in *The Postmodern Condition,* and to its refinements (beyond pragmatics) in *Le Différend.* We saw how, at the end of *Economie libidinale,* Lyotard's analysis required the distinction between 'bodies' of victim and client: in *Rudiments païens* this type of approach identifies three poles or 'instances' of a work, and assesses what is still seen as that work's 'force' in terms of the displacements it operates on those poles: the pole of sending or emission, that of reception, that of reference. These three poles are still here explicitly identified with the narratologist's narrator, narratee and *narré* or diegesis, but are in fact already being used in principle as simply sender, addressee and referent, and the theoretical genre analysed in terms of what it implies of these three poles: this type of analysis is what Lyotard subsequently (IP, 16; CPM, 21-3 [PMC, 9-10]; AJ, 41-84 [JG, 19-43]) refers to as pragmatics. 'To put it briefly, a work is an object of words, images, sounds, endowed with a force capable of displacing either the author – better, authority, which is the collective of authors and the status they enjoy –, or the public, or what it refers to, or several of these points of application together, or all of them.' (RP, 237).

The first pole to be discussed is that of the addressee: taking Plato's dialogues as his exemplary text, Lyotard suggests that the peculiarity of philosophy is to position a figure of the *disciple* in the text, thus controlling the essential unpredictability of the addressee's response by prefiguring it in the statement. Philosophy offers a model of its right reader, and this leads to the creation of a space of the School or University. Philosophy would have us believe that such discipline is simply an indispensable preliminary to the practice of its genre: Lyotard replies that this positioning is immanent to the text of philosophy and not prior to it as a propedeutic – in an attempt to challenge this set-up, *Le Différend* will define its reader as 'philosophical, i.e. anyone at all' (LD, p. 13). On the other hand, the traditional set-up does invite that disciple to take over the position of the master and become the sender or narrator of philosophical discourse him or herself – and Lyotard opposes this to the work of painting or politics, where no such invitation is in principle immanent to the work produced. The other two poles, namely those of sender and reference, are treated as follows:

Where the other arts accept quite happily (even when painfully) the principle that there is no referent which is not signified in a work, whatever the material of the work, the art of theory appears to need the opposite hypothesis: it needs a reference independent of what it can say about it. This reference has borne a good many names from the Idea of the Good to Infrastructure or Being. But all the systems or anti-systems which have been and will be able to make good their right to Truth will only manage to do so at the cost of inverting the relationship of their work of language with what it talks about.

They need to hide from sight (from the sight of their audience but also from that of their own authority) the artifice of their discourse, i.e. the fact which is recognized and demanded by poet and novelist – namely that it is the work made of words which fictions or fashions its reference. *Non fingo* is their most common article of faith. It is by virtue of this that whoever wants to be a philosopher must have himself forgotten as artist, by himself included, that he must disguise the will to fiction which organises his discourse as a will to truth of its reference.

Now this fiction of non-fiction does not take place without a concomitant displacement affecting the [agency of enunciation]. For if the work of theory must not only fashion its reference but relate it, if it must be faithful and not ingenious, then the theorist must play the role of a listener, at most of a spokesperson, rather than that of an author, and it is to the reference of the discourse that real authority will finally devolve. (RP, 243)

And the pragmatic organisation of the genre can now be summarised as follows:

So one can see, however brief this glance, what a bizarre rotation on the pragmatic triangle is set in motion by the philosophical art. While selecting as addressee of the discours a hearer or reader capable of become a master in it, it admits as its mistress only a thought which learns from and listens to its object, thus making itself that object's faithful disciple, while as a matter of principle according to what it talks about supreme authority over its own discourse. (RP, 244)

In theory, then, the apparent sender becomes an addressee of the referent become sender, while the addressee will become a new sender/addressee in turn. The fate of the addressee in this type of analysis will reappear as the focus for the analysis of the ethical genre in the later work: the shifting of sender and referent will determine the later critique of positivisms of all sorts. The effort to avoid such a set-up determines the apparent voluntarism of the 'pagan' work, and its 'philosopher-artist' overtones. These emphases will largely be dropped, as still 'metaphysical', in the more careful elaboration of this new perspective in *Le Différend.*

Reality

Let us approach that more careful elaboration, as worked out in *Le Différend,* by returning to the question of the referent, of the reality that a variety of discourses, but notably those of science and history, in some sense claim to represent, transcribe or otherwise deliver. From the point of view of an analysis of ways of speaking, it ought to be possible to specify the discursive conditions which must be satisfied for a referent to be considered as real, and for us to entertain notions of objectivity, such that reality is thought to be there even when we are not perceiving or talking about it. The most obvious way in which language gets some sort of grasp on the real is through ostensive sentences involving terms such as 'there', 'this', 'that', 'now', and so on, in other words, the very deictic terms which we saw in *Discours, figure* provide a first access to the notion of the *figure*. As we saw, these deictic terms have the peculiarity of not having a stable and specifiable signification within the language system, and of depending on the immediate context of their use in order to signify at all. But this very immediacy also means that they cannot in and of themselves establish a durability of what they are used to pick out, and also that nothing in their use can determine whether what is being pointed to is real or an 'illusion' for example. Designation by means of deictics is essentially fleeting and uncertain. A certain stability of designation can only be secured by a different sort of sentence including a nomination: a word such as 'this' or 'that' changes its designation according to the sentence in which it is used – a name does not. The name is like a deictic in that it designates, but unlike it in that it retains its value from sentence to sentence – only a name can specify the reference of a deictic and allow the 'same' thing to be referred to in different sentences, of different types. Following Kripke (though not in every aspect of Kripke's account), Lyotard thinks of names as 'rigid designators'. But names don't

'Let's call something a *rigid designator* if in every possible world it designates the same object. . . One of the intuitive theses I will maintain in these talks is that *names* are rigid designators. Certainly they seem to satisfy the intuitive test mentioned above: although someone else might have been the U.S. President in 1970 (e.g. Humphrey might have), no one other than Nixon might have been Nixon. In the same way, a designator rigidly designates a certain object if it designates that object wherever the object exists. . . For example, 'the President of the U.S. in 1970' designates a certain man, Nixon; but someone else (e.g., Humphrey) might have been President in 1970, and Nixon might not have; so this designator is not rigid. . . I will argue, intuitively, that proper names are rigid designators, for although the man (Nixon) might not have been the President, it is not the case that he might not have been Nixon (though he might not have been *called* 'Nixon'). Those who have argued that to make sense of the notion of rigid designator, we must antecedently make sense of 'criteria of transworld identity' have precisely reversed the cart and the horse; it is *because* we can refer (rigidly) to Nixon, and stipulate that we are speaking of what might have happened to *him* (under certain circumstances), that 'transworld identifications' are unproblematic in such cases.' (Saul Kripke, *Naming and Necessity* (Oxford, Blackwell, 1980), pp. 48-9). For our present purposes, 'transworld identifications' can be thought of as 'trans-sentence' identifications or even 'trans-universe' identifications – as we shall see, for Lyotard every sentence presents a universe, whereas a 'world' in his terminology is made up of a network of names: 'I call it a world because these names, being "rigid", each refer to something even when that something is not there; and because this something is supposed to be the same for all the sentences which refer to it; and also because each of these names is [unlike a deictic] independent of the sentence-universes which refer to it, and notably of the senders and addressees presented in those universes'. (LD, §60)

mean anything, they are empty, they are not essences, an indefinite number of unpredictable descriptions can be attached to a given name (LD, §74). Whether the referent is real or not depends also on the description it can be given: it is quite possible to name ('It's Caesar') while pointing to a picture of Caesar (LD, §63). Reality is established by the link of a certain description and an ostension: the name, as quasi-deictic or rigid designator, allows the identity of the referent of the description and the ostension to be asserted. So a valid cognition depends on the linking together of three sentences at least: a descriptive, 'the Empire has a capital city'; a nominative, 'it's called Rome'; an ostensive, 'this is it' (LD, §65). A fourth sentence can then affirm that the referent of these three sentences is the same, and that it is therefore real. Of course this link can always be questioned, new descriptions offered, and so on. Reality is, then, neither simply given and awaiting more-or-less adequate transcription, nor is it magically produced by a demiurgic act of creation on the part of a speaker, but is an unstable state attributed to referents on the basis of operations of nomination, ostension and description. These operations do not include narration. Reality is established as the result of playing a language-game with specifiable component parts.

Why do Lyotard's examples here always involve 'proper' names? Surely this does not imply that he thinks that every object has or should have a proper name? Is this a remnant of the 'mad lover of singularities' of *Economie libidinale*? (In *Le Différend*, §55, such an idea is qualified as a 'metaphysical illusion'). Would not the normal test-case for reality involve objects without proper names? Or, perhaps, deictics used adjectivally of common nouns: 'my body', 'this paper', 'this fire'? Lyotard does not ever thematise this as a problem, though not all of his examples involve proper names as such:

> Reality: a swarm of meanings lights in a field located by a world. It is signifiable, showable and namable. The accent is sometimes on one of these aspects, sometimes on another. On showing: 'Look, there it is, the knife Elisa gave you'. In other words, in order: shown, signified, named. On naming: 'That one is Hector, the chairperson's husband' – shown, named, signified. On meaning: 'something that's used to record speech? A microphone, like this one, I bought it in Brussels' – signified, shown, named (LD, §82).

This type of analysis suggests among other things that the use of the term 'language-game' in *The Postmodern Condition* was imprecise: there is was used to refer to types of sentences such as descriptives and prescriptives, but also to regulated ways of linking such sentences together, such as 'science' (a similar equivocation is probably at work in Wittgenstein's *Investigations*). Accordingly, Lyotard drops the term 'language-

---

Review the multiplicity of language-games in the following examples, and in others:
    Giving orders, and obeying them –
    Describing the appearance of an object, or giving its measurements –
    Constructing an object from a description (a drawing) –
    Reporting an event –
    Speculating about an event –
    Forming and testing a hypothesis –
    Presenting the results of an experiment in tables and diagrams –
    Making up a story; and reading it –
    Play-acting –
    Singing catches –
    Guessing riddles –
    Making a joke; telling it –
    Solving a problem in practical arithmetic –
    Translating from one language into another –
    Asking, thanking, cursing, greeting, praying.
(*Philosophical Investigations*, §23)

---

game' (he has another reason for so doing, which will appear shortly), and talks about 'regimes of sentences' on the one hand (descriptives, narratives, prescriptives, ostensives, etc.), and 'genres of discourse' on the other (science, philosophy, tragedy, and so on). Genres involve linking together sentences of a variety of regimes: regimes seem to be irreducible (in the sense that they cannot be translated the one into the other, nor derived the one from the other – whence their heterogeneity).

The idea that knowledge (in the sense of knowing what is real) is unstable and subject to revision and completion is scarcely new, and would traditionally be accounted for by some invocation of the notion of experience, and thereby of a singular or collective subject of that experience. In this type of description, a subject gathers the properties of events as phenomena and constitutes their reality by carrying out the temporal synthesis of that series of events. The partial and incomplete nature of experience can be attributed to the finitude of the individual subject, and the ultimate guarantee of reality transferred to some absolute witness (God), or else to a non-human or possibly collective subject (Spirit, Humanity). Lyotard thinks that neither the notion of a subject nor that of an experience is necessary to the analysis of knowledge, and that both cause unnecessary trouble. A subject is tied to the pronoun 'I' ('I think therefore I am'): but 'I' is a deictic and no more stable than a 'this' or a 'now' – even supposing that 'I think therefore I am' is true every time I 'proffer it or conceive it in my mind', as Descartes says, the identity of that 'I' from occurrence to occurrence of the sentence cannot be presupposed, and can in fact only be asserted on the basis of a name to link

> But the body is real? – The body 'proper' is a name from the family of idiolects. It is, further, the referent of sentences obeying diverse regimes. I've got toothache: this is a descriptive, along with a co-presented demand: Get rid of it for me. The dentist makes of your pain a case which verifies a cognitive sentence. . . – But the toothache is a pain, it's lived, etc! – How do you verify that it's lived? You are the sole addressee of that pain. It is like the voice of God: 'You can't hear God speak to someone else, you can hear him only if you are being addressed' (*Zettel*, §717). Wittgenstein adds: 'That is a grammatical remark'. It circumscribes what an idiolect is: 'I' am alone in hearing it. The idiolect falls easily under the dilemma (§8): if your lived experience is not communicable, you cannot bear witness to its existence; if it is, you cannot say that you are the only one who can bear witness to its existence. (LD, §145)

those occurrences. But names are given, the reality of the supposed subject is established prior to that subject's proffering any sentence at all. Reality is therefore not a result of experience, and subjectivity is not therefore a ground for knowledge. If I do set out to doubt, I can't stop so soon.

Sentences: Presentation

But there is nonetheless a sort of Cartesianism without the subject in Lyotard's later philosophy. The 'object' of *Le Différend* could, apparently, hardly be more different from those of *Economie libidinale* and *Discours, figure:* after the complex imagination of the 'libidinal band' and the ultimately ungraspable 'figure', here we have a disconcertingly simple object for philosophy: the sentence. We may well wonder whether a whole

> In his forthcoming translation of *Le Différend* for the University of Minnesota Press, Georges Van Den Abbeele elects to translate Lyotard's *phrase* (the usual French word for the English 'sentence') by the English 'phrase'. It is true

that the French word does also allow this sense, and translating it thus has the advantage of avoiding possible suggestions of grammatical and/or semantic completion carried by 'sentence', which Lyotard's examples often do not show (silence is a *phrase*, and so too, perhaps, is a storm at sea). Translating *phrase* as 'phrase' also allows the verb *phraser* to be translated in continuity with the noun.

Despite these advantages, I have preferred to translate *phrase* as 'sentence', for the following reasons:

– *Le Différend* quite deliberately entertains an ambivalent relationship with the Anglo-American philosophical tradition: Lyotard's use of *phrase* marks this fact, and 'sentence' retains that mark in a way that 'phrase' does not.

– In avoiding 'sentence''s connotation of grammatical completion and unity, 'phrase' carries a strong sense of designating a *fragment* of such a unity. On balance, it is more accurate to think of Lyotard's *phrase* as a unity than as a fragment of a larger unity.

– It is indeed intuitively odd to think of some of Lyotard's examples as sentences: but intuitively odd to think of almost any of them as phrases instead

philosophy can be supported by such an object. The sentence 'I think' does not entail that I am, but that there has been a sentence. This at least is indubitable. The sentence 'I doubt that there is a sentence' is a sentence. 'There is no sentence' is a sentence. (And ' "There is no sentence" is a sentence' is another sentence). But this does not imply that 'I think' or 'I doubt' or even 'There is a sentence' is the *first* sentence, of course: such a sentence presupposes sentences defining terms and giving examples of usage, and so on. To describe it (in a second sentence) as a 'first' sentence also presupposes the ordinal sequence of numbers (or at least 'second') to give 'first' a meaning. And this supposed 'first' sentence would also presuppose a prior sentence to which it links up, for example a question to which it would propose an answer.

. . . we have to say that the first is not the first if there is not, after it, a second. Consequently, the second is not what comes, like a late arrival, only *after* the first, but it is what allows the first to be a first. So the first cannot manage to be the first by its own strength, by its own means: the second must help it with all the power of its delay. It is through the second that the first is first. The 'second time' thus has a sort of priority over the 'first time': it is present, right from the first time, as the prior condition of the priority of the first time (without itself of course being a more primitive 'first time'): it follows that the 'first time' is in reality the 'third time' (Vincent Descombes, *Le même et l'autre: quarante-cinq ans de philosophie française (1933-1978)* (Paris: Minuit, 1979), p. 170)

What is indubitable about a sentence is not its meaning (further sentences would have to interpret it and spell its meaning out), nor even its existence, its reality (which requires the sorts of procedures I have sketched out, which procedures involve doubt). Simply that there is a sentence is indubitable. That there is a sentence is presupposed in saying anything at all. In this conception, neither reality nor the subject stands prior to and in principle independent of a sentence. Reality is attributed by a sentence to a referent positioned by a sentence, and a subject is also positioned by a sentence. A sentence which declares that a thinking substance or a transcendental ego stands outside the sentence positions that subject as the referent of a sentence, and describes that subject as standing outside sentences in general. Lyotard goes on to argue that all such questions are to be analysed in terms of the presentation by a sentence of what he calls a 'universe', which consists of four poles or posts: the three we saw at work in *Rudiments païens,* viz sender, addressee and referent, but now also the meaning (*sens*). None of these four poles or posts pre-exists the sentence which presents them and their relationship or situation. What we call subjects, reality, meaning are, then, effects of the concatenation of sentences.

'We should say: the sender and addressee are instances, marked or not, presented by a sentence. A sentence is not a message passing from a sender to an addressee both independent of it (. . .). Sender and addressee are situated in the universe it presents, just like its referent and meaning. . . a sentence presents what it is about, the case, *ta pragmata,* which is its referent; what is signified of the case, the meaning, *der Sinn;* that to which or addressed to which this is signified of the case, the addressee; that 'by' which or in the name of which it is signified of the case, the sender. The disposition of a sentence universe consists in the situation of these instances with respect to each other.' (LD, §§ 18 and 25) The inclusion of 'meaning' as a fourth pole in the sentence-universe is clearly decisive. In the earlier conception, meaning's absence from the discussion left it in principle in a transcendent position outside the universe of sentences and presentations. *Le Différend* apparently attempts a radical immanentisation of meaning in the event-sentence: just as the identity of sender, addressee and referent depends on the ability of an event-sentence to present as 'the same' their occurrences in a series of event-sentences, so the identity of meaning requires the same procedure. Previously, meaning would have had to be thought as the milieu in which sentences occurred: now, the postulation of any such milieu itself takes place in a sentence, and cannot therefore be thought of as prior to a sentence. Wittgenstein's notion of meaning as use no doubt helps Lyotard to make meaning apparently immanent to a sentence, but in Wittgenstein this takes place at the price of implying a user outside the sentence – Lyotard's conception refuses any such transcendence. But the idea that meaning is 'immanent' is misleading if it suggests that each event-sentence exists in a pure self-sufficiency, with its meaning 'in' it: meaning is always in fact *imminent*, contingent on the event-sentence which links up with this event-sentence.

A sentence presents a 'universe', consisting of sender, addressee, referent and meaning, and their 'situation' (their relationships with each other). The indubitable 'that' of the sentence is not *the universe presented*, with its situation of instances, but the *presentation of the universe*. A sentence presents what it presents, but cannot present that it presents what it presents. A further sentence (such as Lyotard's in the chapter of *Le Différend* entitled 'La présentation') can make of that *event* of presentation the referent of the universe it presents, in an effort to remember the forgotten presentation: in so doing, it 'forgets' its own event of presentation. 'Memory is lined with forgetting. Metaphysics struggles against forgetting; what is the name of that which struggles for it?' (LD, §124: the 'amnesiac singularity' of the intense event in the libindinal work is itself here remembered).

And if it is indubitable that there is at least one sentence, then, says Lyotard, there are several sentences: if the sentence 'I doubt' cannot be the first sentence then there is more than one sentence. If there is more than one sentence, then there is a series of sentences: the existence of a series presupposes time, which is therefore also indubitable.

But the sentence which formulates the general form of the passage from one sentence to another may well be presupposed as an *a priori* for the formation of the series, it nevertheless takes place after the sentence which formulates the passage. . . How can what is presupposed come after? Do we not have to make a distinction between a logical or transcendental anteriority and a temporal one? – One can always do so and no doubt one must if what is at stake is that the passage from one sentence to another take place under the logical or cognitive regime (and notably that of implication). One rule of this regime is, then, to ignore the fact that *a priori* propositions or definitions and axioms are themselves presented in sentences of ordinary language which are chronologically earlier. One rule is to ignore even the chronism (even if it is a metachronism) which remains unquestioned in the idea of logical anteriority (for example in the operator 'if, then'). Unlike the logician or theoretical linguist, the philosopher has as his rule not to shy away from the fact that the sentence formulating the general form of passage from one sentence to another is itself subject to this same operation of passage. In Kantian terms: that the synthesis of the series is also an element of the series (*Critique of Pure Reason*, 'Critical solution of the cosmological conflict of reason with itself', B525-530). In Protagorean terms: that the debate about the series of debates forms part of that series (. . .). In Wittgensteinian terms: that 'the world is the totality of facts', that 'the image is a fact' and that 'the logical image can be the image of the

world (*die Welt abbilden*)' (*Tractatus Logico-Philosophicus*: 1.1, 2.141, 2.19).
(But the sentence must not be called an 'image'. Wittgenstein later gives this up) (. . .).
Philosophical discourse has as its rule the discovery of its rule: its *a priori* is its stake. It is a question of formulating this rule, and this can only be done at the end, if there is an end. Time cannot therefore be excluded from this discourse without that discourse ceasing to be philosophical. (LD, §§97 & 98)

That there is a sentence, the 'there is' involved in any sentence, is inevitably forgotten in *what* sentence there is, and what it presents. And here, finally, is the event. A sentence is always *a* sentence, *this* sentence, a singular occurrence or event. The status of this event or occurrence is complex, however: presentation (the occurrence of a sentence) happens *now,* but taking that now as the referent of philosophical sentences loses it as event, and inevitably talks of a general form of now-ness (or presentation), which transforms 'now' into *the* now. Lyotard makes this point via a dense discussion of Aristotle's notion of time:

Aristotle thus makes a distinction between the time which, in the universes presented by sentences, situates with respect to each other the instances constituting these universes (the before/after, the now), and the presentation-event (or occurrence) which as such is absolute (now). As soon as this latter is phrased, it is placed in the relations of sentence universes. The presentation is then presented. In order to grasp the presentation comprised in [*comportée par*] a sentence, another sentence is necessary, in which that presentation is presented. The 'present' presentation is not phrasable now, but only as a situation (before/after) in the universe presented by another sentence: it is the presentation [which took place] *then.* Aristotle disconnects the diachronic operators at play in sentence universes and the occurrence of the sentence (or the sentence-occurrence). The 'current' presentation is unpresentable, the event is forgotten as such in so far as it is conserved (the after), anticipated (the before), or is 'maintained' (the now [*le maintenant*]). (LD, p. 114)

If two or more sentences are to be declared identical in any respect, then a further singular event-sentence has to do that declaring. (Event rather than 'speech-act', which presupposes a prior subject to perform the act.) A sentence is always what semanticians would call a 'token': and the identification of 'types' (allowing the assertion that two token-sentences are of the same type) must take place in a further event-sentence which positions such a type as its referent (LD, §104). Or the claim that two or more sentences 'express' the same 'proposition' takes place in a new event-sentence. (Similarly, as we saw in *Discours, figure, langue* in Saussure's sense is always only the referent of a particular act of *parole*). It can easily sound here as though Lyotard were moving into Heideggerian waters and talking about Being with a capital B: Being (which is not an entity and which therefore is not) is inevitably forgotten in the entities the Being 'of' which it 'is'. Presentation (which is not a sentence) is inevitably forgotten in the sentence presentation presents. Lyotard would accept this *rapprochement* up to a point, but against Heidegger (or apparently against Heidegger) Lyotard would stress the *singularity,* the always-only-this-one-nowness of a sentence. ('Could one call the presentation comprised by a sentence, *Being?* But it is *one* presentation, or: what in a case-sentence is the case. Being would be a case, an occurrence, the "fact" that it "falls" [tombe], that it "falls upon" [accourt] (*Fall, occurrence*). Not Being, but *a* being, once' (LD, §113).) It is possible to make of 'Being' the referent of a sentence (even of a sentence which declares it to be the real sender of all sentences, to which we should be attentive), but this is done in a further particular event-sentence. Further, says Lyotard, the Heidegger to whom he is closest would determine presentation as an act of donation the addressee of which is humanity, whose destiny or destination would be secured by heeding to the authenticity of time: 'Destination, addressee [*destinataire,*] sender [*destinateur*], man, are here instances or relations in the universes presented by sentences, they are situated, *to logo.* The *there is* [Il y a] takes place, it is an occurrence (*Ereignis*), but it presents nothing to anyone, it does not present itself, and it is not the present, nor presence. Insofar as it is phrasable (thinkable), a presentation is missed as occurrence' (LD, p. 115).

This type of argument may be more familiar from the work of Paul de Man: in *Allegories of Reading* (Hew Haven: Yale UP, 1979), De Man works with an idea that seems similar to Lyotard's – any cognitive or constative sentence has a performative dimension which it cannot ever take as the object of its cognition or constatation. 'Any speech act produces an excess of cognition, but it can never hope to know the process of its own production' (p. 300). For Lyotard too, any sentence is, as event of presentation, in excess of what it can present and situate in its universe: but whereas De Man reduces this insight to discussion in terms of an opposition between cognition and performance, Lyotard would argue that this situation holds for a sentence of any regime whatsoever, including 'performatives' in Austin's sense. The use of the notion of 'performance' to talk about this *general* property of sentences is difficult (cf. LD, §205), and possibly encourages the (mis)understanding of De Man's work as unduly 'aesthetic' in its orientation. For Lyotard, 'performative' would also have unfortunate links with the 'demiurgic' conception of language which haunted some of the earlier discussion of narrative, and with the 'legitimation by performativity' criticised in *The Postmodern Condition.*

Presentation is not presentable as such. Presentation is unpresentable.

Is it not then just another name, shorn of a certain pathos, for libido or energy? Lyotard would say not: 'By presentation (. . .), I do not mean the act of a *dunamis,* of a power [*puissance*], or of a will of that power, a desire of language to accomplish itself. But only that something takes place. That something is a sentence, indubitably. As a sentence presents a universe, I call [the fact that] the sentence takes place "presentation"' (LD, p. 115).

Let me illustrate some of the perplexities which may arise around this conception of the sentence with a long quote from *Le Différend:*

Give a definition of what you understand by *sentence.* – with a prescription of that type, you presuppose an object called *sentence,* the type-sentence. You also presuppose that a complete description of it must be given so that we can argue and come to an agreement as to the nature of this object, do you not? Allow me to point out to you: 1) that the substitution of a type-sentence (or of the object called 'sentence') for an event-sentence is demanded by a regime of sentences, the definitional regime (only terms taken as objects of a metalanguage, whose definite descriptions have been established are introduced into the discourse), and by a genre of discourse, the genre of dialogue. Your prescription is one of the rules of this regime and of this genre. . . 2) That it does not seem that the genre of discourse (if there is one) followed by the sentences of this book privileges the definitional genre. The question is: how to define definition? Endless regression in the logical order, unless one has recourse to a decision or a convention. Endless procession in the succession of event-sentences, and here there is no exception, there is time.

Give a definition of what you understand by sentence. – A definition is a sentence which obeys logical and cognitive rules. But, for example, your 'Give a definition. . .' is a prescriptive which does not obey these rules. – So be it. But that in no way prevents you from giving a definition of this prescriptive. There is no necessity for what is defined and the definition to come from the same regime of sentences. – Indeed. But there is a necessity that the value of the sentence which is the object of a definition (which is taken as the referent of a definitional sentence) be transformed by the fact that it is taken as the referent of another sentence, the definitional sentence, which is metalinguistic (. . .). In order to validate the order 'Give a definition of the sentence', one must give a definition of the sentence. If one replies by pointing out that this order is a sentence which does not obey the regime of logical or cognitive sentences, one places this order in the situation of a referent of the 'present' sentence, and makes it into a counter-example of a logical or cognitive sentence. This order is not validated, it is used, as referent of an ostensive sentence (*Here is a case of a non-cognitive sentence),* to validate another, descriptive, sentence (*Some sentences come under non-cognitive regimes)* (. . .). Now you are performing the same metalinguistic operation with *A sentence.* You are taking the expression *A sentence* as a sentence. You are depriving it of its 'present-ness' (I do not say of its context, cf. §141), of its referential and pragmatic import as an event, which

> But at least the context ought to allow a decision as to what the sender of the
> first sentence meant and what the addressee, who is the sender of the second
> sentence, would be correct to understand. . . – You'll have to present the
> context, by means of sentences. . . Or else by appealing to the context your
> sentence situates you as addressee in a cognitive universe in which the context
> would be the sender and would tell you the facts about itself. Why do you judge
> this sender to be more credible than that of the first sentence?
> . . . What you call the context is itself only the referent of cognitive sentences,
> those of the sociologist, for example. The context is not a sender. In the confu-
> sion of context as referent and context as sender resides positivism, and notably
> the positivism of the human sciences in general. (LD, §§141-2)

calls for many possible sorts of sentences. You order that I link onto it with a
definitional metalinguistic sentence. You have the right to do so. But be aware
that it is an order. (LD, §§106 & 107)

The complexities of presentation should remove any suspicion of a
'metaphysics of presence' attached to the notion of a sentence. A sentence
is never simply present (to itself) – split on the one hand between presentation and the universe presented (situation), a sentence is also, constitutively, linked to other sentences. The illusion of seizing the event of a
sentence in any or all of its instances is an illusion created retrospectively,
by the following sentence: 'Metaphysical illusion would consist in treating
a presentation as a situation' (LD, p. 96). Thinking that a sentence is an
entity is an illusion created by a cognitive sentence which takes 'a sentence' as its referent. Sentences are on the move, in the possible ways
of linking onto them with more sentences. Lyotard's own description of
a sentence (as presenting a universe with four poles) depends on such
linkages: and it is only the possible ways of linking a sentence with a
sentence which justifies the isolation of those four poles in the 'first' place:

Where do you get the idea that they comprise four instances? – From the ways
of linking. Take the sentence: *Ouch!*. One links by saying: 'Are you in pain?' (on
the sender); by 'I can't do anything about it' (on the addressee); by 'Does it hurt?'
(on the meaning); by 'Gums are always very sensitive' (on the referent). – In
human language, but what of the cat's tail? – One links with the erect tail of the
cat, respectively: 'What do you want?'; 'You're a pain'; 'Still hungry?'; 'They have
such an expressive tail'. I'm deliberately taking sentences in which the instances
are not marked, and neither is their situation. This division is not pragmatic if
the presupposition or prejudice of pragmatics is that a message goes from a
sender to an addressee supposed to 'exist' without it. And it is not humanist:
name non-human entities which could not occupy one or other of these instances!
(LD, §123)

If a sentence is thus vitally dependent upon the sentence which links with it, then it would seem that sentences are not exclusively linguistic. If a referent is always (only) what is situated as such in a sentence-unverise, then saying anything about anything would involve linking onto a (possibly) non-linguistic sentence with a linguistic sentence. This problem leads to some of the most difficult issues raised by *Le Différend*. The question of presentation is an ontological question: sentences 'are' as events or occurrences, and situate entities in their universes – confusion arises because a sentence can *itself* be situated as an entity in a universe.

---

131. 'Every sentence is.' Is everything that is, a sentence? *Is* is not *what is*. And no more is *is*, *is real*. One cannot say: *Every sentence is real*. Reality is a property of the referent to be established (. . .), it is not. Including the reality of a sentence. Everything real is rational, yes, if *rational* signifies, 'in conformity with the procedure of establishing the reality of a referent.' – In 'every sentence is', *every sentence* means *everything that happens [tout ce qui arrive]; is* means: *there is [il y a]*, *it happens [il arrive]*. But *it happens* is not what happens, in the sense that *quod* is not *quid* (that presentation is not situation). So *is* does not mean: *is there*, and still less *is real*. *Is* signifies nothing, it would designate the occurrence 'before' the signification (the content) of the occurrence. Would designate it and does not designate it, since in designating it it situates it ('before' signification) and thus occults *nun [now]* in *husteron proteron* [before/after] (. . .). *Is* would, rather, be *'Arrive-t-il?'* [is it happening, does it happen, is it coming] (the French *il* indicating an empty place to be occupied by a referent). (LD, §131)

The questions around reality, reference, 'the outside world' and so on are still looming. Surely Lyotard cannot be claiming that everything that happens is linguistic? Not if a sentence is not necessarily linguistic. But a common-sense approach, or a reader attracted by *Discours, figure*'s refusal to assimilate the space of the perceived world and the space of language, is still worried here by questions of perception. It can occasionally seem in *Le Différend* that Lyotard is proposing something quite close to an analytical philosophy in the Anglo-American sense: in which, for example, perception would be analyzed via an analysis of perception-sentences, and the grammar of verbs such as 'to see', and so on. This type of analysis leaves the status of perception 'itself' unexamined (or would leave it to psychologists to talk about it): Lyotard, on the other hand, wants to argue that in some sense perception 'itself' (and not just reports of perception) can and must be analysed in terms of sentences. (The aims and methods of this type of analysis should be compared with those of Vincent Descombes, *Grammaire d'objects en tous genres* (Paris: Minuit,

1983) [tr. *Objects of All Sorts: a Philosophical Grammar* (Oxford: Blackwell, 1986)]). This type of analysis is clearly called for by the logic of the book, which is (like all of Lyotard's work) an attempt to exceed and account for a philosophy of the subject, including the subject of perception. We have already seen Lyotard claiming that the notion of experience is unnecessary in an account of reality and knowledge: here he suggests that the notion of *data* in the sense of what is *given* in sensation is itself a reductive negociation of the basic question of presentation. Naturally enough, this analysis cannot present perception in person (because of the argument around the idiolect), but is exercised on Kant's 'Transcendental Aesthetic' from the *Critique of Pure Reason*.

> In whatever manner and by whatever means a mode of knowledge may relate to objects, *intuition* is that through which it is in immediate relation to them, and to which all thought as a means is directed. But intuition takes place only in so far as the object is given to us. This again is only possible, to man at least, in so far as the mind is affected in a certain way. The capacity (receptivity) for receiving representations through the mode in which we are affected by objects, is entitled *sensibility*. Objects are given to us by means of sensibility, and it alone yields us *intuitions*; they are thought through the understanding, and from the understanding arise *concepts*. But all thought must, directly or indirectly, by way of certain characters, relate ultimately to intuitions, and therefore, with us, to sensibility, because in no other way can an object be given to us.
>
> The effect of an object upon the faculty of representation, so far as we are affected by it, is *sensation*. That intuition which is in relation to the object through sensation, is entitled *empirical*. The undetermined object of an empirical intuition is entitled *appearance*.
>
> That in the appearance which corresponds to sensation I term its *matter*; but that which so determines the manifold of appearance that it allows of being ordered in certain relations, I term the *form* of appearance. That in which alone the sensations can be posited and ordered in a certain form, cannot itself be sensation; and therefore, while the matter of all appearance is given to us *a posteriori* only, its form must lie ready for the sensations *a priori* in the mind, and so must allow of being considered apart from all sensation. (Kant, *Critique of Pure Reason*, B33-4)

Lyotard's analysis breaks this account down into an exchange of two sentences: first, a sentence (or 'quasi-sentence', as Lyotard calls it more than once, this apparent equivocation *perhaps* simply respecting a more familiar distinction of linguistic and non-linguistic events) in a 'language' or idiom called 'matter' – of unknown sender, addressed to a receptive addressee. This is a sentence with no referent and of unclear meaning, a 'sentimental' sentence in Lyotard's terms. In the second sentence, the addressee of the first becomes the sender of a sentence in a language or idiom called 'form'. This sentence does have a referent, called 'phenomenon', and this referential function of the second sentence hangs on the capacity to apply criteria of space and time to the first sentence: the second sentence is what Kant calls 'intuition'. This 'dialogue' is complex, not only in that what is given in intuition is thus not in fact 'immediately' given, but in that although the addressee of the first sentence hears it and replies, that addressee does not understand the language in which it is formulated – in Kant's terms, we shall never know the thing in itself, only the phenomenon as organised in the language of our second sentence, of which we are the *sender*. And we shall never know if the sender (if there is a sender) of the first sentence understands in return, i.e. whether space and time are valid in themselves.

The point of this type of reconstruction or transcription of a previous philosophical argument into the language of sentences is not simply to suggest that philosophy in general could be rewritten in these terms, but to prepare for the location of problems. Here Lyotard begins such a location by questioning the notion of *Darstellung* in Kant. Once constituted in this manner as phenomenon, the object (referent of the second sentence) can be the object of a presentation or *Darstellung:* and specifically as an example subsumed under a concept. Kant's notion of presentation is a linking of two sentences of different regimes (a descriptive and an ostensive, in the genre of knowledge). Such a presentation is the work of the subject, not an event come from elsewhere: the first sentence is transformed into the second, as intuition: the deictics of intuition are picked up by further sentences in the process of knowledge (imagination, conception, sensibility). In Kant this process is thought as involving the faculties of a subject:

The subject is thus neither active nor passive, it is both, but it is only one or the other to the extent that, caught in a regime of sentences, it objects to itself a sentence from another regime, and seeks, if not their conciliation, at least the rules of their conflict, i.e. its own always threatened unity. The only exception appears to be sensation, where, through matter, something which does not proceed from the subject seems to affect it. But we have seen that this something is immediately situated as an instance in the dialectic of sentence-universes, and treated as a first sender and second addressee, with the result that its 'donation' is seen as the result of an exchange.

With Kant, a *Darstellung* is not a presentation, but a placing in situation (. . .). The repression of presentation under representation is permitted and encouraged by the doctrine of faculties, and ultimately by the metaphysics of the 'subject'. Cases are [here] not events, but summonses to appear. The question of the *Il y a,* briefly evoked in the shape of sensory data, is rapidly forgotten for the question of what there is. (LD, pp. 100-1)

This problem arose from the insistence on the importance of *enchaîne-ment* or linking of sentences. Lyotard would say that the linkings proposed by the Kant of the 1st *Critique* are such that the question of presentation, of the event, is forgotten. There is of course no *necessity* for Kant's discourse to respect that event (linking is a necessity, but how to link is a contingency): but Lyotard would argue that such a respect is a constitutive rule of the genre of philosophy – and only this gives relevance to the criticism of Kant.

Genres

Philosophy is only one genre among many others, of course. After a sentence, another sentence is inevitable (even if that sentence is a silence): linking is a necessity – *what* sentence comes next is, for Lyotard, a radical contingency. Genres involve an apparent reduction of that contingency by proposing certain sorts of linkings as more appropriate than others: sentences of various regimes (descriptive, prescriptive, ostensive, performative) are oriented by a genre towards a goal to be achieved (persuade, convince, refute, amuse, etc.). 'Teleology begins with genres of discourse, not with sentences. But in so far as they are linked together, sentences are always caught in (at least) one genre of discourse' (LD, §147). Or, genres exercise a generalised seduction on sentence universes: a genre

Inclines the instances presented by this sentence towards certain linkings, or at least it keeps at a distance other linkings which are not fitting with respect to the goal pursued by this genre. It is not the addressee who is seduced by the sender. The sender, the referent and the meaning undergo no less than the addressee the seduction operated by what is at stake in the genre of discourse. (LD, §148)

In this account, any sentence must be the object of this 'seduction' from all sorts of genres: the contingency of what sentence is to come next means just this. The genres must be thought of as proposing rival linkings, or as linking to just one of the universes co-presented by an equivocal sentence (LD, §§137-46) and these rival linkings must in some sense be in conflict. Further, insofar as genres reduce the contingency of the sentence to come, then they can be thought of as potentially suggesting a pseudo-necessity of their sentences as a way of 'winning out' over rival genres. This is the precise point at which the philosophy expounded in

Le Différend encounters ethics, as questions of judgement and justice. We left *Instructions païennes* on questions of piety and justice: having complicated the appeal to narrative in that book, we can suggest that piety (the term no longer appears in *Le Différend*) would now be described as following the rules of one genre as though they were necessary, and justice in the attempt to respect the contingency of each linking – which is the corollary of the attempt to respect the event of each sentence. For insofar as a sentence appears to be programmed by generic rules, then it loses its character as event and becomes recitation.

Presented in this way, it is perhaps not immediately obvious that this is above all another attempt to question Hegel. We saw one attempt so to do in *Discours, figure,* and chapter 4 of *Le Différend* provides a more persistent interrogation. Again, Lyotard patiently attempts to transcribe Hegel's dialectic into his language of sentences before using that transcription to locate problems. In this case the attempt to do this is constantly dogged by the ease with which opposition to the dialectic can be absorbed by the dialectic as itself a dialectical manoeuvre. Through an argument I cannot hope adequately to summarise here, Lyotard suggests that, although speculative discourse would claim to be the self-engendering of truth, it in fact involves a presupposition for which it is unable to account in its own terms. This presupposition is the *Selbst,* the 'Same':

There is an X, and one only. It is the same under the diverse forms, through all the operations, and this is why it is totalised into a single *Resultat,* in turn dissolved into new operations. It is also via the supposition of this same that the linkings of sentence to sentence are reputed to be necessary in their mode and occurrence, and that dialectics is said to be a sublation. Now this presupposition of the same is not falsifiable (. . .). It is a rule which governs metaphysical discourse (it is its closure). Philosophical examination never reveals such a subject-substance. It reveals sentences, sentence universes and occurrences. . .

One clearly cannot object to the presupposition of the *Selbst* that 'in reality this is not how things are'. One *can* object that it is a rule of a genre of discourse, the metaphysical genre which attempts to engender its own rules; but that precisely this rule cannot be engendered from that discourse. (LD, p. 144)

The rule of the speculative dialectic would be formulated by Lyotard as: 'Engender every sentence (including the present sentence) as the expressed identity of the preceding sentences' (LD, p. 145). Logically, such a sentence must be considered as 'first' for the discourse concerned. If it is first, it cannot itself be the result of the identity of the preceding sentences. Hegel of course would say that such a notion of a 'first sentence' has no place in speculative discourse, and that precisely this will emerge at the 'end' of the dialectic, as its result. To which Lyotard replies that this 'beginning' can appear at the 'end', as 'result', only if that result has in fact been presupposed. Speculative discourse conforms to the rule it is seeking before having found it: its linkings are determined by the rule rather than by the search for the rule. The burden of the demonstration is not that speculative discourse is wrong, but that it is one genre among others, with rules that can be formulated. This already undermines its claim to speak the truth of all other genres and to discover a necessity in sentence-links in general.

For Lyotard, it is not that speculative discourse is 'wrong' in the sense of being incorrect, but in the sense of being unjust. This injustice consists in its assigning of hegemonic status to a particular regime of sentence (the cognitive), which, in formulating the speculative 'truth', *quotes* other sentences and in so doing deprives them of their 'immediate' value.

A noteworthy result of the speculative apparatus is that all of the discourses of learning about every possible referent are taken up not from the point of view of their immediate truth-value, but in terms of the value they acquire by virtue of occupying a certain place in the itinerary of Spirit or Life – or, if preferred, a certain position in the Encyclopedia recounted by speculative discourse. That discourse cites them in the process of expounding for itself what it knows, that is, in the process of self-exposition. True knowledge, in this perspective, is always indirect knowledge; it is composed of reported statements that are incorporated into the metanarrative of a subject that guarantees their legitimacy.
The same thing applies for every variety of discourse. . . (CPM, 59 [PMC, 35])

Speculative discourse deals notably with prescriptions not by being obliged by them, but by stating that they are prescriptions. As this seems to be precisely what is going on in §107 (quoted above), we might suspect that Lyotard is still falling back into the hold of the speculative at the very moment we seem to have exceeded it in a non-dialectical way. In fact Lyotard wants to make a distinction between 'impertinence' and 'offence': it is certainly impertinent to link onto an order with a commentary on that order – but it is an offence to assume that such a commentary deals with and neutralises the obligation created by such an order (LD, §§ 45 and 149).

Lyotard spends a lot of time analysing the specificity of prescriptive sentences and the ethical genre (if it is a genre), both in *Au Juste* and in *Le Différend,* and this insistence could easily lead to a misapprehension: analysing and respecting the specificity of the ethical genre is not primarily what is at stake in this work, but part of a more general 'ethics' of analysing and respecting the incommensurability of genres *in general.*

In *Au Juste* this attempt leads to unresolved paradoxes which are linked to the difficult status of 'dissensus' we have already noted at the end of *The Postmodern Condition:* on the one hand there is a 'multiplicity of justices', to do with respecting the rules of each genre, and on the other a 'justice of multiplicity', in which a universal prescription enjoins us precisely to such a respect (AJ, 188-9 [JG, 100]). The tensions and difficulties this involves are, if not resolved (and the value of 'resolution' could only be suspect here), further specified in *Le Différend.* The chapter on obligation is one of the more difficult in the book, and essentially involves, with respect to Levinas and the Kant of the 2nd *Critique,* the type of dense transcription and questioning we have already seen at work.

The re-writing of Levinas into the language of sentences allows a striking formulation of the specificity of prescription:

A sender appears whose addressee I am, and about which I know nothing beyond the fact that it situates me on the instance of addressee. The violence of revelation is the expulsion of the self from the instance of sender from which it pursues its work of enjoyment, power and knowledge. It is the scandal of a me displaced onto the instance of the you. The me become you attempts to take hold of itself again by understanding what unsettles it [*le dessaisit*]. Another sentence forms, in which the me comes back into the position of sender, in order to legitimate or reject, little matter, the scandal of the sentence of the other, and its own dispossession. This new sentence is always possible, like an inevitable temptation. But it cannot annul the event, only tame it and master it, and in so doing, forget the transcendence of the other. (LD, pp. 163-4)

All sorts of things can go on in the 'second' sentence, following the prescription: in principle they do not alter the situation of obligation created by the universe of the 'first' sentence. The 'inevitable temptation' is to return in this second sentence to the primacy of the cognitive, and thus efface the event of the first, rather as (the analogy is difficult but important) in the transcription of the Transcendental Aesthetic, the event of the (quasi-) sentence of matter is forgotten in the ensuing activity of the subject. Such a return would involve, for example, the pretension to ground the prescription (as just or unjust) in a *description* of justice as a state of affairs to be brought about. This apparently 'reasonable' pretension is extensively criticized in *Au Juste,* and in *Le Différend* is described in Kantian terms as a 'transcendental illusion' (the expression will return) (LD, §166). Such an attempt involves a derivation of prescription *from*

The tribunal whose idiom is the genre of discourse of knowledge, and which therefore admits only descriptive sentences of cognitive value, asks of whoever alleges an obligation: what is the authority which obliges you (or will oblige you)? The obliged is placed in a dilemma: either he names the sender of the law and expounds the authority and meaning of that law, and he ceases being obliged by the very fact that the law thus rendered intelligible to knowledge becomes an object of discussion and loses its obligatory value; or else he recognizes that this value cannot be expounded, that he cannot phrase in the place of the law, and this tribunal cannot admit that the law obliges because it is without reason and thus arbitrary. In the idiom of knowledge, either the law is reasonable and it does not oblige, it convinces; or else it is not reasonable, and it does not oblige, it constrains. This tribunal demands that only what the obliged can account for by argumentation should be obligatory. It therefore supposes that I can occupy the place of the sender of prescriptions, that I can 'assume' those prescriptions. They are obligatory because I can understand their meaning and explain it to the tribunal. The value of explanation is the value of truth, it is universal. Through this dilemma, the family of cognitive sentences annexes the family of prescriptives, the I effaces the you. (LD, §176)

description, whereas the account derived from Levinas suggests that prescription occurs as a seizing prior to the possibility of description.

It can seem as though this account creates an unnecessary pathos of dispossession, when all it is in fact doing is describing (in spite of itself it is a description, necessarily) a common feature of genres in general. As we have seen, that another sentence arrive is a necessity: what sentence arrives is not, and can therefore be the object of conflicting prescriptions 'issued by' the various genres in competition. The sender of the prescription would be simply the genre in question, and the 'imperative' would, in Kant's terms, be always 'hypothetical', i.e. of the form 'If you want to achieve x, then do y'. If this were the case, ethics would be dissolved into strategic calculation in terms of desired ends. Lyotard's philosophy would thus collapse into a sort of positivism or even a manual of instructions for how to succeed given certain goals.

To this type of objection, Lyotard would reply that the so-called hypothetical imperative indeed characterises the various genres, but that their capacity to issue prescriptions and place addressees under obligation presupposes a more general possibility of obligation and prescription which they do not interrogate (LD, §174). This is precisely what is at issue. In the transcription of Kant's 2nd *Critique,* Lyotard points out an essential assymmetry encountered by the attempt to derive or deduce obligation along the same lines as the derivation or deduction of knowledge: in the latter case, the sentence of the object-language and that of the critical metalanguage both belong to the descriptive regime – in the case of obligation this is not so: the sentences of the critical metalanguage remain descriptive despite the fact that those of the object-language are prescriptive (LD, p. 175). As is well known, Kant concludes the impossibility of deducing the moral law, but argues that *freedom* can be deduced on the basis of the law become a *Faktum* which is not a fact of experience in the strict sense. The incommensurability of morality and knowledge is, in Kant, negotiated by recourse to the notion of analogy: to prevent morality being a pure abstraction with no effects in the real world (the object of cognitive sentences), we must act *as if* the moral law were a law of nature. Lyotard fears that this reasoning gives rise to another transcendental illusion: in the analogy, the 'you must' of obligation is assimilated, via what Kant calls the 'type' (i.e. the form of conformity to law in general) to the 'I know' of knowledge and to the 'I can' of freedom. By appealing to the Idea of a 'humanity' or a 'community of rational beings', Kant is able to annul the asymmetry, in the sentences of obligation, of 'I' and 'thou' (and posit a 'we' into which they are subsumed). It is this argument which gives rise to the notion of autonomy, which in *Au Juste* Lyotard had opposed to simpler attempts to derive prescriptions from descriptions. Autonomy implies that the addressee of the law is also its sender, and, by extension, that the subject of the state is also a member of the Sovereign or legislator. Kant's categorical imperative demands that I be able to place myself in the position of legislator as well as in that of the subject of the legislator's laws (see AJ, 59-63 [JG, 29-31]). But from the perspective of a philosophy of sentences, this involves presupposing a notion of 'person' (eventually secured by a proper name) which cannot be established by the sentences being analysed – this is a problem similar to that of presupposing a subject with faculties. In Lyotard's terms no such subject can be presupposed. The ethical sentence *immediately* creates the situation of obligation, come what may, regardless of the sentence or action to follow. On Lyotard's reading of Kant, the categorical imperative does not prescribe that one act so as to bring about a community of reasonable practical beings, but *as if* the maxim of the action were to be a law for such a community (for this reading of Kant's *so dass* see LD, p. 182). Kant insists that obligation should give rise to a phenomenon in the world, but this passage to the cognitive realm is not inscribed in the ethical sentence. For Lyotard, there is and will not be an ethical community in reality (LD, p. 186). The implications of such a reading of Kant for political thought will return.

In this account, the abyss or 'gulf' noted by Kant between the realms of the first two Critiques is exacerbated still further. But although the

---

Albeit, then, between the realm of the natural concept, as the sensible, and the

realm of the concept of freedom, as the supersensible, there is a great gulf
fixed, so that it is not possible to pass from the former to the latter (by means
of the theoretical employment of reason), just as if they were so many separate
worlds, the first of which is powerless to exercise influence on the second: still
the latter is *meant* to influence the former — that is to say, the concept of
freedom is meant to actualize in the sensible world the end proposed by its
laws; and nature must consequently also be capable of being regarded in such
a way that in the conformity to law of its form it at least harmonises with the
possibility of the ends to be effectuated in it according to the laws of freedom.
— There must, therefore, be a ground of the *unity* of the supersensible that lies
at the basis of nature, with what the concept of freedom contains in a practical
way, and although the concept of this ground neither theoretically nor practically
attains to a knowledge of it, and so has no peculiar realm of its own, still it
renders possible the transition from the mode of thought according to the
principles of the one to the principles of the other. (Kant, *Critique of Judgment*,
Introduction, §2)

ethical is clearly accorded a specificity resistant to knowledge, Lyotard
would insist that this specificity is the property of all regimes (this is
why they are heterogeneous) and of all genres (this is why they are
incommensurable) (LD, §178). And, again, this is to do with the notion
of dissensus in *The Postmodern Condition*. I suggested that the impression that book may have created, namely that dissensus was a telos
proposed in opposition to the telos of consensus defended by Habermas,
was mistaken. What idea could we possibly have of a pure dissensus?
Dissensus implies conflict, and *pure* conflict is unthinkable. If dissensus
were absolute, then it is difficult to see how the attempted annexation
of the ethical by the cognitive could even begin. This type of point is
raised in connection with the distinction between regimes and genres:

– You say that a genre of discourse imprints upon a multiplicity of heterogeneous
sentences a single finality by linkings aiming to procure the success proper to
that genre. If such is the case, it follows that the heterogeneity of the regimes of
sentences is not such that it would forbid their common subordination to one
and the same end. The abyss separating them would, then, be, if not filled in, at
least covered over or stepped across by the teleology of the genres of discourse.
Let us go further. It would only be if sentences fitted together outside any finality
linked to a genre, and took place without a genre, that their heterogeneity would
disjoin them completely and would leave their linking unforeseeable and inexplic-
able, as you complacently describe them. But that is impossible. As you admit,
the sentences which happen are 'expected', not by conscious or unconscious
'subjects' anticipating them, but because they carry with them their 'instructions
for use', as the linguists say (. . .), i.e. an instruction as to the end pursued through
them. And if one insists, as you do, on the indetermination of linkings, this is still

a function of a stake, so as to persuade your reader of the heterogeneity of regimes and the eminence of the occurrence, thus according to a finality prescribed by a genre or at least a style (...). – What you are reading is indeed a book of philosophy, its sentences are joined together to so that that joining cannot be taken for granted, and that the rule of their joining is to be discovered. (LD, §180)

This again allows us to stress the importance of the linking, the *enchaîne-ment*, as against an impossible atomism of sentences. To the extent that there is linking, there cannot be complete separation. Once the dialectical solution to that linking (namely that the separation between two (types of) sentences can be determined as contradiction and sublated in a third sentence) has been refused, how are we to think the conflict that arises? Clearly neither as the 'peaceful diaspora' evoked by Derrida a propos of Levinas, nor as some equally inconceivable absolute antagonism. In that same essay on Levinas, Derrida suggests that total violence and total non-violence are both unthinkable (I would add that traditionally the idea of a 'state of nature' has served to label such unthinkables as if they were thinkable), and that we must think of an 'economy of violence' with degrees of more and less to be evaluated. And this is precisely what Lyotard attempts to think, in his own rather different terms. In fact the very title of *Le Différend,* and the book's first chapter which bears the same name, begin the attempt to refine on the 'dissensus' of *The Post-modern Condition,* away from any teleological or narrative investment. In disrupting the order of presentation of Lyotard's book and deferring the attempt to explicate the sense of the word 'différend', I have tried to provoke in the reader a sentiment which, for Lyotard, would itself be the sign of the *différend.*

Le Différend

Le Différend in fact opens with a short section entitled 'Fiche de lecture' (a partially ironic 'summary' of the book, aimed among other things to 'allow the reader to "talk about the book", if the fantasy so takes him, without having read it' (LD, p. 13): the notion of 'gaining time' here is explicitly thematised in the book, and I shall return to it), and the first paragraph of that section explains the work's title in a way we are now in a position to approach:

As opposed to a litigation, a *différend* would be a case of conflict between two parties (at least) which could not equitably be decided for lack of a rule of judgement applicable to both argumentations. That one argumentation be legitimate would not imply that the other was not. If however one applies the same rule of judgement to both to decide their *différend* as if it were a litigation, one causes one of them a wrong [*tort*] (to at least one of them, and to both if neither admits this rule). A damage [*dommage*] is the result of an injury done to the rules of a genre of discourse, and can be repaired in accordance with those rules. A wrong results from the fact that the rules of the genre of discourse according to which one judges are not those of the genre or genres judged. The property of a literary or artistic work can suffer a damage (the moral rights of the author are violated); but the very principle that one should treat the work as the object of a property can constitute a wrong (not recognizing that the 'author' is its hostage). The title of the book suggests (through the generic value of the article) that a universal rule of judgement between heterogeneous genres is lacking in general. (LD, p. 9)

So, for example, an argument as to the existence or non-existence of a referent can in principle be decided by using the rules of the cognitive genre; as to the morality or not of an action, by appealing to the rules of the ethical genre; as to the validity or not of an accusation of theft, by appealing to the law of property (involving cognitive and ethical sentences). But such a ruling of an accusation of theft might well also involve a *différend,* if one of the parties does not recognize that the object in question is a legitimate object of property.

We have in fact just come across an example of a *différend* in the discussion of obligation: the rational tribunal demands proof of the obligation and the obliged party is unable to provide any such proof in terms the tribunal will accept. In the quasi-legal terminology which Lyotard uses in *Le Différend,* the plaintiff (i.e. the party alleging that it has suffered a wrong) is habitually placed in a dilemma: if the obliged party adopts the language of the tribunal, then the obligation vanishes ipso facto: if s/he does not, then the obligation retreats into what the tribunal can only see as mysticism or the irrational. The obliged party has no language in which to state his or her case. And this becomes a defining feature of the wrong which results:

A wrong would be this: a damage accompanied by the loss of the means to prove the damage. This is the case if the victim is deprived of life, or of all liberties, or of the freedom to make his ideas or opinions public, or simply of the right to bear witness to this damage, or still more simply if the sentence which bears witness is itself deprived of authority (. . .). In all these cases, there is added to the privation which is a damage the impossibility of bringing it to the knowledge of others, and notably to the knowledge of a tribunal. If the victim attempts to pass over this impossibility and to bear witness nonetheless to the wrong suffered, that victim comes up against the following argumentation: either the damage you are complaining about has not happened, and your evidence is false; or else it has happened and, since you can bear witness to it, it is not a wrong you have suffered, but only a damage, and your evidence is false again. (LD, §7)

More examples: a citizen of a communist state denies that the state is in fact communist. But the authorities of the state are alone empowered to decide as to the reality of communism: insofar as the citizen disagrees with these authorities he is thereby no longer a communist and can have no authority to make a claim as to the reality of communism (LD, §4). A worker suggests that his labour-force is not simply a commodity which can be the object of exchange. But if he does this then he cannot accept a contract to work under conditions which presuppose just this: and if he does not accept such a contract then his condition will be one of slavery (LD, §4). A Martiniquan suggests that he is the victim of a wrong by the fact of being a French citizen: such a complaint cannot be heard in French law. And to have a case against the French state in International law, the plaintiff would have no longer to be a French citizen. It follows that he has no recognized means of proving the reality of the wrong done to him (LD, §36).

In general, these examples suggest that a defining feature of a wrong is that it cannot be proven. The most general form of the dilemma of the victim of a *différend* is as follows:

Either you are the victim of a wrong, or you are not. If you are not, then you are mistaken (or you are lying) in claiming that you are. If you are [the victim of a wrong], then, since you can bear witness to it, it is not a wrong, and you are mistaken (or you are lying) in claiming that you are the victim of a wrong. Let p = you are victim of a wrong; *non-p*: you are not; Tp: the sentence p is true; Fp: it is false. The argument is: either p or *non-p*; if *non-p*, then Fp; if p, then *non-p*, then Fp. The Ancients call this argument a dilemma. It contains the link of the 'double bind' studied by the school of Palo Alto, it is a mainspring of Hegelian dialectical logic (. . .). This link consists in the application of two logical operators: exclusion (*either. . . or*), and implication (*if. . . then*), to two contradictory propositions p and *non-p*. Or, both [(*either p or non-p*) and (*if p, then non-p*)]. As if you were to say at the same time: *either it's white or it is not white;* and: *if it's white, it is not white.* (LD, §8)

It would seem to follow that the inevitable tendency is to treat wrongs as mere damages, *différends* as litigations: this is in fact the only possible course to follow in a thought based on the excellence of dialogue and

There is then a *différend* about the means of establishing reality between the partisans of agonistics and the partisans of dialogue. How to settle this *différend*? The latter say: by dialogue; the former: by *agon*. If one remains at that, the *différend* merely perpetuates itself, becoming a sort of meta-*différend*, a *différend* on the subject of the means of settling the *différend* on the subject of the means of establishing reality. And by this fact the principle of agonistics, far from being eliminated, still wins out. (LD, p. 47)

consensus. It is perfectly possible for an appearance of consensus to reign, troubled only by occasional settlable litigations, despite the persistance of *différends*. Thus strikes by workers and demands by trades unions habitually invoke matters of pay and conditions which accept the language of the employer and argue that the employer is not respecting the terms of that language: arbitration is in principle possible. No such arbitration is possible between labour-force and capital.

Auschwitz

But Lyotard's principal example (if it is an example) in *Le Différend* is provided by Auschwitz. Already in 1980, Lyotard had introduced his 'philosophy of sentences' (to the Colloque de Cerisy around Derrida's work) with a paper entitled 'Discussions, ou: phraser "après Auschwitz"', and this paper, with some modifications, appears as the chapter of *Le Différend* concerned to argue against the Hegelian dialectic. Auschwitz appears in every chapter of the book, and with it comes an assertion and a series of questions which I have deferred until the framework of the 'philosophy of sentences' was in place. The assertion is that 'after Auschwitz' a philosophy of sentences is the only sort of philosophy not to fall into illusion: the questions are many, but include the following – How can there be a continuity between the crime called 'Auschwitz' and the question of the occurrence of a sentence? Is the claim made for such a continuity not inevitably both a trivialisation of the Holocaust and a spectacularization of what is only a book of philosophy? What is the status of a historical event (called 'Auschwitz') for an analysis which has every appearance of being transcendental?

Auschwitz provides *Le Différend* with its first example of *différend*, wrong and victim. Not immediately in the relation of Jew and SS, but in the claim made by revisionist historians (and particularly Faurisson) that the gas-chambers did not exist. Faurisson claims to have been unable to find a single witness able to prove that s/he saw a gas-chamber. The *différend* here is gross: 'to identify that a place is a gas-chamber, I accept as witness only a victim of that gas-chamber; now according to my adversary, the only victims are dead victims, otherwise this gas-chamber would not be what he claims; so there is no gas-chamber' (LD, §2). A more insidious version would conclude, not baldly that there is no gas-chamber, but simply that the plaintiff cannot prove the existence of a gas-chamber (because all witnesses are victims and all victims are dead): here the *différend* would consist in an insistence on the application of rules of the cognitive genre to a postulated referent which the rules invoked can only find to be non-existent (LD, §6). In general, this insistence on the application of the rules of the cognitive genre to cases which might not come under its jurisdiction is the most common form of *différend* discussed by Lyotard (despite his insistence on their multiplicity): and here one reason for his persistence with such cases is simply this: 'If the demand to have to establish the reality of the referent of a sentence is extended to any sentence, and in particular to those which refer to a whole, then that demand is totalitarian in its principle' (LD, §5).

Lyotard, crucially for the whole argument of *Le Différend,* takes over from Kant a distinction between concept on the one hand and Idea of reason on the other: this distinction can be said to motivate the insistence on *différends* based on an illegitimate extension of the cognitive genre, but also the curious position of the ethical we have noted and not resolved, and the appeal to a re-worked notion of the sublime to which we shall come in due course.

Reason concerns itself exclusively with absolute totality in the employment of the concepts of the understanding, and endeavours to carry the synthetic unity, which is thought in the category, up to the completely unconditioned. We may call this unity of appearances the *unity of reason,* and that expressed by the category the *unity of understanding.* Reason accordingly occupies itself solely with the employment of understanding, not indeed in so far as the latter contains the ground of possible experience (for the concept of the absolute totality of conditions is not applicable in any experience, since no experience is unconditioned), but solely in order to prescribe to the understanding its direction towards a certain unity of which it has itself no concept, and in such a manner as to unite all the acts of the understanding, in respect of every object, into an *absolute* whole. . . I understand by idea a necessary concept of reason to which no corresponding object can be given in sense-experience. . . If I speak of an idea, then as regards its object, viewed as an object of pure understanding, I am saying a *great deal,* but as regards its relation to the subject, that is, in respect of its actuality under empirical conditions, I am for the same reason saying *very little,* in that, as being the concept of a maximum, it can never be correspondingly given *in concreto.* (Kant, *Critique of Pure Reason,* B383-4)

Whereas, as we saw, the cognitive genre requires ostensive sentences in its establishment of the reality of a referent, there are referents to which such sentences could never be applicable. In Lyotard's terms, for example, communism is not a possible object of knowledge, but an idea of reason (not, indeed, of pure reason, but of historico-political reason), the reality of which could in principle never be established. It does not follow from this that ideas are a waste of time: respected in their specificity, they allow a certain resistance to the pretensions of the cognitive genre (notably in the field of ethics and politics), but also allow a certain exercise of judgement once those pretensions have been resisted. The dilemmas and *différends* we have seen are largely to do with the unilateral attempt to force non-cognitive referents into the cognitive genre, and correlatively, to assume that any referents which cannot be thus treated are negligible. At a second level of argument, an imaginary interlocutor operates the same type of dilemma on 'Lyotard', in his attempt to argue for the *différend* itself:

How can you judge that there is a *différend* when in this hypothesis the referent of the victim's sentence is not an object of knowledge, properly speaking? How can you even affirm that such a situation exists? Because there are witnesses to it? But why do you believe their evidence when they cannot, *ex hypothesi*, establish the reality of what they affirm? Either the *différend* has as its object an established reality, and it is not a *différend,* but a litigation, or else, if the object has no established reality, the *différend* has no object, and there is no *différend* at all. (LD, §37)

To which the reply is that this is simply to confuse reality and referent: many sentences have non-real referents, but still take place as sentences.

Even with this rough distinction between reality as pertinent to the cognitive genre, and 'ideas of reason' as pertinent to other genres, Auschwitz seems to be a problem. It is difficult to see how it can be thought of as an idea of reason in Kant's sense. Of course the reality of Auschwitz is an important question. But Faurisson, faced with what he claims is the silence of the survivors, interprets that silence unilaterally. In Lyotard's terms, silence is a sentence, and essentially a negative sentence: the negative it involves does not necessarily bear on the referent of the sentence it follows. It can bear on any or some or all of the instances positioned by that sentence: the silence can be transcribed as bearing on the addressee ('it's nothing to do with you'), on the sender ('I have no authority to speak of it'), and on the meaning ('What happened cannot be expressed'), as well as on the referent (LD, §27). But if the reality of the gas-chambers is to be established, then these four negatives must be lifted. It may be thought that Faurisson simply does not want to be convinced of the existence of the gas-chambers, and no doubt this is true. But such an imputation, if it is to avoid psychologizing, has to proceed by the method of showing that what is at stake for Faurisson is not in fact the establishment of reality, that this is not the stake of the genre of his sentences – this cannot be prejudged: only when the rules of the cognitive genre have been followed through can it be asserted that was not the game Faurisson was playing.

But then supposing the rules of the cognitive genre are respected in the form we have already summarised above: Auschwitz will still refuse to be a simple 'fact' in those terms, and the wrong suffered will resist transformation into litigation. In Lyotard's terms, the formation of the State of Israel is a transformation of wrong into damage, *différend* into litigation, an end to the silence in the form of sentences conforming to the idiom of international law and politics. If wrong and *différend* there be, they cannot, by definition, be established as reality. Even the quantity of the crime resists precise establishment because of the destruction of documents necessary for such an establishment. What is essential for Lyotard is that this silence imposed on the sentences of knowledge is not a silence which signals forgetting, but a (quasi-) sentence which signals a sentiment. A sentiment is precisely the sign of an inability to phrase what must be phrased, and is as such the mark in general of the *différend*:

The *différend* is the unstable state and instant of language in which something which ought to be able to be phrased cannot yet be phrased. This state involves silence which is a negative sentence, but it also appeals to sentences possible in principle. What is ordinarily called sentiment signals this fact. 'You can't find the words to say it', and so on. A great deal of searching is necessary to find new rules of formation and linkage of sentences capable of expressing the *différend* betrayed by sentiment, if one does not wish this *différend* to be immediately stifled as litigation, and the alert given by sentiment to have been useless. It is the stake of a literature, a philosophy, perhaps of a politics, to bear witness to *différends* by finding idioms for them.

In the *différend*, something 'asks' to be phrased, and suffers the wrong of not being able to be phrased. So humans who thought they used language as an instrument of communication learn by this feeling of pain which accompanies silence (and of pleasure which accompanies the invention of a new idiom), that they are the object of language's demand, not that they increase to their own benefit the quantity of information which can be communicated in existing idioms, but that they recognize that what is to be phrased exceeds what they can phrase at the moment, and that they must allow the institution of idioms which do not yet exist. (LD, §§ 22-3)

For the case of 'Auschwitz', Lyotard suggests an analogy: an earthquake of sufficient power to destroy the instruments which measure the force of earthquakes would leave science silent, but would certainly provoke a sentiment (linked to what is called 'the negative presentation of the indeterminate'). Again the sentiment should not be thought of in psychological terms, but as linked to what is now called a 'sign' (not at all in a Saussurean sense, as we shall see): 'The fact that in a sentence universe the referent is situated as a sign has as it corrolary that in this same universe the addressee is situated as someone affected, and that the meaning is situated as an unresolved problem, perhaps an enigma, a mystery, a paradox' (LD, §93). It is the indetermination of meaning which 'calls for' phrasing in subsequent sentences and new idioms. Finding such sentences and idioms is a question of justice, because of the chain linking sign to sentiment to *différend* to wrong. Positivist historians are at the mercy of a Faurisson if they imagine that justice consists solely in the application of cognitive rules in such cases. If history were merely a question of such rules, it is hard to know how Faurisson could be accused of injustice.

On the other hand, the account of referents and reality suggests that this situation is generalisable: it will be remembered that names were assigned the function of marking the 'sameness' of the referent across a sequence of sentences from heterogeneous regimes. It was also argued that insofar as names do not signal essences which could be completely expressed in descriptions, then 'reality' was never in fact established for good: new meanings can *always* be attached to names:

Reality involves the *différend*. *It's Stalin, here he is.* One agrees. But as to what Stalin means? Sentences come to attach themselves to this name, which not only describe its various meanings (this can still be discussed in a dialogue), not only place the name on different instances, but obey heterogeneous regimes and/or genres. This heterogeneity renders a consensus impossible, for lack of a common idiom. Assigning a definition to Stalin necessarily does a wrong to the non-definitional sentences relative to Stalin which this definition ignores or betrays, for a time at least. Vengeance stalks round names. For ever? (LD, §92)

So if 'Auschwitz' suggests, almost emblematically, that the historian needs to be attentive to that which cannot be presented according to the rules of the cognitive genre, then, on this account, 'Auschwitz is the realest of realities' (LD, §93). As a sort of emblem, Auschwitz signals the limit of historical competence: but this limit is implied in the structure of 'reality' in general.

How then can Lyotard maintain on the same page that 'with Auschwitz, something new happened in history'? (LD, §93). The question returns in a much later section, commenting on Adorno's claim that 'since Auschwitz, being afraid of death means being afraid of something worse than death' (LD, §152):

> *After* implies a periodisation. Adorno counts time (but what time?) from 'Auschwitz'. Is this name that of a chronological origin? What era begins with this event? The question appears ingenuous when one remembers what dissolution the dialectic operates on the idea of a beginning, in the first chapter of the Science of Logic, and already in Kant's first Antinomy [*Critique of Pure Reason*, B454-61]. Has Adorno forgotten this? (LD, §152)

Has Lyotard forgotten this? Our attempt to explicate this problem will require further detours. Adorno suggests that 'after Auschwitz' speculative discourse in the Hegelian sense is impossible: the deaths at Auschwitz resist all attempts to sublate them into an economy according to which they would have paid for a crime or achieved sanctity by martyrdom. These are *senseless* deaths (and the silence is then taken to bear primarily on the meaning of sentences about Auschwitz). Lyotard wants to link this resistance to an impossibility of giving rise to a 'we', and this implies the impossibility of making the SS's prescription: 'Die!' the object of a norm.

Norms

We saw how the problem of the prescriptive sentence can be elaborated around its focus on the addressee pole of the universe, and how even Kant's stress on the specificity of the moral with respect to the cognitive was reduced by the operator of analogy, allowing that addressee to return to the familiar 'subject-position' of sender. Lyotard explores this problem further by distinguishing between prescription and norm. The shift of the 'same' 'subject' from addressee of the prescription to sender of the norm determines a particular notion of legitimacy, namely autonomy, which is the ground for a republican politics. In the statement of the norm: 'y declares as a norm that "it is obligatory for x to accomplish action α"' (LD, §155, quoting Georges Kalinowski), that autonomy would be secured by replacing y and x with the same proper name: 'The French people declares it to be obligatory for the French people to accomplish action α'. The pronoun 'we' also secures the transfer of addressee to sender, because it can contain both 'I' and 'you'. The normative sentence tends to mask this discrepancy ('we' are not sovereign and subject 'in the same place') by including the prescriptive sentence within itself. This is again the transcendental illusion found in Kant.

'Auschwitz' again provides an exacerbation of this situation. The 'grammar' of the normative sentence already suggests that the 'we' is unstable and potentially split: this possibility is evidently at its height when the obligation is to die. On the other hand, the 'identity' of that 'we' can in fact be strengthened by such an obligation, so long as that obligation is modalised: '(Let us) die rather than be defeated'; '(Let us) die rather than be enslaved'; 'Better dead than red', and so on. Although we saw *Rudiments païens* define death as relegation to the narrated (now we would say 'referent') pole exclusively, the point of such norms is to allow the dead paradoxically to re-appear at the other poles of a sentence-universe,

Socrates [in the *Menexenus*] locates the displacements of instances operated by the funeral oration. The *logos epitaphios*, a species of the epideictic genre, has as its sender an orator proposed by the Council, as its addressee the Assembly of the citizens, as its referent the citizens killed in battle for the fatherland. Its instituted meaning is the praise of the latter. Its effect on the addressee is a 'charm' (the hearer thinks himself transported to the Islands of the Blessed).

To this sentiment there correspond certain displacements of names on instances: death in combat is a 'noble death'; a noble death implies a 'good' life; Athenian life is good; you are good. The situation of names on the instances in the manifest universe presented by the *epitaphios* are: I the orator, I say to you (the Assembly) that the dead on the field of honour are good. In the co-presented (latent) universe, the situations are: 'I say to you that you are good'. And even, taking account of the final prosopopeia (in which the dead heroes speak): by his intermediary (the orator), we (the dead heroes) say to ourselves (the living citizens) that we (the living and the dead) are good. What was addressee in the first universe also occupies the situation of referent in the second. The referent of the first universe also becomes sender in the second. (LD, p. 40)

by means of the pronoun 'we'. At Auschwitz, however, this economy is disrupted. Here the deportee has no alternative: it is not a question of 'die rather than. . .' – there is clearly no question of a commutability of SS and Jew across poles of sentence-universes under cover of a 'we'. The 'we' in the sentence of the Nazis is exclusive of the 'you' of the addressee: further, that 'you' is to be prevented from ever becoming a 'we' (which could in principle recuperate the deaths in the manner described above). What is killed at Auschwitz is also the possibility of a death being noble (this would be the sense of Adorno's 'something worse than death'). If this be a question of obligation, then that obligation is not even addressed by the Nazis to the Jews, who become simply the referents of an obligation to exterminate: there is no possibility of a legitimation of such an obligation for the Jew. The sentence of the SS ('That he should die, such is my law'), and that of the deportee ('That I should die, such is his law') remain radically separate. Any 'we', even that of 'humanity' (which allowed Kant to mask the heterogeneity implied in obligation) is dispersed: which is why Auschwitz is something new, and why it brings down the Self of the speculative dialectic. *Auschwitz is therefore immediately the question of 'after Auschwitz'*, if not even enough of a 'we' remains to ponder the dispersion of the 'we' at Auschwitz (LD, §157).

Except that the resources of the dialectic are far from exhausted by this analysis: of course an 'I' and a 'he' can form a 'we', when that we is the name of a sender addressing itself to a third party (not included in that we). This situation is of course no longer that of legitimation by autonomy, but it is nonetheless a 'we'. The addressee of that 'we' is, precisely, 'us', able to affirm that any 'we' was dispersed at Auschwitz: or, more speculatively, the 'dispersion' (or 'dissensus') of our post-Auschwitz (post-modern) condition comes to self-knowledge and self-possession in the 'we' composed of the sender of the sentences positioned by *Le Différend,* and the sender and addressee positioned by the sentences of this paraphrase of its argument. The heterogeneous regimes and incommensurable genres would still, on this type of account, add up to a totality which is still in fact a Subject coming to be in-and-for-itself in part through the mediation of Lyotard's attempts to deny any such possibility. Hegel himself would allow for the 'sentiment' signalling a *différend* which 'wants' to be phrased in almost literally Lyotardian terms: the in-itself for us coming to be in-and-for-itself.

And yet: if this is so, speculative discourse ought to be able to name speculatively the effect of 'Auschwitz' (which is itself, from the point of view of the dialectic, only a contingent, empirical name). This is difficult, insofar as Nazism cannot be placed into a universal process: the (auto-) legitimation of Nazism is exclusive and tied to the particular name of a particular race (the Aryans). Whereas the rational terror of the French Revolution is in principle generalisable in the name of 'Reason' to the whole of humanity, Nazi 'terror' makes an exception and simply eliminates the rest: just as in the Athenian funeral oration decried by Socrates, where the slippage among the pronouns and sentence-instances allowed a move from 'they were good' to 'we are good', insofar as 'we are Athenians', so here the Aryans recount to other Aryans the story of (all) good Aryans. Here we have a narrative organisation formally identical to that of the Cashinahua Indians, which effectively marks the community of tellers, hearers and heroes as substitutable and exclusive. Nazism returns

A sentence, which links, and is to be linked onto, is always a *pagus*, a zone of borderlands, where the genres of discourse enter into conflict for the mode of linking. War and commerce. It is in the *pagus* that pax and pact are made, and unmade. 'Internal' peace at the price of perpetual *différends* on the edges. (The disposition is the same for the ego, for self-identification). This internal peace is made by the narratives which accredit the community of proper names and draw their credit from it. The *Volk* closes itself in on the *Heim*, it identifies itself in narratives attached to names, blocking the occurrence and the *différends* born of it. Joyce, Schönberg, Cézanne: *pagani* making war between genres of discourse. (LD, §218)

to this 'primitive' and 'mythical' form of legitimation in the middle of modernity: a 'regressive' narrative (recover an original purity which should never have become corrupt) against the 'progressive' narratives of post-Enlightenment Europe.

There is, claims Lyotard, no possibility of taking the sentence of Nazism and that of the Jewish deportee and linking them in a dialectical sublation. The genre of discourse practised by the Jewish people has nothing in common with that of Nazism: the difference between the two cannot be thought of as a contradiction. The mythical narrative organisation is

By annihilating the Jews, Nazism eliminates a regime of sentences in which the mark is on the addressee (*Listen, Israel*) and in which the identification of the sender (the Lord) and that of the meaning (what God means) is a dishonouring and dangerous presumption. The genre of discourse called Kabbala (tradition) is, as interrogation and interpretation, at the antipodes of the savage narrative tradition. The latter is placed under the sign of the already-there, the Jewish idiom under the sign of the *Arrive-t-il?*. Nazism attacks the occurrence, the *Ereignis* (. . .). It thus attacks the time of the whole of modernity. (LD, §160)

repetitive in its circular self-affirmation. It does not sublate what is not it, but ignores or eliminates it. And correlatively, there is no speculative solution to that organisation – Nazism was not destroyed speculatively and dialectically:

The destruction of Nazism also leaves a silence after itself: people dare not think through Nazism because it was put down like a rabid dog, as a police measure and not in conformity with the rules admitted by the genres of discourse of its adversaries (argumentation for liberalism, contradiction for Marxism). It was not refuted. (LD, §160)

'Auschwitz' does not therefore give rise to a dialectical result. In arguing this point, Lyotard goes further and practically exceeds the terms his own book provides: this analysis is not, finally, the 'answer' to the 'problem' of Auschwitz – even the *différend* cannot describe Auschwitz: 'Between the SS and the jew there is not even a *différend*, because there is not even a common idiom (that of a tribunal) in which a damage at least could be formulated, even in place of a wrong' (LD, §160).

If 'Auschwitz' is the name of a silence, a sentiment, then it is not simply a *fact* adequately dealt with by the cognitive genre. Lyotard would say it is a *sign*, and more specifically, a 'sign of history', in a Kantian sense to which we shall return. It is, roughly speaking, a sign of the fission of the *Selbst* of the dialectic or, to maintain an important ambivalence of *Le Différend*, a sign that such a *Selbst* was never there to be fissured. This 'fissuring' is the dispersion or dissensus with which we are concerned.

I have suggested that pure dispersion or dissensus is unthinkable, and we have seen that insistence on the heterogeneity of sentence-regimes and on the contingency of linkings is characteristic of a *particular* genre of discourse, that of philosophy. A sentence is always linked in a generic sequence, and given that the genre proposes an aim and ways of reaching it, then it follows that genres in general function to reduce heterogeneity at the level of regimes. This is true even of the genre of philosophy, which may well take that heterogeneity as its referent, but rarely enacts it in its own linkings. (Remember the dismay of *Discours, figure*, only able to signify 'deconstruction', unable to enact it.) That reduction of heterogeneity takes place at the cost of the incommensurability of the aims proposed by the various genres. With every linking of one sentence onto another, sentences from the diverse genres compete, and that competition is in every case a *différend*, insofar as generic ends are incommensurable (even if all genres aim at 'victory' or 'success', nothing suggests that those terms here name a single outcome). There is no need, and in fact it is a transcendental illusion, says Lyotard, to describe these generic

---

[Generic ends] seize sentences, and the instance they present, i.e., notably, 'we'. 'We' do not aim at them. Our 'intentions' are tensions, to link in a certain manner, exercised by genres on addressees and senders of sentences, on their referents, and on their meaning. We think that we want to persuade, seduce, convince, be fair, make believe, make question, but the fact is that a genre of discourse, dialectic, erotic, didactic, ethical, rhetorical, 'ironic', imposes on 'our' sentence and 'our'-selves its mode of linking. There is no reason to name these tensions intentions and will, except the vanity of giving ourselves credit for what is due to the occurrence and the *différend* it inspires among the ways of linking onto it. (LD, §183)

ends in terms of our intentions: simply the contingency of linkings means that many sentences are possible, but that there can only be one sentence 'at a time' means that most of those sentences will be forgotten or repressed. The diversity of genres is made possible by the contingency of linkings, which in turn depends on the 'absolute' event of the sentence: but genres strive to forget what makes them possible by providing an illusion that linkings are necessary (that there are laws of history).

Lyotard's hostility to the tendency to domination of the cognitive genre (or, in *The Postmodern Condition,* of the performative genre; and later in *Le Différend,* of the economic genre) is now grounded in a logical argument. No one genre can claim to be the genre of all genres, if only because of Russell's set-theory paradox. The philosophical effect of 'Auschwitz' is that the pretension of philosophy to be just such a genre (and the speculative dialectic is the fullest attempt at such a domination) is defeated, but also shown to be constitutively unjust. But the pretensions of other genres to replace philosophy in this respect are no more just than it. Politics presents a peculiarly difficult instance of this: often enough nowadays politics is presented as just such a supreme genre, in the name of which philosophy is contested, and in the name of which all our sentences are called to judgement. This is no doubt particularly true in the context in which this book is written: the Anglo-American response to the recent French thought has regularly raised questions and objections under the sign of the political, demanding political implications and results from the work of Derrida, Foucault, and Lyotard himself. In the contemporary 'crisis of legitimation' addressed by *The Postmodern Condition,* the call is for a totalisation of sentences as political, and a subordination of the contingency of linkings to Ideas of socialism or liberalism, for example.

Politics

In Lyotard's terms, politics has to do with normative sentences: as soon as the (ethical) sentence of obligation is taken up and quoted within a normative sentence, then we move to the political. To this extent, the political immediately masks the heterogeneity of regimes, throwing a bridge across the abyss (LD, §207). The normative sentence removes the addressee from the solitude of the sentence of obligation by constituting a community of addressees all subject to the law. The heterogeneity of the normative regime consists in the impossibility of deducing its authority from other sentences (notably descriptive sentences, as argued especially in *Au juste).* The diverse attempts to legitimate or ground the

Authority cannot be deduced. Attempts to legitimate authority lead to vicious circle (I have authority over you because you authorise me to have it), to *petitio principii* (authorisation authorises authority), to infinite regression (x is authorised by y who is authorised by z), to the paradox of the idiolect (God, Life, etc., designate me to exercise authority, I am the sole witness to this revelation). The aporia of a deduction of authority, or the aporia of sovereignty, is the sign that the sentence of authorisation cannot be the result of a sentence coming under a different regime. (LD, §203)

authority of the normative are therefore bound to fail. These various attempts nonetheless constitute politics in its various types: narrative legitimation from an origin in nationalist politics; narrative legitimation towards the realisation of an Idea in Enlightenment politics; revelatory legitimation (e.g. divine right) in certain royalist politics.

These various figures of politics are, in their different ways, all intolerant of difference and *différend*. This intolerance can be precisely formulated in Lyotard's analysis of the normative sentence. This sentence, it will be remembered, takes the form: 'y declares as a norm that "it is obligatory for x to accomplish action α"'. This declaration positions first of all as its addressee the addressee of the prescriptive it is normativizing. But it has a secondary addressee ('z'), outside the community of those subject to the law, to whom the law is notified. This difference between two sorts of addressee depends on their being given a proper name ('We, the French', 'You, the rest'). Insofar as the norm legitimates the prescription, the restriction of its legitimacy to an empirical named community seems arbitrary and potentially violent: either an imperialist extension tends to assume that 'z' can be included in 'x' and therefore 'y', or else 'z' (the Jews for the Nazis) are ideally forgettable and empirically eliminable. In the first of these possibilities, the tension arises out of legitimations in terms of an Idea, which cannot in principle be limited to an empirical community: in such cases the proper name of the nation concerned is absorbed into the Idea of humanity (or, for example, the Idea of Englishness, precisely because it is an Idea, becomes synonymous with (true) humanity). Lyotard provides a detailed analysis of these mechanisms on the basis of the French Declaration of 1789 (LD, pp. 209-13; compare Derrida's analysis of the American Declaration of Independence in *Otobiographies: l'enseignement de Nietzsche et la politique*

If the sender [of the norm] has a historico-political name [the French people], its declaration has no scope beyond that corresponding to the extension of that name. If it is to exceed this, and if the Declaration is to extend to all names,

the sender should not have a proper name [and will claim to represent humanity]. . .
The split of the sender of the Declaration into two entities, French nation and
human being, corresponds to the equivocality of the declarative sentence: it
presents a philosophical universe [positioning the referent 'humanity'] and
copresents a historico-political sentence [positioning the referent 'the French
people']. The revolution in politics which the French revolution is comes from
this impossible passage from one universe to the other. Henceforth, no one
will know whether the law thus declared is French or human, whether the war
waged in the name of rights is a war of conquest or emancipation, whether the
violence exercised under the name of liberty is repressive or pedagogical (progressive), whether the nations which are not French are to become French or
become human by giving themselves a Constitution which conforms to the
Declaration, even if they do this against the French. The confusion permitted
by the Constituants, which was to propagate throughout the historico-political
world, makes of any national or international conflict an insoluble *différend* about
the legitimacy of authority. . . The Constituants. . . hallucinate humanity in the
nation (LD, p. 212)

du nom propre (Paris: Galilée, 1984), pp. 13-32). In the second possibility,
the name of the nation is predominant and exclusive, repeated in
narratives of the origin. Conflict here is born of the concomitant
recognition of (national) boundaries and their maintenance:

This is what the Right ceaselessly valorises. The Left accredits a counter-narra-
tive, a history of humanity as a whole, the narrative of its emancipation, of international scope, without popular roots, cosmopolitan. But they are always accused
of ruining the fatherland, and always condemned to safeguard it nonetheless
during wars (civil, foreign and economic) because authorisation by myths, which
is immanent (the heart of the country) does not yield to the authorisation which
has recourse to the ideal, transcendent meta-norm (rights of man). There is no
Supreme Being to reconcile them. (LD, p. 213)

As always in Lyotard's work, political questions are most urgently worked
out in relation to Marxism. Here, for example, Lyotard suggests that the
legitimating set-up to be found in the *Communist manifesto* or *The Civil
War in France* is essentially the same as that of the French Declaration,
with the exception that the initial appeal to the Nation has disappeared,
to be replaced with an appeal to the worker (as universal, an Idea or
Ideal of Reason). The problem is that of knowing how such a non-real
entity can ever acquire a historico-political reality in the absence of
national proper names: the subsequent difficulties of the workers' movement, at least in its Internationalist aspect, can, according to Lyotard, be
assigned to the incommensurability between the Idea and the reality.

The problems located here could easily be illustrated from an 'exemplary' recent
Marxist work which attempts to discuss and invalidate recent French thought
(in which Lyotard is, however, given the very briefest of mentions): Perry Ander-

son's *In the Tracks of Historical Materialism* (London: Verso, 1983) suggests that the attack by E. P. Thompson on the work of Althusser had the beneficial effect of breaking down the tendency of Western Marxism to concentrate on national context, 'to the detriment of any genuinely internationalist discourse' (pp. 26-7), while celebrating the new predominance of 'intellectual production' (i.e. Marxist thought, defined by means of the operation of the dilemma outlined above with respect to the communist state) in English-speaking countries. The question as to whether the Thompson-Althusser debate is a struggle over national boundaries rather than an instance of 'internationalist discourse' is conveniently elided.

Let me try to give some further substance to this type of position by summarising some of Lyotard's remarks about Marx at the end of *Le Différend*. Marx identifies a wrong done to workers under a capitalist organisation of production (Lyotard would formulate this wrong, as we have seen, as a deprivation of their ability to phrase their labour-power as anything other than a commodity to be exchanged for a salary, and in principle approves of Marx's attempt to formulate rules for a genre in which that work could be described otherwise). But the operations Marx then proceeds to carry out are unsatisfactory, according to Lyotard. First, Marx transforms the empirical working-class (referent of cognitive sentences) into the presumed sender of a prescriptive sentence (a demand for communism): this operation involves a hidden transformation of that real referent into something rather different, the proletariat, an Idea or Ideal of reason, demanding the means to bring about its self-fulfillment and universalization in the form of liberated laborious humanity. In order to make the real working-class into a speaking incarnation of the proletariat, political organisations are set up to relay the message sent, to quote the prescription. The authorisation of this prescription as a norm runs into the problems just described. The philosophically inconsistent task of the party is to establish the reality of the proletariat, which is not in principle amenable to any such establishment of reality. It does this by writing off any difficulty in achieving its task of identifying a reality (the working-class) and an Idea or Ideal (the proletariat: liberated laborious humanity) to the operations of ideology, confidently defined from a position of science or knowledge – this simply implies that the party has claimed the right and ability to define what counts as reality, and on that basis to proceed to the derivation of a prescription from that reality. Further, as this reality is placed in a process of universalisation, then in principle it tends to the effacement of the particularity of proper names, necessary to any reality. Whence the difficulty Marxism has with national differences, for example. In practice the party deals more or less opportunistically with political reality, while repeating the initial error of treating that reality as the sender of authoritative sentences it should be sufficient to heed and transcribe (LD, §§ 236-9).

To the inevitable reaction to this type of analysis: namely, 'that's all very well, but what alternative do you propose?', Lyotard would still almost answer with the statement from *Economie libidinale* quoted earlier. But that type of answer is here given a little more specification. No *alternative* would be proposed if 'alternative' here implied the proposal of a rival genre for legitimation or a different Idea as telos for a narrative. The unthinkable 'dissensus', which certainly guides Lyotard's political judgement (as a regulative Idea), returns here: the reason I have repeatedly described this term as 'unthinkable', and denied that is should be conceived as a telos, is that far from suggesting a political goal within

---

In deliberative politics, that of modern democracies, the *différend* is exposed, although the transcendental appearance of a single finality which would bring it to an end persists in having it forgotten, in making it tolerable. . . The deliberative is more 'fragile' than the narrative (. . .), it allows a glimpse of the abysses separating the genres of discourse among themselves and even the regimes of sentences among themselves, and which threaten the 'social bond'. . . Put briefly: the narrative is a genre, the deliberative an assemblage of genres, and this suffices to allow occurrences and *différends* to appear in it. (LD, §§ 210, 217: a detailed analysis of the regimes and genres involved in deliberative politics is to be found in §§ 210-7)

a genre or group of genres, 'dissensus' is the name for the heterogeneity of regimes and the incommensurability of genres. If politics is conceived of as a genre, Lyotard offers no political 'solution' at all. But if politics (or perhaps, though Lyotard does not make this distinction in these terms, 'the political') is taken as a name for that heterogeneity and that incommensurability, as 'the threat of the *différend*' (LD, §190), 'the possibility of the *différend* on the occasion of the slightest linking' (LD, §192), then the determination of the political as politics is the problem, and the resistance to that determination the (dis)solution. Lyotard accepts the proposition that 'everything is political' if the political is described as above, but refuses the apparent corollary ('politics is everything') insofar as that suggests a genre containing or subordinating all other genres.

The universe presented by a sentence is immediately 'social' if by 'social' one understands that a sender, an addressee, a referent and a meaning are situated together in it. By 'immediately' I mean that none of these instances can be deduced from another as from an origin. . . A 'deduction' of the social presupposes the social. . . . The social is always presupposed because it is presented or co-presented in the least sentence. . . . Even when the social is explicitly taken as referent in the sociologist's sentence, it is also presupposed in the situation of all the instances presented by that sentence. (LD, §§ 193-4)

All of which could look like a prescription for a sort of revolutionary politics, in the sense of a politics constantly questioning the legitimacy of whatever tribunal happens to be in place, constantly questioning the legitimations offered. Or it could seem to imply an anarchism, and a defence of violence and war as somehow more 'just' in themselves than established justice, insofar as they do not mask *différend* as litigation. But a revolutionary politics would undertake such violence (or legitimate such violence) as showing that different tribunals are preferable to existing ones. Once instituted, such tribunals could only proceed to mask

---

All we wish to suggest here is that any philosophy of non-violence can only, *in history*, — but would it have any meaning elsewhere? — choose the lesser violence in an *economy of violence*. . .

The thought of being is thus never, in its unveiling, foreign to a certain violence. The fact that this thought always appears in difference, that the same (thought *(and) (of)* being) is never the identical, means primarily that being is history, dissimulates itself in its production and, originarily, does itself violence in thought to say itself and appear to itself. A being without violence would be a being producing itself outside entities: nothing; non-history; non-production; non-phenomenality. Speech producing itself without the slightest violence would de-termine nothing, would say nothing, would offer nothing to the other; it would not be *history* and would *show* nothing: in all the senses of this word, and first of all in its Greek sense, it would be speech without *sentence*. . .

But why history? Why does the sentence impose itself? Because, if one does not violently drag the silent origin from itself, the worst violence will cohabit in silence with the *idea* of peace? Peace is made only in a *certain silence*, determined and protected by the violence of speech. Saying nothing other than this silent peace by which it gets itself called, which its mission is to protect and prepare, speech *indefinitely* keeps silence. One never escapes the *economy of war*. . .

Our own reference to history is here only contextual. The economy we are talking about fits no more [than it does with ahistory] with the concept of history as it has always functioned and which it is difficult, if not impossible, to remove from its teleological or eschatalogical horizon. (Jacques Derrida, 'Violence et métaphysique', in *L'écriture et la différence*, pp. 136 n 1, 218, 220)

---

différend as litigation:

This is why politics cannot have as their stake the good, but ought to have the lesser evil. Or, if you prefer, the lesser evil ought to be the political good. By evil

I understand and one can only understand the forbidding of sentences possible at each moment, a challenge opposed to the occurrence, contempt for being. (LD, §197)

It would follow that justice is not an achieved state, nor a state that ever could be achieved. Justice (as respect for the occurrence, and therefore for heterogeneity, dissensus) is scarcely even an Idea of reason: it

> In Kant, the Idea that will serve as regulator for the decision of justice is that of a unity or a totality. In morality, totality of reasonable beings, in politics the unity of humanity. . . For Kant the idea of justice is linked to that of finality. Now, 'finality' means a sort of convergence, or organisation, of a general congruence of a given multiplicity moving towards its unity. . . If we abandon this idea of congruence and put it its place the idea of a 'discrepancy' instead, the question it of knowing whether one can make a moral and political law out of it. . . a politics of Ideas in which justice is not placed under a rule of convergence, but rather of divergence. I believe it is that theme that is constantly to be found in contemporary writers under the name of 'minority'. Basically, minorities are territories of language. Each of us belongs to several minorities and what is important is that none of them should win out. (AJ, 177, 179, 181 [JG, 93, 94, 95])

regulates political judgement *now,* 'on the occasion of the least linking'. It is not the end-point of a narrative of progress. For narrative, which at the beginning of this chapter appeared to be the place to look for the event, turns out to be the genre which best *hides* the event. By coming to an end and organising the temporality of events retroactively (as has been known at least since Sartre's *Nausea),* narrative suggests that there could be a last sentence making sense of all preceding sentences. Narrative hides now as 'the now' in the diachronic series it proposes (in however complicated a fashion: narrative cannot do without such a series) (LD, §219).

And yet we are 'in history', as the possibility of violence and *différend.* How are we to think that history given the suspicion weighing on the narrative genre, which swallows the event we are enjoined to respect? Any serious sense we might be able to give to the term 'postmodern' would depend on addressing this question. Modernity ('which is not an epoch, but rather a mode' (PE, 46) – Nazism, for example, is not modern) is distinguished by a narrative organisation of time, determined teleologically (retroactively from the anticipation of the arrival of that telos as last sentence) by an Idea of emancipation:

[This Idea] is of course differently argued according to what are called the philosophies of history, the grand narratives under which one attempts to order the crowd of events: Christian narrative of redemption through love of the Adamic fault, *aufklärer* narrative of emancipation from ignorance and servitude through knowledge and egalitarianism, speculative narrative of the realisation of the universal Idea through the dialectics of the concrete, Marxist narrative of emancipation from alienation through the socialisation of work, capitalist narrative of emancipation from poverty through techno-industrial development. Between these narratives there is scope for litigation and even for *différend*. But all situate the data brought by events in the course of history whose end-point, even if it remains out of reach, is called universal liberty, acquittal of humanity as a whole. (PE, 47)

These narratives recount a universal history of humanity: as we have already seen, the process of universalisation has trouble with the particularities of proper names which mark, for example, national narratives. It is, of course, possible to presuppose that the senders and addressees of such narratives *already* belong to the subject 'humanity' and that their narratives can thus in principle be integrated into a universal history: but this presupposition falls foul of Lyotard's analysis of the dialectic – no sentence which presents particular narratives as co-presenting the history of humanity can prove itself to have been engendered by that history from the particular narratives it takes as its referent. (LD, §§223-5)

For, told as a narrative, universal history could not avoid proper names to allow the linking of sentences of heterogeneous regimes positioning the 'same' referent: if these proper names are to be acceptable as part of universal history, they must be accepted by all its addressees (who are all its potential senders too), who are therefore 'universal' addressees, already beyond the particularity of proper naming. To avoid begging the question of the possibility of such addressees, an account of how they could be engendered from the particular addressees and senders of particular narratives would have to be given. This universalisation cannot avoid conflict between different national traditions: this conflict is not a *différend*, in that the genre in question is the same on both sides – narrative. But if it is therefore a litigation, it is one which cannot be settled, as there is no tribunal to which appeal could be made for judgement. Such a tribunal would already have to be universal history, and thus again presupposes what is at stake (LD, §227). It would follow that there is not one world (but many different worlds of names), and not one humanity: and no more can there be – the particularity of sentences and genres remains irreducible. This is another way of saying that there is not 'language in general' (as, say an instrument of communication and dialogue), but sentences. Further, Lyotard would say that certain names have blocked the credibility of these various narratives of emancipation struggling for universal history. As we have seen, 'Auschwitz' is seen to block the speculative machine, to stick as an irreducible name which cannot be named speculatively: and Lyotard rather brutally gives a further list:

All that is proletarian is communist, all that is communist is proletarian: 'Berlin 1953, Budapest 1956, Tchequoslovakia 1968, Poland 1980' (I pass) refute the doctrine of historical materialism: workers rise up against the Party. – All that is democratic is by the people and for it, and vice versa: 'May 1968' refutes the doctrine of parliamentary liberalism. The everyday life of the social defeats the representative institution. – Everything that is free play of demand and supply is propitious for general enrichment, and vice versa: the 'crises of 1911 and 1929' refute the doctrine of economic liberalism, and the 'crisis of 1974-9' refutes the post-Keynesian modification of that doctrine. The passages promised by the grand doctrinal syntheses end up in bloody impasses. (LD, §257)

Just like Auschwitz, these names are not simply names of facts solely susceptible to being placed as referents of cognitive sentences. Lyotard is of course not asserting that these 'refutations' have led to the total empirical collapse of the doctrines involved. When, in *Le postmoderne expliqué aux enfants,* he goes on to say, 'The grand narratives have become scarcely credible' (PE, 53), or even when, in *The Postmodern Condition* he claims that 'Most people have lost the nostalgia for the lost narrative' (CPM, 68 [PMC, 41]), it is better, despite the obvious invitation in the second of these quotations (which can itself be referred to the 'somewhat sociologizing slant' (CPM, 9 [PMC, xxv]) deprecatingly pointed out in that book's introduction), not to read such sentences as empirical claims at all, but as locating 'signs of history' which the last chapter of *Le Différend* attempts to explicate, again via a dense reading of Kant.

The Sign of History

'Reality', in the domain of the historico-political, still depends on the rules we have laid down: but the *totality* of the series of historical facts (which, like all phenomena, are essentially linked into the causal chains of natural mechanism), and the beginning of that series (i.e. a cause which is not itself an effect of a prior cause) cannot be intuited: they are the objects of Ideas. Reality on its own does not give much to go on in history and politics: at most repetitive sequences can be established by statistical regularity.

Kant suggests that if one remains at this level, then it appears that political history is a mess, a chaos. This is distressing for reason, and that

> Since men neither pursue their aims purely by instinct, as the animals do, nor act in accordance with any integral, prearranged plan like rational cosmopolitans, it would appear that no law-governed history of mankind is possible (as it would be, for example, with bees or beavers). We can scarcely help feeling a certain distaste on observing their activities as enacted in the great world-drama, for we find that, despite the apparent wisdom of individual actions here and there, everything as a whole is made up of folly and childish vanity, and often of childish malice and destructiveness. The result is that we do not know what sort of opinion we should form of our species, which is so proud of its supposed superiority. The only way out for the philosopher, since he cannot assume that mankind follows any rational *purpose of its own* in its collective actions, is for him to attempt to discover a *purpose in nature* behind the senseless course of human events, and decide whether it is after all possible to formulate in terms of a definite plan of nature a history of creatures who act without a plan of their own. (Kant, 'Idea for a Universal History with a Cosmopolitan Purpose', in H. Reiss, ed., *Kant's Political Writings* (CUP, 1970), 41-53 (41-2))

distress is itself a *sign* of the power of the reason, which conceives of Ideas (and notably the Idea of freedom), and thus can hope for progress and improvement. In Lyotard's terms, distress is a sentimental sentence which signals a *différend* between the cognitive sentence, which presents chaotic events, and the sentence of Reason, which expects progress. Kant believes that rather than assume a nature in contradiction with itself (allowing man the seeds of progress through reason, but preventing their development by the disorder of reality), we should postulate a purpose in nature and see if such a postulation gets us any further. A historical discourse which remains within the cognitive genre will never establish an order in history: and a discourse which takes the idea of such an order as its 'guiding thread' will not operate according to the rules of establishing reality, but by analogous presentations which are for Kant proper to 'dialectical' sentences, i.e. those taking Ideas as their referent. If the discourse of order assumes it can proceed by direct presentation, then it falls into the transcendental illusion: in Lyotard's formulation, acting *as if* it were referring to phenomena, when in fact it is referring to 'as if phenomena' (LD, p. 191). The 'order' is only supposed to exist, as a guiding thread: the authorisation for such a supposition is no more than that of the Idea of freedom. In Kant's terms, the *reflective* judgement,

> Judgement in general is the faculty of thinking the particular as contained under

the universal. If the universal (the rule, principle, or law) is given, then the judgement which subsumes the particular under it is *determinant*. This is so even where such a judgement is transcendental and, as such, provides the conditions *a priori* in conformity with which alone subsumption under the universal can be effected. If, however, only the particular is given and the universal has to be found for it, then the judgement is simply *reflective*. (Kant, *Critique of Judgement*, Introduction, §4)

in the absence of a given law under which to subsume the singularities of history, judges *as if* there were such an order. This order implies a teleology, and the type of retroactive causality we have seen at work in narrative: but Kant says that there is no question of according *reality* to such an Idea. (The illusion of attributing a (potential) reality to such an Idea is the illusion of revolutionary politics.)

The odd type of 'philosophical history' (which, as Kant makes clear in the 9th proposition of the 'Idea for a Universal History' is not at all supposed to *supplant* empirical history) (Kant's *Political Writings*, p. 53) suggested here is 'validated', not by the direct presentation of phenomena, but by indirect or analogical presentation of 'as-if' phenomena. And this is where Lyotard focusses on the notion of the 'sign of history'. This 'sign' is invoked by Kant in a discussion of the question as to whether the human race is continually improving: here, insofar as the question bears on the future, it is clear that no direct presentation (as experience or matter of fact) is possible. Kant's idea is complicated: insofar as humans are not merely parts of a natural mechanism, but freely acting beings, then their actions cannot be foreseen with any certainty. If then we are to defend the proposition which posits a continual improvement, we must work differently. We must still, says Kant, look for an *event* (the German word is *Begebenheit*, which Lyotard glosses as a sort of *delivery* or 'deal' in a card-playing sense; but he is also pleased to find Kant using the word *Ereignis* in a draft of the *Idea for a Universal History*), which would suggest that man has the possibility of being the cause of his own improvement (*The Contest of Faculties*, §5, *Kant's Political Writings*, p. 181, LD, p. 236). This type of causality (by freedom rather than mechanism) cannot be situated in the diachronic series of a factual history, and can happen anytime – and is to this extent unpredictable. But if such an event can be discovered, then the inference of progress can be retroactively applied to the past as well: but in that case the event in question could not be thought of as the *cause* of progress, but as an indication of it, a sign of it, a historical sign. The difficult status of such an event is that it must apparently reconcile the *différend* between the cognitive and the speculative, the claims of determinism (which sees everything in terms of mechanical causality) and the claims of freedom. Insofar as it attempts such a reconciliation, it must be linked to the general question of *judgement* as the 'faculty' which Kant hopes will be able to throw a bridge across the abyss separating the cognitive and the ethical. And insofar as this is true, then the question of judgement (how to judge in the absence of given criteria for judgement), which is the focus of Lyotard's later work – the 1982 Colloque de Cerisy organised around his work was entitled 'Comment Juger?', how to judge – links the aesthetic and the political in a way which is bound to worry all those who immediately scent Fascism in the association of those two terms. It

---

Mankind, which in Homer's time was an object of contemplation for the Olympian gods, now is one for itself. Its self-alienation has reached such a degree that it can experience its own destruction as an aesthetic pleasure of the first order. This is the situation of politics which Fascism is rendering aesthetic. Communism responds by politicizing art. (Walter Benjamin, 'The Work of Art in the Age of Mechnical Reproduction', in *Illuminations*, ed. Hannah Arendt (New York: Schocken Books, 1968), 217-51 (p. 242))

naturally remains to be seen whether Lyotard is aestheticizing politics or politicizing aesthetics, or whether those two terms are sufficient for what is at stake in this work.

The Aesthetic and the Political: the Sublime

For Kant himself immediately looks to an 'aesthetic' event to validate his thesis; not spectacular actions in history, but the reaction of 'spectators' to the French Revolution:

We are here concerned only with the attitude of the onlookers as it reveals itself *in public* while the drama of great political changes is taking place: for they openly express universal yet disinterested sympathy for one set of protagonists against their adversaries, even at the risk that their partiality could be of great disadvantage to themselves. Their reaction (because of its universality) proves that mankind as a whole shares a certain character in common, and it also proves (because of its disinterestedness) that man has a moral character, or at least the makings of one. And this does not merely allow us to hope for human improvement; it is already a form of improvement in itself, in so far as its influence is strong enough for the present. (*Kant's Political Writings*, p. 182; quoted LD, p. 237: Lyotard's version of the last clause has 'within the limits fixed by the present on the capacity for progress'.)

Whatever the actual outcome of the Revolution, however great its atrocities, whatever the conflicting interpretations of rights and wrongs to which it may give rise, Kant finds his 'sign of history' in the passion of the spectators, their sympathy or *enthusiasm*. The immediacy, disinterestedness and universality of the spectator's judgement allows this to be thought of in terms of an 'aesthetic' reaction: but the affect of enthusiasm marks this reaction as coming under, not the aesthetic of the beautiful (marked according to Kant by disinterested pleasure, or pure delight in the free and harmonious play of the faculties), but the aesthetic of the sublime, which involves a 'negative' pleasure, or an oscillation of attraction and repulsion, pleasure and pain. In the sublime, the imagination struggles and fails to find a direct presentation for the Idea: that failure produces the pain, but the pleasure comes from the realisation of a capacity to conceive of ideas precisely beyond any intuitive presentation. Any phenomenon, however large, seems small in comparison with the Ideas of Reason.

In a literal sense and according to their logical import, ideas cannot be presented. But if we enlarge our empirical faculty of representation (. . .) with a view to the intuition of nature, reason inevitably steps forward, as the faculty concerned with the independence of the absolute totality, and calls forth the effort of the mind, unavailing though it be, to make the representation of sense adequate to this totality. This effort, and the feeling of the unattainability of the idea by means of imagination, is itself a presentation of the subjective finality of our mind in the employment of the imagination in the interests of the mind's supersensible province, and compels us subjectively to *think* nature itself in its totality as a presentation of something supersensible [i.e. unpresentable], without our being able to effectuate this presentation *objectively*. (*Critique of Judgement*, p. 119)

The 'enthusiasm' invoked by Kant is an extreme form of the sublime, involving a 'negative presentation' which is a 'presentation of the infinite' [i.e. the unpresentable] (*Critique of Judgement,* p. 127; LD, p. 239). Kant's examples (of the Jewish law forbidding representation, and of 'our' 'representation' of the moral law) heighten this paradoxical 'presentation of the unpresentable', and begin to suggest the links between the aesthetic, the ethical and the political.

It is not that this sublime sentiment has any ethical validity as such, insofar as it has the spectator in the grip of affect: but that affect is sublime in the 'tension' if provokes – it is no accident that, commenting on this description in the *Critique of Judgement,* Lyotard momentarily returns to the language of *Economie libidinale:* 'the enthusiastic pathos in its episodic unleashing. . . is an energetical *sign,* a tensor of the *Wunsch'* (LD, p. 240). For Lyotard, the bridge across the abyss is never crossed, and this tension marks a sort of agitated suspension over the void, an 'experience' of incommensurability *as such.* The ethical suspicion depends on the location of an illusion in this type of reaction: the demand for a presentation of what cannot be presented – in the case of the French Revolution, the confusion of a direct presentation of common being (even communism?) and the indirect presentation of the Idea of the cosmopolitan republic. For Lyotard, politics would reside in the unavoidability of such an illusion.

The aesthetic is political not just because in this case it involves judgement on a political referent, but because any aesthetic judgement, in Kant's description, demands universalisation, anticipates a *sensus communis,* a community, a consensus. This is not like the demand for consensus that might emanate from a cognitive judgement, insofar as the aesthetic judgement is not conceptual and cannot therefore be *proved.* The

The judgement of taste does depend upon a concept (of a general ground of the subjective finality of nature for the power of judgement), but one from which nothing can be cognized in respect of the Object, and nothing proved, because it is in itself indeterminable and useless for knowledge. Yet by means of this very concept it acquires at the same time validity for every one (but with each individual, no doubt, as a singular judgement immediately accompanying his intuition): because its determining ground lies, perhaps, in the concept of what may be regarded as the supersensible substrate of humanity. (*Critique of Judgement,* §57, pp. 207-8)

aesthetic judgement in general is a call for community. In the case of the sublime, which demands a capacity of attentiveness to Ideas of reason, this call is the more difficult to satisfy, insofar as Kant would claim that an openness to ideas requires a certain culture (culture conceived of as the ultimate aim of nature for humanity, and consisting in humanity's capacity to choose its *own* ends). Kant thinks that such a culture can only develop through a certain neutralization of conflict (eventually at the cosmopolitan level, via a confederation of states). Given all these preconditions, he is able to conclude that the enthusiasm of the spectators for the French revolution is a sign of progress. Q.E.D. This is not at all the same as suggesting, cognitively, that the French Revolution shows that societies are close to achieving the confederation of states which would ensure perpetual peace, but that there is progress in humanity's faculty of judgement, revealed in the public 'utterance' of the 'sentence' of enthusiasm, showing a capacity for Ideas which can only be achieved by a progress of 'culture'. It is cognitively impossible to predict when such signs will appear in history; and to this extent the philosophical history Kant proposes is not a philosophy of history.

Despite Lyotard's evident attraction for Kant's analyses of the historico-political, which avoid the trap of positivism and point out the location of illusion while accounting for its inevitability, he is suspicious of them too. All of Kant's argument here rests on the free supposition of the guiding thread of a natural teleology of humanity. This alone allows the antinomy between the argument for determinism (which treats humanity as part of a mechanical universe) and the argument for freedom (which stresses the supersensible) to be resolved. The critical philosopher's authorisation for this supposition which allows the *différend* to be negotiated (in however complex a fashion) depends on his own sentiment of distress at the chaotic picture provided by empirical history. He interprets this sentiment as a sign only by already presupposing the nature emitting the sign which is then used to validate the postulation of that same nature:

The value of signs for the critical watchman... presupposes a sort of intention (finality) on the side of what makes the sign. An as-if subject is thought to signal to the philosopher, by means of a sentiment he feels, that a quasi-sentence takes place in the shape of this sign, a sentence the meaning of which cannot be validated by the procedures applicable to knowledge, but which must nonetheless be taken into consideration. Is it possible to judge on the basis of signs without presupposing (even as problematical) such an intention? That is, without prejudging that an unknown sender not only delivers them to us but addresses them to us for our decipherment? ... Even a denatured nature and signs of nothing, even a post-modern a-teleology, would apparently not escape this *circulus* (LD, p. 196).

And the next paragraph of *Le Différend* goes on to wonder, apparently in some dismay, about this apparent circle:

Is it in this sense that we are not modern? Incommensurability, heterogeneity, the *différend,* the persistence of proper names, the absence of a supreme tribunal? Or is it on the contrary still Romanticism, the nostalgia that accompanies the withdrawal of... etc.? Nihilism? Successful labour of mourning for Being? and the hope that is born with it? All of that still inscribed in a thought of a redeeming future? Is it possible that 'we' no longer tell ourselves [or each other] anything? Are 'we' not telling ourselves [or each other] the grand narrative of the end of the grand narratives? Does it not suffice that thought think according to the end of a history for thought to remain modern? Or else is post-modernity that old man's occupation, rummaging in the dustbin of finality to find remains, brandishing unconsciouses, lapsus, edges, borders, gulags, parataxes, nonsenses, paradoxes, and making of this its glorious novelty, its promise of change? But that too is a goal for humanity. A genre. (Bad pastiche of Nietzsche. Why?) (LD, §182)

Temporal Economy

And possibly this apparent hopelessness could be linked to the last generic analysis in the book, that of the economic genre: for more than the cognitive, more even that the performative (as was the case in *The Postmodern Condition)*, it is the economic which is now seen, in its efforts at achieving generic domination, as the biggest threat to justice. The peculiarity of the economic genre is that it requires two sentences to define its minimal unit:

Sentence 1: x (sender) gives up to y (addressee) the referent a, this (ostensible). Sentence 2: y (sender) gives up to x (addressee) the referent b, that (ostensible). Economic genre: the giving up of that must cancel out the giving up of this. Sentences 1 and 2 are linked with a view (stake, finality of the genre) to 'liberate' the two parties, to unbind them. What is this and what is that, their meaning, is important only for a sentence seeking to describe this and that correctly (the sentence of the anthropologist, of the economist, of the sociologist, of the psychoanalyst). In the economic sentence (which is not that of the economist), the meaning is not that of the objects exchanged, the meaning is the exchange. By sentence 1, x is immediately placed in the situation of creditor and y in that of debtor. Sentence 2 cancels out these situations, and this is the sentence called for by sentence 1 in the economic genre. The linking of 2 onto 1 constitutes exchange itself. In the absence of 2, 1 does not take place. Thus time t + 1 (occurrence of 2) is the condition for time t (occurrence of 1). A didactic sentence 'waits for' acquiescence, but that acquiescence is not the condition of that sentence. A prescriptive waits for accomplishment [of the action prescribed], but that accomplishment is not the condition of the prescriptive. Etc. The economic sentence of giving up does not wait for the sentence of acquittal (counter-cession), but presupposes it. (LD, §240)

The economic genre thus presupposes commensurability of the referents exchanged, and the symmetry of sender and addressee, who reverse roles from one sentence to the next. It would seem that the important feature of this genre is that its minimal cell consists of *two* sentences, linked by a necessity within the genre. It is not of course necessary that after completion of this minimal exchange (or after enough exchanges for parity to be restored), further exchanges take place: at this point the contingency of linkings returns.

To the obvious question as to how the equivalence of referents be ascertained (which is no less than the whole question of value), Lyotard rejects the solution that the estimate of the exchangers decides – this 'anthropological' answer would presuppose a prior debate and consensus as to a scale of values, but cannot account for how x could ever know that y evaluates b as he does a: this question retreats into the radical incommunicability of idiolects. Appealing to prices equally begs the question. To Marx's answer, in terms of social labour-time, Lyotard replies that this too involves a metaphysical assumption around production (taking notions of *energeia* and *dunamis* uncritically from Aristotle), and attributing these powers to a human subject. This account is rejected, as it was in *Economie libidinale*. But whereas in that book Lyotard himself remained in thrall to the language of energy, now he suggests that time alone, not yet determined as 'labour-time', accounts for value: value is simply *time* stocked in an object.

This radical solution is all too rapidly laid out in the very closing pages of *Le Différend*. It requires that 'production' be seen as a genre, or set of genres, separate from and incommensurable with exchange. Production in this account requires analysis into an 'imaginative' sentence which has as its referent the (as yet unreal, non-ostensible) object required, and a 'metaphorical' sentence which makes one referent (raw material) into another (product): this product can be the object of an ostensive. This genre takes time which is 'stocked' in the object when it is presented for exchange in a new ostensive sentence: production loses time with respect to exchange, when, as in capital, the economic sentence is granted hegemony over the productive. The time involved is not essentially labour time, insofar as time spent after production simply waiting for exchange also raises costs. This 'lost time' is what has to be recuperated in the exchange. When this rule of recuperating lost time is extended across other genres, then the acceleration and saturation of time characteristic of capitalist organisation results. 'All debts (of love, of work, even of life) are thought of as payable. For example, when he dies, x will leave cycles of exchange incomplete, before the cancelling out of exchanges in which he is implicated. By insuring his life, a company relays his ability to pay off. He is not in debt for his life to the Gods or his family, but to the insurance company, i.e. to exchange' (LD, §245).

In this analysis, money is not the equivalent of commodities, but of time: according to Lyotard, money demonstrates that neither property of objects nor use/enjoyment of objects is pertinent to the economic genre, but that exchange is a 'negotiation of time'. Money is the sign of an 'abstract' time which can be placed at any moment in the cycle of exchange. It follows that wealth is the possession of such abstract time, and that it allows the time between the two sentences of the economic genre to be lengthened. Those who do not have such time at their disposal have to speed up the succession of the two sentences: workers in capitalist conditions, notably, have, basically, no such abstract time, and can put into exchange only their 'real' time. Their time is chained to the deictics of the calendar and clock – and even if they were to earn more 'abstract' time in the form of money than the 'real' time taken to earn it, it is unclear that they would have enough real time remaining in which to spend it. This collapse of the real time of work and the abstract time gained in exchange is the mark of the *différend* between work and exchange: this is the *différend* signalled by the frustration and anger to which Marxism is attentive (and why it continues), but which Marx's analysis mishandles, as we have seen (LD, §250).

Capital becomes defined as the exchange in the shortest possible real time of the greatest possible abstract time. The spectacular success of the economic genre in hegemonising regimes and genres in general can be given two reasons. The first is that, as we have seen, time is a necessity of sentences, and the economic genre takes that time as its object. Further, insofar as it has seemed possible to submit sentences in general to a calculation (apparently possible and necessary in the 'computerisation of society' scenario discussed in *The Postmodern Condition*) in terms of

---

11. Essentially, the new technologies concern language. They are continuous with previous technologies in that they substitute automats for natural agents (humans, animals, etc.). They are different in that the substitution bears on sequences previously accomplished by the higher nervous systems (cortex). They presuppose the analysis of operational sequences, their encoding in artificial language, the constitution of artificial memories, the formation of automats obeying orders given in this language.

12. The language thus treated is informational: it is made up of messages going from a sender to an addressee, both of them in possession of the same code (with or without translation). . . Information is evaluated in terms of probability (between 0 and 1). It can be calculated. Its cost can be laid out. Science, technology and economy find in it a common unit for measuring knowledge, power and price. (TI, 48-9)

'bits' of information, this type of calculation would suggest that sentences in general can be objects of exchange:

The heterogeneity of their regimes and of the genres of discourse (stakes) finds a universal idiom, the economic genre, a universal criterion, success (having gained time), a universal judge, the strongest (i.e. the most credible) currency, which is the one best able to give and therefore receive time. Speculation on currency which short-circuits production is the procedure for accumulating time which turns out to be the quickest: one buys weak currency on Friday, one sells it on Tuesday, when it has been supported, or simply when it has escaped devaluation. (LD, §251)

Further, the internal 'necessity' of the economic genre enables it to forget the contingency of linkings, and thus to mask the event of a sentence under an apparent inevitability: the void between sentences is rapidly filled by the demands of the economic.

It is perfectly possible for the economic genre to be commented on by an apparent philosophy of history leading to emancipation through universal wealth. But the genre itself does not imply consideration of the ethical question 'What ought we to be?' or attentiveness to Ideas of Reason. The multiplicity of incommensurable ends proposed by the various genres is rapidly forgotten by the imperative to gain more and more time: the idea of a humanity able to be attentive to its possible ends is suppressed. A last chance for universal history seems to reside in the possibility that enthusiasm is not the only sublime sentiment: anger can also be sublime, according to Kant at least – perhaps a 'vigorous melancholy' could still be a 'sign of history' proving progress. For example, the recent proliferation of attempts to phrase a variety of diverse *différends* previously masked as litigations (e.g. feminism, gay rights, the peace movement, ethnic minorities – all of these *différends* had previously been piously subordinated to the authority of a canonic narrative by Left and Right alike) might be taken as the sign that 'culture' in judgement has progressed to such an extent that we must assume a more refined ability to detect the *différend*. This is at least arguable: Lyotard wonders whether any such progress could be asserted – 'culture' takes time which is lost to exchange: in this sense the hegemony of the economic tends towards the suppression of culture, or to its subordination to exchange (remember the brief analysis presented in the introduction). More importantly, how could we still maintain a belief in the 'quasi-subject' called nature signalling to us? The 'ends' imputed to such a subject are distant and imply a deferral to which the economic genre is fundamentally inimicable. Lyotard himself had previously wanted to oppose the apparently triumphant spread of capitalism by a stress on the local and the minority, but now is wary:

People count on the resistance of communities huddled around their names and their narratives to create an obstacle to the hegemony of capital. This is an error. First, this resistance maintains that hegemony as much as it opposes it [insofar as capitalism requires national differences to function, multi-nationalism not-withstanding]. Secondly, it distances the Idea of a cosmopolitan history, and gives rise to the fear of a retreat onto legitimation by tradition, or even by myth, even if it also gives rise to the resistance of peoples to their annihilation. Proud struggles for independence issue in young Reactionary states (LD, §262).

As Lyotard made it clear in a comment at a London conference, with reference to his own involvement in the Algerian fight for independence from France, this perception would not imply that there is no ethical duty to support such struggles, simply that there is no question of inserting them into some global dialectical history, and thereby of assuming they will give rise to 'progressive' political regimes (*Postmodernism*, ICA Documents 4 §5 (1986), pp. 11-12)

All of which would appear to be pessimistic to say the least: the economic genre is deaf to Lyotard's own insistence on heterogeneity and incommensurability. The book in which that insistence takes place is itself an object of exchange for the economic genre. That book attempts to phrase a *différend* with the genre which nonetheless takes it as an object: the *différend* is not even really to do with what the book says, but with its basic quasi-ethical assertion, namely that one be attentive to the *différend*, the event. As the opening 'Fiche de Lecture' states and ironically enacts, this stress demands that time be taken in reflection: this is time fundamentally useless to the economic genre. It is also a time which is open insofar as it opens the question of the event (to come): the *Arrive-t-il?* of the occurrence of a sentence. The economic genre presupposes the next sentence in its first sentence, and to that extent anticipates it as *already* arrived. *Le Différend* proposes sentences for linking in ignorance of what that linking will be: Lyotard claims (LD, p. 15) to have felt in writing the book that his addressee was the *Arrive-t-il?* itself. Elsewhere he would insist that the sender of a philosophical sentence has no obligation towards the empirical addressee of that sentence, but to 'thought'. The philosopher is responsible to the question 'What is thought?', or, the stake of the genre of philosophy is the discovery of its own rule: which will not be discovered once and for all. This cannot then be a book calling for one particular linking (and, notably, not prescribing political action in the normal sense of the words – certain linkings here are perfectly predictable, unfortunately): but that is precisely its stake. Still in the 'Fiche de Lecture', Lyotard states that his ignorance as to whether his sentences have 'arrived at their destination' is the final resistance of the event to the economic genre. This ignorance cannot be the object of exchange, what a cover-note to the *Faculté de juger* volume (Paris: Minuit, 1985) which came out of the 1982 Cerisy conference calls 'invincible weakness'. It is this assertion which underlies the last two paragraphs of the work, which I quote in full:

The only insurmountable obstacle encountered by the hegemony of the economic genre is the heterogeneity of the regimes of sentences and of the genres of discourse, the fact that there is not 'language [in general]' and 'Being', but occurrences. The obstacle does not depend on the 'will' of human beings one way or the other, but on the *différend.* The *différend* reappears even out of the settling of supposed litigations. It puts human beings in the position of having to situate themselves in unknown sentence universes, even if they do not feel the sentiment that there is something to be phrased. (For it is necessity, not obligation). The *Arrive-t-il?* is invincible in the face of any will to gain time.

But the occurrence does not make a history? – It is not a sign, indeed. But it is to be judged, even in it incomparability. One cannot make a 'programme' out of it. – And if no-one hears you bear witness to it, etc.? – You are prejudging the *Arrive-t-il?*. (LD, §§263-4)

Postscript

It would seem that the idea put forward in the Introduction, that Lyotard's thought is fundamentally political, has in a sense been vindicated. This is to be sure not a politics of programmes and prescriptions, and could almost be described as a systematic frustration of politics, through its refusal of the transcendental illusion which pretends to present in the real what can only, or at best, be an Idea of reason acting regulatively on political judgement. To the extent that this type of insistence appears also to be identified by Lyotard with the task of philosophy itself, then philosophy would be politics in this description.

> By showing that the linking of a sentence with a sentence is problematic and that this problem is politics, set up philosophical politics apart from that of the 'intellectuals' and the politicians. Bear witness to the différend. (LD, p. 11)

It remains to complicate this apparent identification of the philosophical and the political: this complication will also return us to the question left hanging about the object of this later thought, namely the sentence, as to whether it could bear the weight apparently being placed upon it.

Let me recapitulate rather brutally. There is a sentence. Another sentence must follow, necessarily. What sentence is to follow is a contingency, although the various genres propose an appearance of necessity to help over the abyss separating two sentences. Judgement as to the following sentence engages questions which are, broadly, ethical or political in nature.

Judgement becomes the problem, as we have said, and Lyotard increasingly turns toward Kant's *Critique of Judgement* for help in elaborating that problem. He points out that although Kant describes judgement as a 'faculty' (of a subject), it is not clear even on Kant's terms that this is an appropriate designation, insofar as this seems to be a 'faculty' without a specified object or domain of objects. Lyotard would say that judgement already has to intervene in the delimitation of any faculty at all or, in his retranscription, in the delimitation of 'a potential of sentences subject to a group of rules of formation and presentation (in Kant's sense)' (LD, p. 189). Judgement is involved in any claim that 'it is the case', in the

presentation of an object to validate a sentence as belonging to a particular regime or genre. This assignation of sentences as belonging to
particular regimes, and of the regimes as belonging to particular genres,
suggests that that 'belonging' is not simply given, but also that it is never
finally determined once and for all. In this respect, *Le Différend* marks
an important refinement on *Au juste:* in the earlier book, the impasse at
the end came of a conception of 'language-games' as somehow having a
purity or propriety which separated them absolutely from each other:
we can now suggest that such an idea is due to a transcendental illusion
on Lyotard's own part, in the desire to present the dispersion which
cannot be presented as the object of a cognitive presentation.

In *Le Différend,* however, Lyotard recognizes that this dispersion cannot be so presented: it cannot be a concept of the understanding, for it
cannot be validated by an intuition. As idea of reason, it can be the object
only of an *analogical* or symbolic presentation: Lyotard suggests that a
reasonable symbol for this dispersion is an archipelago: the genres are
islands, and are as such indeed separated from each other – but they
have a potential means of communicating by sea, and that sea is the
milieu of judgement. If there were no such communication between
genres (and that communication can be thought of as warfare), then there

---

Compare with the slightly earlier (and equally analogical) presentation of this
problem (LD, p. 180) in terms of the juridical terminology which is no doubt the
dominant analogy of Kantian philosophy, that of the courtroom : 'If the abyss
between the world determined by knowledge and obligation cannot be crossed,
then Kantian morality remains an abstraction. You do indeed hear "Close the
door!", but the door will never be closed. (Or, conversely, the world of knowledge remains an abstraction compared with that of morality?) – What is really
abstract is to pose the question of the abyss as though in an alternative way,
such that it would have either to be filled or deepened. But there is no abyss,
and in general no limit, except because each party – to use the symbolics of
lawcourt or war – allows itself the right to look over the other's argumentation,
[and thus] extends its pretensions beyond its frontiers. It is only at this price
that it finds its frontiers'.

would be no genres, no establishment of generic 'proprieties', which are
thus never properly proper.

Judgement, in finding the appropriate rule for the case and the appropriate case for the rule, is the activity defining critical philosophy as such.
Philosophy in this sense is *itself* not an object that can be intuited, but
the object of an Idea of Reason. This seems to clarify some of the problems
and perplexities raised by the sentence as object of philosophy: there is

a sentence, indubitably, but, apparently, no language in general and therefore no sentence in general. A sentence is the case, but not a case subsum-
able under a concept of the understanding: it can be taken as referent of
cognitive sentences, but not exhaustively so, because of the excess of
presentation over situation. It would seem to follow that 'a sentence' is
itself an analogical or symbolic presentation, rather than a positive object.
Small wonder, then, that we do not know *what a sentence is,* but merely
that there are sentences. The sentence is an analogical presentation of
the event, which is as such unpresentable. This is why Lyotard's stress
on the sentence as his object does not involve any linguistic positivism
or anthropologism, and allows non-linguistic events to be presented
analogically in terms of sentences. By stressing the contingency of linkages and the injustice of pretensions to generic hegemony, philosophy
respects that event by treating it in each case as a matter for judgement,
without prejudging the rule of judgement appropriate in that case. In
their very different ways, the 'libidinal band' and the 'figure' were also
analogical presentations attempting to respect the event: but in the end,
the apparently simple 'sentence' is the most complex presentation of the
unpresentable that Lyotard has discovered, because it disallows any
repose in psychic or naturalistic notions of energy.

In this conception, injustice is inevitable. Paradoxically, the obligation
to judge justly does not project an achieved state of justice as the end
of history, but encourages the critical watcher (guided by a regulative
Idea – which is scarcely even an Idea – of dispersion) to discover ever
more *torts* and *différends*, in the very effort made to find idioms to phrase
those *torts* and *différends* already discovered. 'Bearing witness' to the
unpresentable does not prove progress of humanity for the better, but
attests to the activity of thought. This is political in a radical sense (though
not as a programme of 'radical politics'), insofar as it constantly invokes
a 'realm of freedom' in, through and against a 'realm of necessity' (whereas
politics, as a genre, is constantly trying to wrest a realm of necessity
from this realm of freedom). Such 'freedom' is not specifically a human
attribute, but positions humans as *responsible* towards the *différend*.
That responsibility is itself a sentimental sentence, signalled by a silence:
but this silence does not bear on one of the instances situated in a sentence-universe, but on the occurrence of the event 'as such' – Lyotard
would say that this is a sublime sentiment (and we should probably have
to say that it is the sublime sentiment *itself),* as the sentiment that nothing
might happen, that no further sentence might arrive, that there might be
no more to be said or done, along with the 'knowledge' that another
sentence is nonetheless necessary. This suspension in the question

'Arrive-t-il?' (the question mark itself, as Lyotard would say ('The Sublime and the avant-garde', p. 2)) is a sort of pre-judgement that cannot be prejudged. This would be the place to *enchaîner* with Derrida's 'Préjugés: devant la loi' in the *Faculté de juger* volume: pending that, with an earlier comment from 'Violence and metaphysics':

Community of the question, then, in that fragile instance where the question is not yet determined enough for the hypocrisy of a reply to have been already invited under the mask of the question, for its voice to have been allowed fraudulent articulation in the very syntax of the question. Community of decision, of initiative, of absolute initiality, but threatened, where the question has not yet found the language it has decided to seek, and has not yet reassured itself in that language of its own possibility. Community of the question on the possibility of the question. This is not much – it is almost nothing – but in it today there takes refuge and is resumed an unbroachable dignity and duty of decision. An unbroachable decision. (*L'Ecriture et la différence*, p. 118)

'Mais elle ne se fera jamais, cette communauté! s'écria le Rabbi' (LD, p. 186)

Bibliography

(I have been greatly assisted in compiling this bibliography by being able to consult the *Bibliographie zu Jean-François Lyotard* by Reinhold Clausjürgens and a selected bibliography compiled by Eddie Yeghiayan. The bibliography aims to be exhaustive at least to the end of 1985, including details of all of Lyotard's publications in French and English.)

I. BOOKS

La Phénoménologie (Paris: Presses Universitaires de France, 1954)

Discours, figure (Paris: Klincksieck, 1971) [tr. forthcoming, Cambridge University Press. Partial translations. 'The Dream-Work does not think', tr. Mary Lydon, *The Oxford Literary Review*, 6:1 (1983), 3-34 (= DF pp. 239-70); 'Fiscourse Digure', tr. Mary Lydon, *Theatre Journal*, 35:3 (1983), 333-57 (= DF, 327-54); 'The Connivances of Desire with the Figural', in *Driftworks*, (New York: Semiotext(e), 1984), 57-68 (= DF, 271-9)]

Dérive à partir de Marx et Freud (Paris: Union générale d'éditions, 1973) [Contains 'Dérives' (5-21) [partial translation, 'Adrift', tr. Roger McKeon, in *Driftworks*, 9-17]; 'Préambule à une charte' (22-9); 'Désirévolution' (30-5); 'Un Marx non marxiste' (36-46); 'Cadeau d'organes' (47-52) ['Gift of Organs', tr. Richard Lockwood, in *Driftworks*, 85-9]; 'Principales tendances actuelles de l'étude psychanalytique des expressions artistiques et littéraires' (53-77); 'La Place de l'aliénation dans le retournement marxiste' (78-166); 'Oedipe juif' (167-88) ['Jewish Oedipus', tr. Susan Hanson, in *Driftworks*, 35-55]; 'Nanterre: ici, maintenant' (189-209); 'Sur la théorie' [interview with Brigitte Devismes] (210-29) [partial translation, 'On Theory: An Interview', tr. Roger McKeon, in *Driftworks*, 19-33]; 'Notes sur la fonction critique de l'oeuvre' (230-47) [partial translation, 'Notes on the Critical Function of the Work of Art', tr. Susan Hanson, in *Driftworks*, 69-83]; ' "A Few Words to Sing": Sequenza III' [with Dominique Avron] (248-71); 'Leçon d'impouvoir' (272-5); 'Espace plastique et espace politique' [with Dominique Avron and Bruno Lemenuel] (276-304); 'Le 23 Mars' (305-16)]

Des dispositifs pulsionnels (Paris: Union générale d'éditions, 1973), [2nd edition with a new preface and some revisions (Paris: Christian Bourgois, 1980)] [Contains 'Capitalisme Energumène' (7-52 [7-49]) ['Energumen Capitalism', tr. James Leigh, *Semiotext(e)*, 2:3 (1977), 11-26]; 'L'Acinéma' (53-69 [51-65]) ['Acinema', tr. Paisley N. Livingstone and the author, *Wide Angle*, 2:3 (1978),

52-9]; 'Freud selon Cézanne' (71-94 [67-88]); 'La Dent, la paume' (95-104 [89-98] ['The Tooth, the Palm', tr. Anne Knap and Michel Benamou, *Sub-Stance* 15 (1976), 105-10]; 'Esquisse d'une économie de l'hyperréalisme' (105-13 [99-107]); 'Adorno come diavolo' (115-33 [109-125]) ['Adorno as the Devil', tr. Robert Hurley, *Telos* 19 (1974), 127-37]; 'Sur une figure du discours' (135-56 [127-47]); '"L'Eau prend le ciel": proposition de collage pour figurer le désir bachelardien' (157-78 [149-69]); 'Petite économie libidinale d'un dispositif narratif: La Régie Renault raconte le meutre de Pierre Overney' (179-224 [171-213]); 'En Attendant Guiffrey (Quatre pièces pour un abstrait)' (225-36 [215-26]); 'La Peinture comme dispositif libidinal' (237-80 ['. . . (genre parlé improvisé)' 227-67]); 'Plusieurs silences' (281-303 [269-90]) ['Several silences', tr. Joseph Maier, in *Driftworks,* 91-110]; 'Notes sur le retour et le capital' (304-19 [291-305]) ['Notes on the Return and Kapital', tr. Roger McKeon, *Semiotext(e),* 3:1 (1978), 44-53]

Economie libidinale (Paris: Minuit, 1974) [Partial translations: 'For a Pseudo-Theory', tr. Moshe Ron, Yale French Studies, 52 (1975), 115-27 (= EL, 288-90, 292-6, 302-8); 'Use me', tr. Michel Feher and Tom Gora, *Semiotext(e),* 4:1 (1981), 82-5 (= EL, 77-84); 'The Tensor', tr. Sean Hand, *The Oxford Literary Review,* 7:1-2 (1985), 25-40 (= EL, 57-77)]

Sur cinq peintures de René Guiffrey (Paris: Galerie Stevenson et Palluel, 1975)

Instructions païennes (Paris: Galilée, 1977)

Récits tremblants (with Jacques Monory) (Paris: Galilée, 1977)

Rudiments païens: genre dissertatif (Paris: Union générale d'éditions, 1977) [Contains 'Prière de désinsérer' (7-8); 'Apathie dans la théorie' (9-31); 'Humour en sémiothéologie' (32-59); 'Rétorsion en théopolitique' (60-80); 'Faux-fuyant dans la littérature' (81-114); 'Expédient dans la décadence' (115-56); 'Futilité en révolution' (157-212); 'Féminité dans la métalangue' (213-32) ['One of the things at stake in women's struggles', tr. D.J. Clark, W. Woodhull and J. Mowitt, *Sub-stance,* 20 (1978), 9-17]; 'Dissertation sur une inconvenance' (233-46) ['Theory as Art: A Pragmatic Point of View', tr. Robert Vollrath, in Wendy Steiner, ed., *Image and Code* (Ann Arbor: University of Michigan Press, 1981), 71-7]]

Les Transformateurs Duchamp (Paris: Galilée, 1977)

Le Mur du pacifique (Paris: Galilée, 1979) [partial translation, 'Passages from *Le Mur du pacifique',* tr. P. Brochet, N. Royle and K. Woodward, *Sub-stance,* 37-8 (1983), 89-99]

Au Juste (with Jean-Loup Thébaud) (Paris: Christian Bourgois, 1979) [*Just Gaming,* tr. Wlad Godzich (Minneapolis: Minnesota University Press/ Manchester: Manchester University Press, 1986)]

La Condition postmoderne (Paris: Minuit, 1979) [*The Postmodern Condition,* tr. Geoff Bennington and Brian Massumi (Minneapolis: Minnesota University Press/ Manchester: Manchester University Press, 1984)]

La Constitution du temps par la couleur dans les oeuvres récentes d'Albert Ayme (Paris: La Traversière, 1980)

La Partie de peinture (with Henri Maccheroni) (Cannes: Maryse Candela, 1980)

Monory: Ciels: Nébuleuses et galaxies; Les confins d'un dandysme (Paris: Galerie Maeght, 1981)

Monogrammes/Loin du doux (Paris: Galerie le Dessin, 1982)

Le Différend (Paris: Minuit, 1983) [partial translation, 'The Différend, the Referent and the Proper Name', tr. G. van den Abbeele, *Diacritics*, 14:3 (1984), 4-14; full translation forthcoming]

L'Assassinat de l'expérience par la peinture, Monory (Paris: Le Castor Astral, 1984) [contains 'L'Expertise' (7-10); 'Economie libidinale du dandy' (11-109); 'Esthétique sublime du tueur à gages' (113-154)]

L'histoire de Ruth (with Ruth Francken) (Paris: Le Castor astral, 1984)

Tombeau de l'intellectuel et autres papiers (Paris: Galilée, 1984) [contains 'Tombeau de l'intellectuel' (11-22); 'Le différend' (25-31); 'Pour une non-politique culturelle' (35-40); 'Nouvelles technologies' (43-56); 'Wittgenstein, "après"' (49-66); 'Les Modes intellectuelles' (69-73); 'Appendice svelte à la question postmoderne' (77-87)]

(ed., with Annie Cazenave), *L'art des confins: mélanges offerts à Maurice de Gandillac* (Paris: PUF, 1985)

(ed.), *Les Immatériaux: Epreuves d'écriture* (Paris: Centre Georges Pompidou, 1985)

Le Postmoderne expliqué aux enfants: Correspondance 1982-1985 (Paris: Galilée, 1986) [contains 'Réponse à la question: qu'est-ce que le postmoderne?' (13-34) ['Answering the Question: What is Postmodernism?', tr. Régis Durand, in *The Postmodern Condition*, pp. 71-82]; 'Apostille aux récits' (37-42); 'Missive sur l'histoire universelle' (45-64); 'Memorandum sur la légitimité' (67-94) [tr. Cecile Lindsay, *The Oxford Literary Review*, 9 (1987)]; 'Dépêche à propos de la confusion des raisons' (97-103); 'Post-scriptum à la terreur et au sublime' (107-15); 'Note sur les sens de "post-"' (119-26) [transcription of earlier English version, 'Defining the Postmodern', ICA Documents 4&5 (1986), 6-7]; 'Billet pour un nouveau décor' (129-34); 'Glose sur la résistance' (137-51); 'Adresse au sujet du cours philosophique' (155-166)]

L'Enthousiasme: la critique kantienne de l'histoire (Paris: Galilée, 1986)

Peregrinations: Law, Form, Event (New York: Columbia University Press, forthcoming)

II. UNCOLLECTED ARTICLES AND INTERVIEWS (Interviews are preceded by an asterisk). Some early articles in *Socialisme ou barbarie* were published under the pseudonym of François Laborde: these are preceded by '(FL)'. (Pre-published fragments of forthcoming books are only exceptionally included in this list)

'Rencontre avec la jeunesse allemande', *L'Age nouveau*, 24 (1948), 62-6

'La Culpabilité allemande' (review of Karl Jaspers, *Die Schuldfrage: Ein Beitrag sur Deutschen Frage), L'Age nouveau*, 28 (1948), 90-4

'Nés en 1925', *Les Temps modernes,* 32 (1948), 2052-7

'Texte', *Imprudence,* 3 (1949), 78-82

Review of Elliott Jacques, *The Changing Culture of a Factory, Cahiers Internationaux de Sociologie,* 12 (1952), 179-81

(FL) Review of Victor Alba, *Le Mouvement Ouvrier en Amérique latine, Socialisme ou barbarie,* 17 (1955), 72-7

'Note sur le Marxisme', in *Tableau de la philosophie contemporaine* (Paris: Fischbacher, 1956), 55-6

(FL) 'La situation en Afrique du nord', *Socialisme ou barbarie,* 18 (1956), 87-94

(FL) 'La Bourgeoisie Nord-Africaine', *Socialisme ou barbarie,* 20 (1957), 188-94

(FL) 'Nouvelle phase dans la question algérienne', *Socialisme ou barbarie,* 21 (1957), 162-8

(FL) 'Les comptes du "gérant loyal"', *Socialisme ou barbarie,* 22 (1957), 148-52

(FL) 'Mise à nu des contradictions algériennes', *Socialisme ou barbarie,* 24 (1958), 17-34

(FL) 'La guerre contre-révolutionnaire, la société coloniale et le Gaullisme', *Socialisme ou barbarie,* 25 (1958), 20-7

'Le Contenu social de la lutte algérienne', *Socialisme ou barbarie,* 29 (1959), 1-38

'L'Etat et la politique dans la France de 1960', *Socialisme ou barbarie,* 30 (1960), 45-72

'Le Gaullisme et l'Algérie', *Socialisme ou barbarie,* 31 (1961), 24-32

'En Algérie, une vague nouvelle', *Socialisme ou barbarie,* 32 (1961), 62-72

'L'Algérie, sept ans après', *Socialisme ou barbarie,* 33 (1962), 10-16

'L'Algérie évacuée', *Socialisme ou barbarie,* 34 (1963), 1-43

'Algeria', *International Socialism,* 13 (1963)

'Les Indiens ne cueillent pas les fleurs', *Annales, E.S.C.,* 20 (1965), 62-83

'Les Formes de l'action', *Cahiers de philosophie,* 2-3 (1966)

'A la place de l'homme, l'expression', *Esprit,* 383 (1969), 155-78

'Psychanalyse et peinture', in *Enclyclopaedia Universalis,* Vol. 13 (Paris, 1971), 745-9

*'En finir avec l'illusion de la politique' (Entretien avec Gilbert Lascault), *La quinzaine littéraire,* 1-15/5/72, 18-9

'Ante diem rationis', in Boris Eizykman, *Science-fiction et capitalisme* (Paris: Mame, 1973), 225-43

'Les filles machines folles de Lindner', *L'Art vivant,* 41 (1973), 8-9

'Par-delà la représentation', in Anton Ehrenzweig, *L'Ordre caché de l'art* (Paris: Gallimard, 1974 [= French translation of *The Hidden Order of Art* (London: Paladin, 1970)]), 9-24 [tr. Jonathan Culler, *The Human Context,* VII, 3 (1975), 495-502]

'Marcel Duchamp, le grand sophiste', *L'Art vivant,* 56 (1975), 34-5

'A propos du département de psychanalyse à Vincennes', *Les Temps modernes,* 342 (1975), 862-3

'Sur la force des faibles', *L'Arc,* 64 (1976), 4-12 [tr. Roger McKeon, *Semiotext(e),* 3:2 (1978), 204-14]

'The Unconscious as mise-en-scène', tr. Joseph Maier, in *Performance in Post-modern Culture*, ed. M. Benamou and C. Caramello (Madison: Coda Press, 1977), 87-98

'Leçon sur la condition secrète des langues: genre didactique', *Erres*, 3-4 (1977), 69-74 [tr. Ian McLeod, *The Oxford Literary Review*, 3:1 (1978), 35-7]

*'De la fonction critique à la transformation' (entretien avec Jean Papineau), *Parachute*, 11 (1978), 4-9

'L'Autre dans les énoncés prescriptifs et le problème de l'autonomie', in *En Marge: L'Occident et ses 'autres'* (Paris: Aubier, 1978), 237-56

'L'Endurance et la profession', *Critique*, 369 (1978), 198-205 [tr. C. Gallier, S. Ungar and B. Johnson, *Yale French Studies*, 63 (1982), 72-7]

'Notes préliminaires sur la pragmatique des oeuvres (en particulier de Daniel Buren)', *Critique*, 378 (1978), 1075-85 [tr. T. Repensek, *October*, 10 (1979), 59-67]

'Pour faire de ton fils un Baruchello', in Gianfranco Baruchello, *L'Altra casa* (Paris, 1979), 9-15

'Petites ruminations sur le commentaire d'art', *Opus International*, 70-1 (1979), 16-7

'La Micrologie de Lascault, ou la grandeur du petit' (review of Gilbert Lascault, *Voyage d'automne et d'hiver*), *La Quinzaine littéraire*, 16-31/5/1979, 8-9

*'Entretien avec Christian Descamps', *Le Monde*, 14/10/79

'Logique de Levinas', in F. Laruelle (ed), *Textes pour Emmanuel Lavinas* (Paris: Jean-Michel Place, 1980), 127-50 [partial publication: tr. of full text by Ian McLeod, in *Face to Face with Levinas*, edited by Richard A. Cohen (Albany: SUNY Press, 1986), 117-58]

'Tromeur', *La Quinzaine littéraire*, 15-30/6/80, 2021

*'Le Jeu de l'informatique et du savoir', *Dialectiques*, 29 (1980), 3-12

'Faire voir les invisibles, ou contre le réalisme', in B. Buchloh, ed., *Daniel Buren: Les Couleurs, Sculptures; Les Formes, Peintures* (Paris: Centre national d'art et de culture Georges Pompidou, 1981), pp. 26-38

'Discussions, ou: phraser "après Auschwitz"', in P. Lacoue-Labarthe and J-L. Nancy, eds., *Les Fins de l'homme: à partir du travail de Jacques Derrida* (Paris: Galilée, 1981), pp. 283-310 [most of this paper reappears in LD pp. 130-58, and a translation by G. Van Den Abbeele (Center for Twentieth Century Studies, University of Wisconsin-Milwaukee, Working Paper No. 2 (Fall 1986)]

'Introduction à une étude de la politique selon Kant', in P. Lacoue-Labarthe and J-L. Nancy, eds., *Rejouer le politique* (Paris: Galilée, 1981), 91-134 [parts of this text reappear in *Le Différend* and *L'Enthousiasme*: partial translation, 'The Sign of History', tr. Geoff Bennington, in D. Attridge, G. Bennington, R. Young, eds. *Post-Structuralism and the Question of History* (Cambridge: Cambridge University Press, 1987), pp. 162-80]

'Essai d'Analyse du dispositif spéculatif', *Degrés*, 9:26-7 (1981), 1-11 [roughly = LD, 137-45: tr. Geoff Bennington, *The Oxford Literary Review*, 4:3 (1981), 59-67]

'La Philosophie et la peinture à l'ère de leur expérimentation: contribution à une idée de la postmodernité', *Revista di Estetica,* 21:9 (1981), 3-15 [tr. *Camera Obscura,* 12 (1984), 110-25]

'Pierre Souyri: Le Marxisme qui n'a pas fini', *Esprit* 1982:1 (1982), 11-31 [rpt. in Pierre Souyri, *Révolution et contre-révolution en Chine* (Paris: Bourgois, 1982), 7-37; tr. Cecile Lindsay as Afterword in *Peregrinations*]

'Presenting the Unpresentable: the Sublime', tr. Lisa Liebmann, *Artforum,* 20:8 (1982), 64-9

'Presentations', tr. K. McLaughlin, in A. Montefiore, ed., *Philosophy in France Today* (Cambridge: Cambridge University Press, 1983), 116-35

'Un Succès de Sartre' (review of Denis Hollier, *Politique de la prose* (Paris: Gallimard, 1982)), *Critique,* 430 (1983), 177-89 [tr. Jeffrey Mehlman in D. Hollier, *The Politics of Prose* (Minneapolis: University of Minnesota Press, 1987), pp. xi-xxii]

'Le Seuil de l'histoire' [1966], *Digraphe* 33 (1983), 7-56 and 34 (1984), 36-74

'On dirait qu'une ligne...: Préface à "Adami: Peintures récentes"', *Repères: Cahiers d'art contemporain,* 6 (1983), 3-38

'La Peinture du secret à l'ère postmoderne: Baruchello', *Traverses,* 30-1 (1984), 95-101

*'Interview with Georges van den Abbeele', *Diacritics* 14:3 (1984), 16-21

'Longitude 180° W or E', in *Arakawa: Padiglione d'arte contemporanea* (Mailand: Edizione Nava Milano, 1984)

'The Sublime and the Avant-Garde', tr. Lisa Liebmann, *Artforum,* 22:8 (1984), 36-43 [revised rpt. in *Paragraph,* 6 (1985), 1-18]

*'Langage, temps, travail' (Entretien avec Giairo Daghini), *Change International,* 2 (1984), 42-7

'Le Concubinage du savoir et de l'état', *Le Monde,* 1-2/7/84

*'Plaidoyer pour la métaphysique' (Entretien avec Jacques Derrida), *Le Monde,* 28-9/10/84

*'Le design au-delà de l'esthétique' (Entretien avec F. Burckhardt), *Le Monde,* 4-5/11/84

'Judicieux dans le différend', in Lyotard et al., *La Faculté de juger* (Paris: Minuit, 1985), 195-236

'Discussion avec Richard Rorty', *Critique,* 456 (1985), 581-4

*'A Conversation with Jean-François Lyotard', *Flash Art,* 121 (1985), 32-5

'Retour au postmoderne', *Magazine littéraire* 225 (1985), 43

'Sites et récits de sites', in *Traitement de Textes: Cartes et Brouillons de Michel Butor* (Gourdon: Dominique Bedou, 1985), 9-14

'Anamnèse du visible, ou: la franchise', in *Adami* (Paris: Musée national d'art moderne / Centre Georges Pompidou, 1985) [catalogue], 50-60

'L'Obédience', in *In Harmoniques,* 1 (1986), 106-17

'Quelque chose: "communication... sans communication"' in *Art and Communication,* ed. Robert Allezand (Paris: Osiris, 1986), 10-17

Index